Spanish Texas

Gerald Ashford was born in St. Paul in 1907 and began his newspaper career as a reporter at the age of sixteen in Red Wing, Minnesota. He became the publisher of a weekly paper at Goodhue, Minnesota. In 1942 he entered the Army as a private and became an intelligence officer by 1945. Upon leaving the service in 1946 he joined the *Express-News* in San Antonio, Texas and is presently the fine arts editor there.

Mr. Ashford recently published *Everyday Publicity: A Practical Guide,* and has published many columns and articles supporting historical preservation.

Spanish Texas

Yesterday
and
Today

by Gerald Ashford

JENKINS PUBLISHING COMPANY
The Pemberton Press
Austin and New York   1971

Design by Larry Smitherman

Contents

Spanish Texas

Introduction

The Spanish Heritage

A few people may still imagine that the history of Spanish Texas is a closed chapter, a mere prologue, of interest only to antiquarians who like to poke about the old missions of San Antonio or to decipher faded documents in the archives. But actually, Spanish Texas is very much alive today. The Spanish period, in a sense, has not ended here and is not likely ever to end. The story of Spanish Texas even has a profound significance for the understanding of American culture as a whole, and especially the culture of the Southwest, for Texas was the focal point for the fusing of the Southwestern States, all of them, into the American Commonwealth, where they have produced under continuing Spanish-Mexican influence a type of civilization which, though as thoroughly American as the civilization of New York or Virginia, is yet subtly different.

The Spanish regime, though it ended more than a century ago, has left more than a trace, enduring to this day, not only on the laws of Texas, but on its governmental policies, its social customs, its farming and ranching practices, its language, its place-names, its architecture, its religion,

1

and on the character of every inhabitant, from whatever nation descended.

Under the favorable land policy which was virtually continuous under the successive governments of Spain, Mexico, the Republic of Texas and the State, it is not surprising that the whole vast cattle industry of the United States had its beginning in Texas.

In the other states, according to Walter Prescott Webb, "All legislation was made in favor of the farmer; none was ever made for the cattleman, so far as disposal of the public domain was concerned, except in Texas." Whatever progress the cattlemen made in the other states, says Dr. Webb, they made by evading the law.

By the middle of the 18th century, as we have seen, much of the land south of the San Antonio River had been laid out in ranches of a healthy size. Cattle, horses and sheep, guarded by Mexican *vaqueros,* dotted these vast areas. At that time, and for a hundred years afterward, there was virtually no large-scale stock-raising anywhere in the United States, but only the diversified farm to which cattle were incidental.

In the Texas Revolution and the troubles that followed, many of the Mexican ranchers were driven out through one device or another, notwithstanding their rights under law and treaty. Yet for a time the new Texans made few or no systematic efforts to operate ranches. "From the time of the Texas Revolution until the end of the Civil War," says Webb, "cattle grew wild in Texas and multiplied at a rapid and constant rate." In the country between the Nueces and the Rio Grande, they multiplied so rapidly that they became a pest. After the Civil War, however, the surplus was drained away by the great cattle drives which not only supplied the northern markets but spread Texas cattle to take the place of the vanishing buffalo on the rangeland of the West, all the way to Montana and Idaho. With the cattle went the cowboy, a new figure on the American landscape who was a compound of the Texas frontiersman and the Mexican *vaquero.*

So it was in Spanish territory near the Rio Grande that the cattle industry, the most typical feature of the American West, had its beginning. Even the custom of branding cattle, though not consistently practiced in the early days, was introduced to the United States through Spanish Texas, as records still used in the courthouse at San Antonio will witness.

The American horse and sheep also had their origin in Spanish America and came into the United States partly, but not exclusively, by way of Texas. The wild horse, descended from stock abandoned by De Soto, Coronado and other explorers, and strayed from the Spanish settlements, had spread to the Canadian border well before the end of the 18th century, and his taming by the Indians had effected a revolution in tribal culture as far-reaching as that later brought about by the automobile among white Americans. The sheep, first introduced from Mexico into New Mexico, did not become a major industry in Texas until long after the end of the Spanish regime.

Irrigation was introduced into Texas by the first white settlers. Some of these early works, the best known of which are the San Juan and Espada ditches leading to the missions so named near San Antonio, can still be seen. Methods of irrigation which were originally developed in Spain and handed down by tradition were scarcely improved upon until very recent years and are still used by farmers who cannot afford the latest engineering refinements.

The Spanish language is spoken daily, as the mother tongue, nearly two million Texans of Mexican descent, a number which has greatly increased since 1900 and is growing at an accelerated rate since the industrialization of the state has opened new opportunities for employment. Many of these people, including some whose families have lived in the state for generations, speak little or no English. Their Spanish, spoken with a distinctive accent which is said to amuse the people of the interior of Mexico, contains many words adapted from the English, like *metcha* for *match* and *troka* for *truck*. In San Antonio and many smaller cities where "Chicanos" live in large blocs, nothing but Spanish is spoken in many homes, so that the children reach school age without knowing more than a word or two of English.

As a means of communication with their fellow-Texans and the Mexicans across the border, large numbers of English-speaking Texans have learned Spanish as a second language. Although statistics are lacking, it is certain that Spanish is learned by more people in Texas than any foreign language in any other State, and that more Texans learn Spanish than any other foreign language. Interpreters are regularly employed in the courts of many counties in Southwest Texas, and Spanish-speaking employes are indispensable in every store or office of considerable size in that region.

Just as English words have crept into Spanish along the border, so have Spanish words found their place in the English spoken in Texas. Such borrowings, of course, took place all the way from England to California. A whole romantic picture of the old West can be built up with a list of words like those cited by H. L. Mencken: "Rancho, alfalfa, mustang, sombrero, canyon, desperado, poncho, corral, bronco, plaza, peon, alcalde, burro, mesa, tornado, presidio, patio, sierra and adobe," all applying to objects which were strange to the westward-moving American pioneers and to their language.

But it is only in Texas and perhaps in New Mexico that the average person would understand and use such words and phrases as *Yo tambien* (Me too); *vamonos* (let's go); *frijole* (bean); *muy borracho* (very drunk). With no thought of anything exotic, city squares are naturally and unaffectedly called *plazas*; paved areas adjoining houses are called *patios*—a usage which has spread to the rest of the country. The political columnist of the San Antonio *Light* calls himself Don Politico, and formerly dubbed the personages of whom he wrote, to the vast delight of his readers, with Hispanicized versions of their given names, such as Carlos Harrell, Tomasito Tucker, Gustavo Mauermann and Enrique Hein. Perhaps Don Politico's most brilliant inspiration occurred when the former police commissioner, George M. Roper, who was given to smoking cigars of questionable quality, received the sobriquet of "El Ropo," although this is only pidgin Spanish. Actually the Mexican-American voters referred to Mr. Roper as *El Mecate,* from the common Mexican word for *rope.* Both Spanish and English-speaking people sometimes refer to the Bexar County Courthouse as the Casa Colorada, in allusion to the red stone of which it is built, and the City Hall, built of white stone, is sometimes called the Casa Blanca.

Spanish names for plants and animals peculiar to the Southwest are known to every resident of the regions where these flora and fauna flourish. Among trees, there are the mesquite, the retama (or palo verde), huisache and huajillo, to name only a few. Various species of desert plants bear Spanish names which are well understood, such as the ocotillo, lechuguilla, guayule, maguey and various species of yucca and cactus. Well-known shrubs are the ceniza, agarita and several species lumped under the name of chaparral. Of the hundreds of wildflowers found in Texas, many bear Spanish names also.

The map of Texas would be half empty if it were deprived of all the geographical features that bear names of Spanish origin. The hastiest glance at the map reveals the Rio Grande, the Colorado, the Nueces and Brazos Rivers and the cities of San Antonio, El Paso, Corpus Christi and Laredo. Closer inspection yields 41 Spanish names among the state's 254 counties; and numbers of cities, rivers, bays and mountains which it would be futile to count. The tendency extends to street names in San Antonio and elsewhere in Southwest Texas.

Physical remains of the Spanish occupation in Texas are few in number but of great interest. There are the five missions at San Antonio, in various states of repair; the so-called Spanish Governor's Palace in San Antonio; two missions and a presidio with its chapel at Goliad (La Bah*ia); a* restored presidio at Menard; the foundations of the completely rebuilt Cathedral of San Fernando in San Antonio, and that is all, except for a few heaps of rocks marking the sites of other buildings, and a few old houses in San Antonio, Goliad and Nacogdoches which may or may not date back to the colonial period.

Trent E. Sanford, who visited every Spanish architectural landmark in the Southwest in preparing to write his book, *The Architecture of the Southwest,* reported that "Nowhere else in the country [but at San Antonio], within such a small radius, is there so much of architectural interest dating back more than two hundred years and of historical interest dating back even farther." Of the Mission San José, Sanford said, "No group of buildings in this country contains more of historical and architectural interest."

Even if not all of the five missions at San Antonio had been finished 200 years ago, they are older than the more numerous but more widely scattered missions of California, which date from the late 18th and early 19th centuries. San José, "The Queen of the Missions," was restored with excellent taste under the direction of the late Harvey P. Smith in the 1930's, and better than any other of the remains it can today present a clear notion of what life was like for the *Indios reducidos* and their Franciscan pastors. Concepción, on the other hand, unrestored except for minor repairs, is better preserved than any other Texas mission as far as the church is concerned, although most of the other buildings that appertained to it have disappeared. Espada and San Juan, farther down the river, are smaller and still undergoing restoration, but are well worth a visit. At all of these missions, Catholic services are still regularly held, and at Espada a parochial school keeps alive the atmosphere of the days when Indian neophytes received instruction. Some of the people living about the missions, though now called "Mexicans," are descendants of the original Indian converts, to whom land was alloted when the missions were secularized after 1794.

The Alamo (Mission San Antonio de Valero), in the heart of San Antonio both geographically and sentimentally, is a case apart. After secularization it was taken over by the Spanish government. For a time it served as the first hospital in San Antonio, and it was also a garrison for troops, nicknamed "The Alamo" after the *Compania Volante del Álamo de Parras.* Before the famous battle in 1836 it had fallen into ruins. In 1849, when it became a U.S. Army quartermaster warehouse, the officer in charge had the present well-known curved parapet added to the ruined front. When the government gave up the building, there began an intermittent battle between patriotic Texans and commercial interests who sought to use the site for a hotel or other commercial purposes. The patriots finally won, and the Alamo is a historic shrine visited by Texans with profound awe and veneration.

At Goliad, the Mission Espíritu Santo is a restoration which is practically all new construction. The Mission Rosario, a few miles beyond the town, is a heap of stones, and the one object of real historical interest is the presidio with its chapel, built of rough stones on a hill with a commanding view over the valley of the San Antonio River. At Menard, the presidio is almost all new construction.

Otherwise, the missions and presidios which the Spaniards built in Texas have vanished. Those that were of log or adobe construction melted away, and those of stone were wrecked by early settlers who wanted the material to build their own houses. The pioneers, everywhere in the United States, were great builders, but they also were great destroyers. They destroyed the forests, they destroyed the buffalo and other wild game, and where, as in Texas, they came upon the remains of an earlier civilization, they destroyed that too. Even in more sophisticated circles, our interest in historical or architectural remains usually takes second place to more practical considerations. If it were not so, Trinity Church in New York would still be surrounded with the picturesque little brick houses of the Dutch burghers.

Aside from buildings, some of the irrigation ditches dug by the Indians for the Spanish padres can still be picked out by a knowing eye in the heart of San Antonio. Another, more abstract, relic is the *Camino Real* or Old San Antonio Road, the path followed by the first explorers and improved into some semblance of a real road as early as 1719. Although definite information is lacking as to why the Spaniards followed this route rather than some other, it is safe to presume that the track had already been marked by the Indians, who had crisscrossed the entire continent with established trails long before the white men arrived. Today, the approximate route of the Old San Antonio Road is known as State Highway No. 21 from San Augustine, near the Louisiana border, to San Marcos, passing through Nacogdoches, Bryan, Caldwell and Bastrop; U.S. Highway No. 81 from San Marcos to San Antonio; U.S. Highway No. 281 from San Antonio to Pleasanton, and thence across country, following no modern highway, by way of Cotulla to the old presidio of San Juan Bautista on the Mexican side of the Rio Grande, thirty-two miles south of Eagle Pass. The route between San Marcos and San Antonio can be traced more comfortably and perhaps more accurately along several Farm-to-Market roads which parallel the highway.

Living descendants of the Spanish colonial settlers in Texas are present in numbers which cannot be determined accurately or even approximately because, although scions of the more prosperous Spanish-Mexican-American families are well-known and influential, the rank and file of Spanish-descended Texans have almost disappeared in the mass of "Mexicans" of a later immigration. The entire Spanish-speaking element in Texas is separated from the Anglo-Americans more by language, religion and social customs than by priority of settlement.

Some of the descendants of the first comers are acutely aware of their ancestors, and others hardly at all. When a well-educated living descendant of Vicente Alvarez Travieso, a member of the first *ayuntamiento* of San Fernando in 1731, recently read a mention of that doughty Canary Islander in the San Antonio *Express,* he was delighted to learn, for the first time, why the name *Vicente* was often given to the male children in his family. Yet this same man was well aware of a family tradition that one of his female ancestors had been the seventh child baptized in the parish church of San Fernando.

Intermarriage between English-speaking and Spanish-speaking families is somewhat unusual in Texas at the present day, but it was common in the early days of American settlement, when many young men, going to seek their fortunes in the new country, were fascinated by the Spanish girls. Hence many of the oldest families in San Antonio and elsewhere in Southwest Texas, bearing English, German, French and Irish names, have a considerable admixture of Spanish "blood." In San Antonio the Spanish ancestors are commonly spoken of as "Canary Islanders," both to distinguish them from "Mexicans" and because, in the general vagueness of knowledge concerning early Texas history, it is mistakenly thought that the Islanders were the first settlers, some sort of Plymouth Rock equivalent.

The Catholic Church, which came in with the first explorers, continues to flourish, drawing parishioners from later German, Irish, Czech, Italian and Polish immigration as well as from the Spanish-speaking people. Young priests still serve as "missionaries" under the Archbishop of San Antonio, even though their missions are neat clapboarded chapels and their spiritual wards are no longer Indians.

The visitor to Southwestern Texas even today is continually reminded of Spain and Mexico by the prevailing architecture, both because of direct Spanish influence and because the climatic problems have called for similar solutions regardless of what architectural tradition was being followed. The straight tradition has been more often abused than well used, in Texas as in the rest of the United States, and too much of the Spanish architecture has made a detour by way of California, shedding its functional characteristics and retaining only pointless details.

On the other hand, probably without conscious influence, many of the good, simple "ranch type" houses in the new subdivisions bear a striking resemblance to an early indigenous Texas architecture which was developed by adding pitched roofs and verandas to the flat-roofed, featureless Spanish house resembling those still seen in Mexico. Arranged to catch the prevailing southeast breeze, and with overhanging eaves to fend off the sun, nothing could be more comfortable in the Texas climate than this type of dwelling. Motels and small one-story business establishments still favor the flat-roofed Mexican type. Churches of various denominations are patterned after the Spanish missions, which is very well, although the missions have been imitated less happily in building railroad stations, movie houses and skyscrapers.

The Spanish word *patio,* which originally denoted an enclosed courtyard, now means, in Texas and other warm portions of the United States, any paved outdoor area which is used for such activities as eating and lounging. A regular feature of the backyards of Texas houses is the "patty-o," perhaps only twelve or sixteen feet square, often separated from the house to catch the maximum breeze, and equipped with tables and chairs with a barbecue pit at one side. Here the family and its guests gather on warm summer evenings, when the southeast breeze usually cools the outdoors before the heat of the day has quitted the walls of the house. Though different both in form and purpose from the Spanish-Mexican *patio*—which was designed to provide an outdoor area of safety from bandits, wild Indians and rebellious peons—the Texas patio can hardly be denied its name, for it is a logical development from its Mexican prototype. The protective features are no longer necessary, and its removal from the guardian walls makes it all the more suitable for its prime purpose of refuge from the heat.

The patio tradition of "outdoor living" is closely related to the development of such facilities as drive-in theaters and outdoor restaurants. San Antonio even has two annual outdoor art shows, and restaurants sometimes present plays and operettas, arena-style, in their patios. It would be a mistake, of course, to assign all these phenomena to the Spanish tradition, but the continuity of climatic influence is interesting.

The climate, as well as the Spanish heritage, probably has important bearings on another aspect of Texas life—the tendency to go slow, take it easy, and put off doing whatever will keep until *mañana.* This tendency was evident both in the original Spanish inhabitants and in the people from the Old South who flocked into Texas a hundred or more years ago, and the attitude is one which has been easily imitated by later arrivals from the North and East—many of whom, if the truth were known, were probably attracted by that very thing. Texas, even in its southern part, has its share of go-getters, as the economic development of the State will attest, but even these are a little less quick in their movements, a little less subject to ulcers, than their equivalents in New York or Chicago. Certainly they are disinclined to any action which does not have clear-cut advantages enough to overbalance the comfort of delay.

In deliberately setting out to write a chapter on the Spanish influences in modern Texas, there is some danger of exaggerating their importance. On the other hand, this Spanish heritage has too long been minimized by people who would prefer to think that everything good and significant in the State came in with Stephen F. Austin. A balanced view would seem to indicate that, while Anglo-American culture has been dominant in Texas since 1836, the Spanish influence is stronger here today than in any other state except New Mexico, and will become stronger still as the Mexican-descended minority, already growing in numbers at a more rapid rate than the Anglo-American, gains also in education and political awareness. We must bear in mind, however, that the newer and often militant generation of Mexican-Americans, taking their cue from the advocates of *Indianismo* in Mexico itself, emphasize their Indian heritage and minimize or ignore the traditions long since implanted by the Spanish overlords, even though in fact Mexican cultures today is at least as far removed from Montezuma as from Ferdinand and Isabella. To labor these facts would lead us far afield into questions that are disputed among the Mexican-Americans themselves, but the point should be noted.

1

The Search for the Cities of Gold

The real discoverer of Texas, though others before him had sailed along the coast, was a mild-mannered hidalgo named Alvar Nuñez Cabeza de Vaca. He was a sober, conscientious gentleman, 37 years of age and a stay-at-home during the most adventurous years in Spanish history, now sent along by the king as a sort of duenna to the wild conquistadores who composed the expedition led by *Panfilo de Narváez* to the North American mainland in 1528. This man, sneered at though he was by some of the officers of the Indies as a prig and a carpet soldier, was one of only four men who survived an ordeal that took the lives of three hundred, and who then went on to eventual safety through eight years of wandering naked in the wilderness.

In return for financing his expedition, Narváez was granted the usual rights of exploitation in the new land. With him as royal treasurer, to collect the king's share of newfound wealth, went Cabeza de Vaca, a genteel native of Jerez de la Frontera who thus far had done nothing of any note, but who through incredible hardship, was soon to win the distinction with his

10

companions, of being the first explorer of Texas and the first man to cross the North American continent by a route lying partially within what is now the United States.

Cabeza de Vaca received his odd surname (Cow's Head) through the exploit of an ancestor who saved the king's army by marking an obscure mountain pass with the skull of a cow, and was ennobled for his thoughtfulness. The ancestor was on the distaff side, but by a custom of the time young Alvar had had the option of taking either his father's name or his mother's, and he apparently chose the one which he considered the more distinguished, although his paternal grandfather, Pedro de Vera, had been the conqueror of the Canary Islands. (Incidentally, the three parts of the surname are inseparable in the documents of the time, so apparently it is incorrect to refer to the man as "Vaca" or "De Vaca.")

Little is known of Cabeza de Vaca's early life, but it is evident from his later actions and utterances that he must have come under the influence of Bartolome de las Casas. That saintly priest of the Indies had made two trips to Spain during Cabeza de Vaca's young manhood, and a meeting is not improbable. In any case, Las Casas' teachings—that the Indians had souls and must be treated as human beings—were accepted by the royal court and were common talk in Spain at this period. Cabeza de Vaca's role in the expedition is also significant. As the treasurer, he had a direct obligation to the king. Besides prescribing his routine duties, his royal warrant for the expedition included the words, "Informing us . . . especially how our commands are obeyed and executed in thos lands and provinces, of how the natives are treated, our instructions observed, and other of the things respecting their liberties that we have commanded. . . ."

What these instructions meant can be deduced from the fact that Narváez's *cedula* for the expedition rigorously stipulated that the Indians should not be enslaved, nor taken from their homes nor put to labor against their will; that clerics should go along to instruct and convert the natives and protect them from the Christian laity; that barter should not be forced, and fortresses should be built only for security, not for aggression: and other things of similar tenor which sound like the voice of Las Casas.

After a short start and many reverses, the Narváez expedition landed in Florida on Good Friday, April 10, and Governor Narváez ceremonially took possession of the country, having no doubt that he would be able to add tangible reality to the ritual. Against the advice of Cabeza de Vaca, who wanted the expedition to stay with its ships, Narváez led three hundred men on an inland expedition to search for the rumored city of Apalache, which

11

the Indians had told them was rich in gold. They at last found the city, a miserable Indian village lacking the reported wealth, near the Apalachicola River in West Florida.

Harassed by Indians, the Spaniards returned to the sea, hundreds of miles from the bay where they had left the ships. By this time so many men were sick that the forty horses could not carry all of them. Finally, in desperation, the company decided to build some kind of craft in which to strike out along the coast for the Spanish settlement of Santiestevan on the Pánuco River in Mexico, which they believed to be not far distant.

"It seemed impossible," writes Cabeza de Vaca, "as none of us knew how to construct ships. We had no tools, no iron, no smithery, no oakum, no pitch, tackling; in fine, nothing of what was indispensable. Neither was there anybody to instruct us in ship-building, and above all there was nothing to eat while the work was going on."

The food problem was solved by raiding an Indian village for corn and by killing a horse every third day for meat. By September 20, seven weeks after the work started, five barges of twenty-two "elbow lengths" had been hammered together and caulked with palmetto oakum and tarred with pitch made from the local pines. More than forty men had died from disease and starvation, and all but one of the horses had been eaten. Ten other men had been killed by Indian arrows which went right through their chain-mail armor. In the five make shift barges embarked the 251 officers and men left alive out of more than three hundred who had left the ships so bravely four months before.

"So great is the power of need," says Cabeza de Vaca in his *Relacion*, "that it brought us to venture out into such a troublesome sea in this manner, and without anyone among us having the least knowledge of the art of navigation." All of the sailors had stayed with the ships. Where were the ships? No one knew.

Seven days the barges floated through the inlets along the coast, where the water was only waist deep. At last they found the open Gulf and set out toward the Pánuco. After thirty days of painfully slow travel there came a terrific storm, and the pitiful little fleet hid under the lee of a small island. Here five men died from drinking salt brine, for no fresh water could be found. So the party went on, having decided that they would "rather risk the perils of the sea than wait there for certain death from thirst."

At sunset they turned a point of land and found an Indian village where the inhabitants first feasted them with fish and corn, then fell upon them with savage war-whoops. In a nightlong battle, at least fifty of the Spaniards were wounded, but apparently none was killed. Three days later there was another landing and another battle, in which the Spaniards lost two hostages.

A little farther on, they dipped fresh water out of the sea at what must have been the mouth of the Mississippi. They tried to land, but the powerful current carried them out to sea. Soon Cabeza de Vaca could see only two barges besides his own. The men on these three remaining barges took to their oars and pulled hard all day for the land, without success. Toward sunset Cabeza de Vaca asked Narváez, who had the healthiest and strongest men, to allow the barges to be tied together so that they could pull in unison. But the Governor refused, saying that "each one should do the best he could to save himself."

Soon the Governor's barge, too, was lost to sight, Cabeza de Vaca's and the one other remaining barge traveled together for four days, until the other was lost in a storm. There were now left, with Cabeza de Vaca, the Inspector Alonzo de Solis and forty-nine men under their joint command. Even these few, fortunate enought to survive, were in great suffering from cold, hunger and the buffeting of the waves. "The next day people began to break down, so that when the sun set all those aboard my barge had fallen in a heap and were so near dying that few remained conscious, and not five men kept their feet."

For these many days the frail, crazy craft had been out of sight of land, with no means of setting a course but the will of God. Before dawn of the day following that dreadful sunset, Cabeza de Vaca thought he heard the sound of breakers. Incredulous, he woke the skipper, who agreed. They took a sounding and found seven fathoms. They tried to keep off shore till daylight, but a wave caught the little barge and hurled it the distance of a horseshoe pitch out of the water on a flat, sandy beach.

"With the violent shock nearly all of the people who lay in the boat as if dead came to themselves and, seeing we were close to land, began to crawl out on all fours. As they took to some rocks, we built a fire and toasted some of our maize. We found rain water, and with the warmth of the fire people revived and began to cheer up."

The date was November 6, 1528. The place was Galveston Island, on the coast of Texas.

Lope de Oviedo, the strongest of the survivors, managed to climb a tree for a better view. He shouted down that the place was an island and that the ground was pitted with the tracks of cattle, from which fact the castaways, not yet knowing the buffalo, concluded that this must be a land of Christian men. Oviedo also found a footpath which he followed for a mile or so to a small cluster of Indian huts whose occupants were evidently out hunting. So he picked up a cooking pot and all the edible stuff he could find—a little dog and a few fish.

Soon afterward the Spaniards were confronted by a hundred Indian braves who, although they were not very big fellows, looked like giants to the terrified castaways. Fortunately Cabeza de Vaca still had some trade goods—beads and bells—with which he pacified the savages. They promised to come back next morning with food, for they had none at the time. This promise they kept with plenty of fish and some roots, with a nutlike taste, which they had dug up out of the shallow water along the shore. Strengthened by the food, the castaways decided to put to sea again and try to beat their way to the Pánuco. So they took off all their clothes, put them on the barge and waded into the water to dislodge the craft, which had become embedded in the sand. Two crossbow shots from shore, a wave caught the barge and threw the naked men into the Gulf, killing Solis and two others who were caught underneath.

This new predicament, without the barge and naked against the north wind, appeared hopeless, and so it turned out to be for the great majority. "It was in November, bitterly cold, and we in such a state that every bone could easily be counted, and we looked like death itself," Cabeza de Vaca recalled. When the Indians saw the Spaniards in this desperate condition, they ran away in fright. But when Cabeza de Vaca explained by signs what had happened, the Indians sat down and wept loudly for half an hour. Later visitors found that weeping was a social ritual among the Indians of the Texas Coast, who "wept indifferently for good or evil," according to Simars de Bellisle.

The huddled group of castaways debated whether they should ask for shelter in the homes of the Indians. Some, who had been in New Spain, opposed this plan, saying that if they entrusted themselves to the Indians they would be sure to meet death in a bloody sacrifice. Cabeza de Vaca, however, decided that possible death in an Indian village was preferable to sure death on the beach, so he asked the Indians to take the castaways to their homes. With expressions of pleasure, the savages agreed. They immediately began gathering firewood with which they built a series of fires along the trail to their village, while the shivering Spaniards wondered if they were to be delivered from the fury of the north wind only to meet death as burnt offerings.

14

The real purpose of the fires soon appeared, however, for the Indians picked up the castaways—light loads because of their long starvation—and carried them from fire to fire, warming them at each one before they hurried on to the next. At the village a newly built lodge was ready with many fires in it. Here the still terrified and suspicious castaways uneasily rested while the Indians danced and howled in a nightlong ceremonial which the Spaniards thought must be a prelude to human sacrifice. In the morning, however, the castaways were again fed and were treated so kindly that they were somewhat reassured.

It was probably at this point, though he does not quite say so, that the theories learned from Las Casas began to be a living reality for Cabeza de Vaca. Surely, beings without immortal souls could not be imbued with such kindness, and there must be much good in a people who could so tenderly care for these naked strangers, sharing their own meager subsistence with the hairy, light-skinned men from another world, who could reasonably have been regarded as enemies.

That same day Cabeza de Vaca's party found the Captains Andres Dorantes and Alonso del Castillo, with all their crew, who had been cast ashore a day earlier and four miles away. Here was hope again, for the other barge had not been lost, so a plan was worked out whereby those members of both parties who were strong and willing should put to sea again, while the rest would remain on the coast until they were restored to strength or until a rescue party could come for them. If this seems like a plan to desert the weaker ones, we must remember that the distance and difficulties of the overland journey to Santiesteban were still being greatly underestimated.

But a new shock of disaster came when the barge proved to be full of holes and sank almost as soon as it touched the water. So the party of eighty men, half of them naked and all starved and sick, decided to winter on the island, which they named Malhado (Ill Fortune), while four of the most able-bodied should go overland to the Pánuco in search of help. These four departed, taking an Indian as a guide.

In a few days the weather on Malhado Island became so cold and stormy that the Indians could neither fish nor pull roots. Still more people died of starvation, and five of the Spaniards, who had made their camp a little apart from the rest, "were driven to such an extremity that they ate each other up until only one remained, who being left alone there was nobody to eat him."

The story of European penetration into the Americas is largely a history of friendly Indians whose good will is turned to hostility by the acts of the invading "Christians." So it was on Malhado Island. At the cannibalism of the white men "the Indians were so startled, and there was such an uproar among them, that I verily believe if they had seen this at the beginning they would have killed them, and we all would have been in great danger."

To these simple Indians, hunger was a normal state, and they would no more have thought of eating their companions than of devouring their own arms and legs. Later travelers report cannibalism among the coast tribes of Texas, but this was of a ceremonial nature, for spiritual rather than physical sustenance, and the victims were captured enemies, not members of the tribe. Strangely enough, in all his wanderings, Cabeza de Vaca reports no instance, not even a rumor, of cannibalism among the Indians. If the Karankawas of the Texas Coast were cannibals at a later date, can it be that the custom was introduced among them by the "Christians?" Though this be a fantastic speculation, the thought cannot be kept back.

What with hunger and disease, in a little while only fifteen of the eighty castaways were left alive. The natives also fell sick so that half of them died; among those who remained, the suspicion grew that the Spaniards—evil men who ate each other—were in some magical way responsible for the death of the Indians. Some of the headmen of the village argued that it would be expedient to kill the few Christians who still survived. But the Indian who was Cabeza de Vaca's host replied that, if the Spaniards had so much power, they would not allow so many of their own men to die. So the castaways were spared.

But although they acquitted the Spaniards of black magic, many of the Indians still insisted that the strange men from out of the sea must have miraculous powers, for they evidently knew many things that the Indians had no idea of. So "they wanted to make medicine men of us without any examination or asking for our diplomas," says Cabeza de Vaca with a rare flash of humor. The Spaniards tried to laugh off the suggestion, but the Indians would not be gainsaid, and insisted that since their guests were useless in hunting and fishing they must be doctors to earn their keep. So the Spaniards reluctantly agreed.

The Indians' own medicine men would make a few cuts at the site of any pain, suck the blood for a time, cauterize the wound with fire, then breathe on it. Cabeza de Vaca agreed with the Indians that this technique was very effective, but, perhaps impelled by aesthetic as well as religious considerations, he adopted a more European method. "The way we treated the sick was to make over them the sign of the cross while breathing on them, recite a Pater Noster and Ave Maria, and pray to God, Our Lord, as best we could to give them good health and inspire them to do us some favors."

This method of healing proved to be surprisingly effective. "Thanks to His will and the mercy He had upon us, all those for whom we prayed, as soon as we crossed them, told the others that they were cured and felt well again. For this they gave us good cheer, and would rather be without food themselves so as to give it to us, and they gave us hides and other small things."

Food was so scarce, however, that Indians and Spaniards alike sometimes went without eating for as much as three days at a time.

These Indians, said Cabeza de Vaca, were tall and well formed. The men decorated their bodies with long pieces of cane thrust through perforations in their nipples and their lower lips; they were otherwise naked except when they wore robes of buffalo hide, deerskin or fur against the cold. The women covered the private parts of their bodies with Spanish moss, while the girls went about in deerskins. The coast tribes had no rulers: they clustered together in clans, and were extremely generous in sharing.

After separating in search of food during a part of the winter, the castaways reassembled on Malhado Island on the first of April, 1529. Cabeza de Vaca was not with them, for he was sick almost to death at a place on the mainland. Twelve of the survivors crossed over to see him, leaving two on the island who were too feeble to go along. On the way the twelve picked up another Spaniard, raising the total number of known survivors to sixteen. After visiting Cabeza de Vaca, the thirteen able-bodied men set out to beat their way along the coast toward the Pánuco.

Apparently Cabeza de Vaca's illness cost him his reputation as a faith-healer. At any rate the Indians now required him to go out and do women's work, for he seems to have been incompetent in the masculine arts of war and hunting. "Among many other troubles I had to pull the edible roots out of the water and from among the canes where they were buried in the ground, and from this my fingers had become so tender that the mere touch of a straw caused them to bleed." Cabeza de Vaca refers to his condition at this period as that of a "slave." However, he does not indicate that these Indians ever tried to restrain him from going where he would; all they did was require him to earn his keep. But the work was too hard for him, so he joined another tribe on the mainland and became a trader.

This was a welcome service to the aborigines, among whom trade was extinct—if it had ever existed—because of the continuous intertribal wars. So the *hidalgo* of Jerez de la Frontera became a peddler with a pack, carrying seashells and cockles, shell beads and other specialties of the Coast which he exchanged in the inland areas for buffalo and deer hides, red ochre, flint for arrow points, glue and hard canes to make arrows, and red-dyed tassels of deer hair. He was well treated and fed wherever he went, and became such a famous character that the Indians would flock out, merely to see him, when they had nothing to trade. Wherever he went, he kept a sharp eye out for a trail that might lead to Christian lands.

Despite his improved situation and the hardening that must have come during his four years as a trader, Cabeza de Vaca's lot was still not easy. "My suffering, while trading thus, it would take me long to tell; danger, hunger, storms and frost overtaking me often in the open field and alone, and from which through the mercy of God, Our Lord, I escaped." He was as naked as the Indians, and like them he did not venture out in cold weather except under strict necessity.

Once every year he went back to Galveston Island to plead with Lope de Oviedo, the lone survivor of the two who had stayed there, to go with him "in search of Christians." Each year, Oviedo put off his departure until the year following, apparently because he had found an Indian woman and was too content with the simplicity of his animal existence to attempt the hazardous quest for civilization. Finally, however, he agreed, and the two went with several Indians down the coast to Matagorda Bay.

Here they got news of the party of thirteen which had left them on Galveston Island four years before. Farther on, the Indians told Cabeza de Vaca and Oviedo, there were three white men survivors from a larger party, of whom three had been killed by the Indians and the rest had died of cold and hunger. Here, among the Indians who knew the other Christians, Cabeza de Vaca met his first ill treatment at the hands of the savages. "They threw mud at us, and put arrows to our chests every day, saying they would kill us in the same way as our other companions." At this the faint-hearted Lope de Oviedo decided to go back to Malhado Island with some Indian women who were traveling that way, and he was never heard of again.

Left alone, picking pecans for food, Cabeza de Vaca found Andres Dorantes, Alonso del Castillo and Dorantes' Moorish or Negro slave, Estebanico. "That day was one of the happiest we enjoyed in our time," says Cabeza de Vaca. They talked of joining forces to make their way to Mexico, but the trio were slaves of the Indians, who would kill them if they tried to escape. So they decided to wait for a more opportune time.

The newfound survivors brought news of Governor Narváez and the passengers on the two barges that had disappeared with him. Various

18

members of these parties had died in various ways, after their barges had landed on the Texas Coast. The Governor, staying overnight on his beached barge with a pilot and a sick page, had been swept out to sea by a sudden norther. The rest continued overland for some time, racked by cold and hunger. "Thus they perished one after another, the survivors slicing up the dead for meat."

So it became horrifyingly evident that, of the 300 men who had gallantly marched into Florida five years before, the only ones left alive were Cabeza de Vaca, the king's treasurer; the Captains Alonzo del Castillo and Andres Dorantes, and the slave Estebanico, all reduced to substantial equality on the lowest level of existence as naked castaways and slaves of the miserable Indians of the Texas Coast, from whence they could return to civilization, if at all, only by traveling unknown distances through too easily imagined hardships and dangers.

2

The Children of the Sun

Cabaza de Vaca, being evidently a man of more energy of mind than the rest, easily took the lead, and soon the aimless wandering of the four castaways turned to a purposeful journey. The treasurer's higher official position may have helped him a little in gaining the ascendancy, but not much, for distinctions of rank must have been pretty well washed out after five years in the wilderness, with no certainty of ever returning to Christian lands. Even Estebanico, technically a slave of slaves, seems to have reached a position relatively near equality to the whites, and his superior aptitude for languages made him the interpreter of the expedition. It is not quite certain, by the way, whether he was a Negro or an Arab Moor, for the Spanish word *negro* was then used indifferently for both. However, he was a large man, which would be remarkable in an Arab but not in a Negro, and the Indians marveled at his blackness, which they would hardly have done if he had been an Arab, no darker than the Indians themselves.

The castaways decided that the most opportune time to escape would be the annual migration of the Indians to the tuna (prickly pear) fields southeast of the site of modern San Antonio. The diet of these Indians was as astonishing in its variety as it was unappetizing. Their principal foods were two or three kinds of roots, mostly bitter and carminative. "Now and then they kill a deer and at times get a fish, but this is so little and their hunger is so great that they eat spiders and ant pupas, worms, lizards and salamanders and serpents, also vipers the bite of which is deadly. They swallow earth and wood, and all they can get, the dung of deer and more things I do not mention; and I verily believe, from what I saw, that if there were any stones in the country they would eat them also. They preserve the bones of the fish they eat, of snakes and other animals, to pulverize them and eat the powder."

Not many hundreds of miles away there were far more advanced tribes, who cultivated the soil, wove cotton, and lived in permanent houses. These wretched coast people had probably, long since, been forced outward to the periphery of the continent by the pressure of stronger and more efficient tribes in the interior.

In spite of their chronic semi-starvation, Cabeza de Vaca tells us, the Indians of the Coast were strong enough to run after a deer until it was worn out. He adds, "They are a very merry people, and even when famished do not cease to dance and celebrate their feasts and ceremonials." Cabeza de Vaca never seemed to learn that these "celebrations" were not the expression of sheer exuberance but were religious affairs designed for definite purposes, often for the magical bringing of the very food which the Indians lacked.

At last came the time when the tunas were ripe. The fruit of the tuna, which is bright red when it is "green," is purple when ripe, resembling a fig in appearance and a watered-down huckleberry in flavor. Tunas are still eaten and made into jam by the Mexicans in South Texas. Cabeza de Vaca's Indians would squeeze them open and set them out to dry. When dried they were carried in baskets to be eaten on the way. The peelings were ground and pulverized. What was done to prevent injury from the viciously sharp spines is a mystery which this writer has not been able to fathom.

The tuna fields were full of mosquitoes, so the Indians built smudge fires all about their camps. Sometimes the smoke and heat were worse than the mosquitoes, and when the Spaniards managed to fall asleep the Indians would waken them with blows to go and rekindle the fires.

In this country Cabeza de Vaca's party became the first white men to meet with the bison or American buffalo, which Cabeza de Vaca described accurately although he called them simply "cows."

Plans for escape went all awry when the Indians split up after a

21

fight over a woman, taking their slaves with them in opposite directions. So it became necessary to wait another year for the next tuna harvest. Badly treated and ill fed, Cabeza de Vaca tried three times to escape by himself, but was brought back each time. Between the lines one can read that Cabeza de Vaca had deep religious scruples against the practice of faith healing, for he must have known that a little judicious quackery at this stage might have gone far to relieve his own suffereings.

Next year the four castaways met on the same spot as before, but were immediately separated. Thirteen days later, Cabeza de Vaca, Dorantes and Estebanico managed to come together, found Castillo, and fled with him into the wilderness. It was in September, 1534, nearly six years from the day when they had been cast ashore on Malhado Island, that the three Spaniards and the African slave began the incredible journey which brought them to a meeting with other Christians near the west coast of Mexico eighteen months later.

Two days after leaving the tuna camp, the party saw the smoke of an Indian village and hurried toward it. Soon they found an old Indian who, frightened at the apparition of three white men and a black, ran away. Cabeza de Vaca sent the Negro ahead by himself as evidence of peaceable intent, and finally the Indian agreed to guide the strangers to the dwelling place of his people, a different tribe from that which the Spaniards had left. Here they were hospitably received because, in the words of Oviedo y Valdes, the contemporary historian who talked with Cabeza de Vaca, these Indians "were very gentle and had some knowledgge of the Christians, though little, because they did not know how badly the others had treated them (which was a very fine thing for those sinners)."

These new Indians, whom Cabeza de Vaca called the Avavares, may just possibly have been the 16th-century inhabitants of San Antonio. The people who lived around San Pedro Springs in what is now San Antonio a century and a half later were called Payayas, but since all these Indians were somewhat nomadic, the Payayas are not necessarily the same people who lived there at an earlier date, and in any case none of the early explorers can be trusted to reproduce Indian names with even the distant approach to accuracy that European alphabets permit. On purely geographical grounds, it is not unlikely that the village of the Avavares was at San Antonio, for it is fairly certain that the tuna fields were southeast of the present city, and that the course which our travelers now took was toward the northwest.

The Avavares had heard of the miraculous cures worked by the bearded medicine men, and the same night that they arrived in the village the

Spaniards were besieged with sick Indians begging for relief. With prayer and the sign of the cross, the patients promptly felt better, and by way of reward gave the Spaniards so much venison that they did not know where to store it all.

Cold weather was coming on, so the Spaniards decided to spend the winter with the Avavares. The venison must have given out, for the tribe now went in search of the seeds of the "ebony-tree." (Possibly the persimmon, a member of the ebony family.) Castillo apparently was the most successful of the four as a faith-healer, though they all took part, justifying their unorthodox conduct (only a priest was supposed to perform cures) on the ground that "there was no way of getting these people to help us so that we might be saved from our miserable existence." Many times the cures worked, or at least the sick men felt relief, and Cabeza de Vaca, though he had more than an inkling of the power of suggestion, attributed his success as a healer simply to the mercy of God.

As the Spaniards moved from tribe to tribe, "nothing was talked about in the whole country but the wonderful cures which God, Our Lord, performed through us, and so they came from many places to be cured." In one case Cabeza de Vaca administered his spiritual treatment to a man who was supposed to be already dead, and later it was reported that the man had returned to life. In return for such ghostly services the Indians pressed upon the Spaniards all their possessions, which were pitifully little. During the eight months that the Spaniards remained among the Avavares, Indians came to them from all points of the compass and hailed them as verily "Children of the Sun." (In the same general area, in 1948, a Negro called Elder A. Bonds drew thousands of persons, some of them perhaps descendants of the Avavares, to his faith-healing meetings in the San Antonio parks.)

"I was the most daring and reckless of all in undertaking cures," says Cabeza de Vaca. "We never treated anyone that did not afterward say he was well, and they had such confidence in our skill as to believe that none of them would die as long as we were among them."

But despite the generosity of the Indians, the Spaniards, like their hosts, were always hungry. While waiting for the tunas to ripen again, they were reduced to eating some sort of green fruit that contained a burning, milky juice. Water was as scarce as food. The naked travelers froze in winter, and in summer their sunburned skins ulcerated in great sores, while the ropes which held their heavy loads of water and firewood cut into the flesh of their shoulders and arms. Scraping a skin for the Indians was the greatest luxury he enjoyed, says Cabeza de Vaca, for he could eat the parings and save enough of them to last two or three days. When someone gave the Spaniards a piece of meat, they would eat it raw "because if we broiled it the first Indian coming along would snatch and eat it."

Though the narrative is vague on this point as on many others, it is evident that there were wide fluctuations in the demand for the Spaniards' services as healers and in the treatment which they received from the Indians. It seems likely that the more difficult periods through which they passed may have been the result of failures in their healing efforts, which took them a while to live down. It is also probable that they encountered varying temperaments in the different tribes among which they traveled.

Their strength restored a little by the flesh of two dogs which they had bought from the Indians, the Spaniards decided it was time to go father on—*mas allá,* a poetic phrase which runs like a refrain through all the chronicles of Spanish exploration. After becoming lost in the woods, they came up to another village where the inhabitants were afraid of them at first but soon begged for medical aid and feasted the travelers with tuna leaves and the baked green fruit. After a few days here, the Spaniards moved on again, though the Indians fell on their knees and begged them to stay.

The same drama was repeated in another village, where the Spaniards became acquainted with the mesquite bean, which the Indians mixed with carth to sweeten it before eating. Four leagues beyond this village the travelers reached a spring which Cleve Hallenbeck has identified as Big Spring, near the modern town of that name. They were far into West Central Texas, having crossed two-thirds of the state, if Hallenbeck's reading is correct. Cabeza de Vaca's itinerary is so vague that the several scholars who have tried to determine his route have come up with widely different conclusions. However, Hallenbeck has done the most thorough job and, being the latest, had the benefit of the mistakes of his predecessors, so his account has been accepted for the purposes of this simple narrative. In any case the exact route is unimportant beside the great human story of these first travelers through North America.

Word of the healers' coming must now have traveled ahead of them, for at the next village after Big Spring there were no signs of fear, but the Indians nearly squeezed the Spaniards to death in their eagerness to touch them. After this there arose a new custom. When the Spaniards moved on, their hosts went with them to the next village and took away from the people of the next place their bows and arrows, their shoes and beads, such as they had, plundering their homes. The victims took this in good part, "saying that we should not worry, that they were so happy at seeing us as to gladly lose their property," and besides they would recoup their losses by repeating the procedure, still farther on. "On that whole journey we were much worried by the number of people following us."

Then they saw the mountains, sweeping down rank on rank from the North. These were (says Hallenbeck) the Guadalupe Mountains, which rise to 6,000 feet above sea level and 3,000 feet above the plateau west of the Pecos River. The travelers, seeking Mexico, kept on toward the west, for as long as the streams ran south they imagined the Gulf was still south of them as it had been when they were slaves of the Karankawas, and they wished to avoid the cruel tribes of the Coast. After crossing the divide where the streams began to run toward the West, they would turn south into Mexico.

During this stage of the journey the Spaniards were given two gourd rattles by the native medicine men—objects which were held in such respect that they increased the owners' authority among the Indians. At another village Dorantes was given a large rattle of copper, decorated with a face, which appeared to have been moulded in a foundry. This was the highest evidence of civilization that the Spaniards had seen since they left their barges. It was supposed to have come from the North, where much more of the same material was said to exist.

In this area, near the intersecting borders of Texas, Mexico and New Mexico today, the Spaniards continued their triumphal progress among so many tribes that Cabeza de Vaca, writing his story later, could not attempt to remember all of them. At times as many as three or four thousand Indians traveled with the Children of the Sun, quite out of control because of their sheer numbers, although they showed such veneration for the healers that they would not eat a morsel without first having it blessed by one of the four. Besides blessing the food, the Spaniards were constantly called upon to give their specific benedictions to many other activities of the Indians.

Once, just when the Spaniards had become angry because the Indians were afraid to show them the way into a trackless stretch of country, it happened that many of the redskins fell sick, and eight of them died. All of the Indians who saw or even heard of this portentous occurrence were so frightened, it seemed as if a mere look from the Spaniards would kill them. In another place, Cabeza de Vaca laid aside his spiritual role to perform a real surgical operation on an Indian who suffered from an old arrowhead stuck close to his heart. Cabeza de Vaca opened the man's chest with a stone knife, pried out the arrow, and sewed up the incision with a needle of deer bone.

In this region the four travelers saw things and heard rumors which were to have far-reaching consequences when they carried the story back to Mexico. First Dorantes and his slave made a side trip to "a river which flows between mountains" (evidently the Rio Grande) where they found people who lived in permanent houses and raised beans, squash and corn—the highest type of civilization the castaways had yet seen. The rest of the party, overjoyed, quickly went to these houses, but Cabeza de Vaca does not describe them in detail in his written narrative. After thirty-four more days of slow travel, seventeen of them up the river and seventeen more to the west, the travelers found other permanent houses, where the people raised cotton from which they made blankets. At the end of another hundred leagues, which took them into Mexico, they were given five "emeralds" (probably malachite), shaped into arrow points, which the Indians used in their ceremonials, and many turquoises, both of which were said to come from a region of high mountains in the North, where there were populous villages with great houses. When Cabeza de Vaca's party returned to Mexico, as we shall see, these villages were immediately identified as the fabled Seven Cities founded by seven bishops who had fled from the Moorish invader of the Iberian Peninsual 800 years before.

At last, while the eager travelers were waiting for a swollen river to go down so that they could cross it, came a thrill the like of which few men can ever have experienced. After these eight years of wandering naked in the wilderness, with only the vaguest idea of where civilization might be found, Castillo saw an Indian wearing on a buckskin thong around his neck a little buckle from a Spanish sword-belt, and in it was sewn a horseshoe nail.

The Indian said his trinket had come "from heaven." Pressed for further details of its manner of arrival, he answered "that some men, with beards like ours, had come from heaven to that river; that they had horses, lances and swords, and had lanced two of the Indians."

Surely these must be Christians! With new hope, mingled with certain qualms, Cabeza de Vaca and his companions pressed on. They found the whole country almost deserted, for the people had fled to the mountains in fear of the Christians, who had come burning, pillaging, killing and taking slaves. "This filled our hearts with sorrow, seeing the land so fertile and beautiful, so full of water and streams, but abandoned and the villages burned down, and the people, so thin and wan, fleeing and hiding."

When Cabeza de Vaca, tired and worn, asked the others to go ahead and make contact with the Christians, they all excused themselves, "although any one of them might have done it far better than I, being younger and stronger." So Cabeza de Vaca took the Negro and eleven Indians and after a day's journey he came upon a party of Spaniards on horseback, led by Diego de Alcaraz, a lieutenant of the cruel governor Nuño de Guzman of Culiacán.

"They stared at me for a long time, speechless," says Cabeza de Vaca. "So great was their surprise that they could not find words to ask me anything." Even so might a space traveler of the twenty-first century stare at an earthly castaway found on the moon.

Diego de Alcaraz himself was in a bad way; for many days now he had not been able to catch any slaves, and his men were starving for lack of loot. Yet Cabeza de Vaca, backed even in his isolation by the authority of Church and State, prevailed upon the captain not to make slaves of the Indians who had followed the Children of the Sun from the North. Among themselves the Indians decided that Cabeza de Vaca and his party were really not Christians at all, for they did not ride horses, or wear clothes, or steal, or kill.

The travelers were hardly out of sight on their way to Culiacan, however, before Alcaraz fell upon the helpless Indians. The three Spaniards and the Negro went on to confront Melchor Diaz, the chief alcalde and captain of the presidio at Culiacán, who appears to have been a just man, although a man of his time and place. Impressed with Cabeza de Vaca's arguments, Diaz pledged himself before God, Our Lord, to take no more slaves—at least not until he was ordered to do so by Governor de Guzmán or the King.

So, at the first outpost of civilization in New Spain, ended Cabeza de Vaca's eight years of unpremeditated exploration through Texas and the adjacent regions, an adventure the like of which can hardly be found anywhere else in history. It was undoubtedly due in great part to Cabeza de Vaca's stubborn force of character that the four "Children of the Sun"— themselves the only known survivors of the three hundred in the Narváez expedition—were able to go on, for it was Cabeza de Vaca who had found the three others wandering aimlessly and had begun to lead them in a purposeful expedition. All four, of course, must have been physically rugged to withstand the hardships of cold and starvation and disease that had killed their companions. They must also have been of strong character to avoid the temptations of suicide and cannibalism and the situations that led to some of the Spaniards' being killed by the Indians. But Cabeza de Vaca was undoubtedly the real leader, though he does not say so and there is no clear indication that he was so regarded.

At the same time Cabeza de Vaca was evidently a man of only moderate intelligence, not a philosopher or a man of profound insight. The late Haniel Long, in his excellent little book, *The Power Within Us*, tries to read into Cabeza de Vaca's story a spiritual growth of realization of the brotherhood of man, an odyssey of the soul as well as of the body, but Long's attempt is successful only in the way that highly significant fiction can be successful. While it is certainly true that Cabeza de Vaca set out as a member of an expedition of conquest and ended, after his experience of living among the Indians, by defending them against "Christian" attempts at enslavement, there is no indication either in his own book or in other contemporary documents that he underwent any radical change of heart. If anything, his increased understanding of the savage mind only reinforced the ideas of justice which he had acquired in Spain long before he sailed with Narváez—ideas which, although rejected by many of the men of action in the New World, became more popular the farther one traveled away from the frontier toward the royal court. And he had gone as a direct representative of the King to see that the humane laws were not broken.

He certainly knew, too, after his experience in Texas, that the Indians, highly though he regarded them, were not altogether the lovable, pure-hearted people that Las Casas, anticipating Rousseau by more than two hundred years, had alleged them to be. Said Las Casas: "God created them simple, lacking in malice and duplicity, very obedient and faithful to their own natural lords and to the Christians whom they serve; they are humble, patient and calm-tempered . . . The best people in the world if only they knew God."

Las Casas, too, knew the Indians at first hand, and he must have been aware of the dangers of generalization. But such niceties went by the board in the face of the priest's overmastering interest in winning sympathy for his Indians and thereby ending their vicious exploitation.

Cabeza de Vaca, on the other hand, speaks of the cruelty and viciousness of some of the tribes he encountered, and there is nothing in his *Relacion* to match Las Casas' idealistic view of the race as a whole. In fact there are few abstractions of any kind in Cabeza de Vaca's book. When he departs from straight narrative to describe the Indians, he deals with little more than their physical appearance and their specific customs. In one place, though, he says, "Whoever has to fight Indians must take great care not to let them think he is disheartened or that he covets what they own; in war they must be treated very harshly, for should they notice either fear or greed, they

28

are the people who know how to abide their time for revenge and to take courage from the fears of the enemy."

Although Cabeza de Vaca took a realistic view of the Indians, he believed strongly enough in justice to attempt to put his ideas into practice when he became governor of Paraguay a few years after his return from Texas. In Paraguay he failed miserably to curb the riffraff who made up his little army, and he was sent back home in chains by his rebellious followers. Cabeza de Vaca was a good corporal but a bad general.

Dorantes and Castillo stayed in Mexico, the former serving honorably in the subjugation of Jalisco. Estebanico, who chose to remain a slave when he could easily have escaped to become his own master in the wilderness, provides the connecting link between the journey of the four castaways and the later history of Texas. He was acquired as a chattel by the Viceroy, Antonio de Mendoza, who saw in him a convenient instrument for the discovery of the fabled Seven Cities, now identified in speculation with the great towns from whence had come the copper, turquoises and emeralds found by Cabeza de Vaca. Not that the Spaniards, on the upper levels at least, believed they would actually find any cities that had been founded by seven fugitive prelates from Portugal, but the legend served to throw a romantic haze over the quest for another treasure trove like those of Mexico and Peru, and was probably credited by many of the simple soldiers in the ranks, who believed that anything written in a book must necessarily be true.

Meanwhile Cabeza de Vaca added to the furore of speculation over what might be found in the interior of North America. Besides filing his complaints against the slave-catcher Nuño de Guzmán (who was soon tried and condemned on this and other charges), Cabeza de Vaca kept a close mouth concerning what he had seen and heard, and his silence fed the snow-balling rumors that he carried a rich secret—that he knew of the Seven Cities, and the lands of the Amazons, the Island of California, the westward passage to India, and of rich mines of gold and jewels.

Such rumors were rife throughout Christendom in the half-century following the discovery of America—rumors even more fantastic than the modern myth that all Texans have grown rich in cattle and oil. But until 1519, when Alonzo Alvarez de Pineda sailed down the Gulf Coast in search of a westward passage to India, the land that is now Texas, larger than any country in Europe west of Russia, lay unknown to the wider world, baked by the sun in summer, swept by bitter northers in winter, sparsely populated by a few tribes of wandering Indians who were far more primitive than the Zuñis and Hopis to the west or the swarming tribes of Mexico to the south. Not until almost 200 years after Pineda's voyage was the first permanent Spanish settlement erected where the San Antonio River takes its source at the foot of the Balcones Escarpment.

Yet, by a quirk of legend, the history of Spanish Texas can be said to have its origin at a time long prior to the discovery of America. In the year 711, it is said, Roderick, the king of the West Goths in Spain, violated Florinda, the daughter of Count Julian of Ceuta. Her father sought vengeance by calling in the Moors, and Roderick was overcome by these invaders in a seven days' battle. When the Arabs swept on into Portugal, the terrified Archbishop of Lisbon gathered six bishops and a number of their parishioners into seven ships in which they fled westward toward the setting sun to an unknown island called Antilia, where they founded seven noble cities. So the legend says.

The infidels stayed in Spain for nearly 800 years, until the last of them were driven out by Ferdinand and Isabella in 1492, the same year that Columbus sighted land in the Bahamas. In the next few years the Atlantic and the Caribbean became thoroughfares for numberless ships. Colonies and exploring parties were sent into all the West Indian islands and many of the coasts of North and South America, but nowhere did the conquistadores come upon the seven majestic cities, resplendent with gold and jewels, of which the ever-growing legend told.

By 1514 the new Spanish colonies had begun to exhibit the diseases of civilization, and Bartolomé de Las Casas in Cuba was inveighing against Indian slavery and what we would now call the sadistic cruelty of the conquerors.

The colonies were almost like independent principalities, and their governors competed for more territory. Soon after Cortés had begun his conquest of Mexico in 1519, a rival fleet under Pineda was sent to the mainland of North America by Francisco de Garay, the governor of Jamaica. These four vessels set sail in the spring of 1519, rounded the end of Cuba, touched the peninsula of Florida, and traced the entire Gulf Coast as far as Vera Cruz, making frequent landings to trade with the Indians and take formal possession of the territory. It is highly probable that Pineda landed in Texas on this voyage, though there is no specific evidence to that effect.

Finding that Cortés had preceded him, burned his ships to prevent desertion, and organized the civil government of "La Villa Rica de Vera Cruz," Pineda turned back toward the North. On "a very large river," which could have been either the Mississippi or the Rio Grande, the fleet stopped for forty days to repair its ships, meanwhile exploring the country

30

round about and going six leagues up the river. In the area that they explored, Pineda's men found some forty Indian villages. The expedition soon returned to Jamaica to present a report which, at face value, indicated that Pineda found more in this country than anyone ever saw afterward. There were many rivers whose sands were heavy with fine gold, he averred, and the Indians wore golden ornaments all over their bodies. There were giants as much as nine feet high, and dwarfs of no more than four feet. However, Pineda was unable to report the finding of any strait that led toward India, nor was anything heard of the Seven Cities.

Fired by Pineda's report of gold and giants, Garay in 1520 sent a second expedition to the Gulf Coast under the command of Diego de Camargo, with 150 men, artillery, and bricks and lime with which to build a fort. This fleet of three ships landed at a river which again is of uncertain identity, but is believed to have been either the Rio Grande or the Pánuco, 250 miles down the coast in Mexico. In any case, the conquistadores turned tail after being worsted in a battle with the Indians, and the proposed settlement came to nothing.

Two years later, armed with a royal grant which included detailed instructions for the humane treatment of the Indians, Garay himself led a third attempt to conquer the vaguely delimited territory in and about Texas, which was now designated as Amichel. By June, 1523, he had assembled a fleet of sixteen vessels, carrying 600 foot soldiers, 150 horsemen, 200 guns, 300 crossbows, and some artillery. This fleet seems to have landed first at the Rio Grande, from which Garay and most of his men went overland to the Pánuco while his ships sailed down the coast. On his arrival at Cortés' new settlement of Santiestevan de Pánuco, however, Garay was presented with a royal order which commanded him to leave that region in the undisputed possession of the conqueror of Mexico. Conceding his defeat, Garay went to Mexico City and soon died, a guest in the home of his victorious rival.

The Coronado and De Soto Expeditions

After hearing the report of Cabeza de Vaca's party, Viceroy Mendoza ordered an exploring expedition under the command of Fray Marcos de Niza, a rugged French priest and disciple of Las Casas, "skilled in cosmography and the arts of the sea, as well as in theology," with Estebanico as a guide. The party left Culiacan early in March, 1539. When the expedition reached the frontier in far northwestern Mexico, Fray Marcos ordered Estenbanico to go ahead, and to send back an Indian courier with a small, medium-sized or large cross as a symbol of what reports he might hear concerning new lands. The largest cross was to be sent only if he heard of a country greater and better than Mexico. Only four days later, the messenger staggered into camp bearing a cross higher than a man. The word was that Estebanico had heard news of "the greatest country in the world," a region called the Seven Cities of Cíbola. A few days later Estebanico sent back another large cross with a message urging the friar to hurry. Soon afterward he sent a third cross with the same message.

Finally, when Fray Marcos had arrived at a point which he

believed, or at least said, to be very near Cíbola, two badly wounded Indians from Estebanico's party came staggering into the main camp. They told a hair-raising story. As Fray Marcos reported it later, Estebanico and many of his party had been killed by the Indians of the Cíbola pueblo because they believed him to be a spy for an advancing army, because he had arrogantly demanded turquoises and women, and because he must have been lying when he said he was an emissary of white men, since he was so obviously black.

Fray Marcos went on to climb a mountain and look down on Cíbola, he says. His veracity was challenged even in his own time for he said the pueblo (presumably Háwikuh, the westernmost of the Zuñi pueblos on the Arizona-New Mexico line, where Estebanico was killed), was "larger than Mexico," but Cornoado soon found that this was far from the truth.

It remained for the late Cleve Hallenbeck, in his last book, *The Journey of Fray Marcos de Niza,* published in 1949, to prove conclusively that the Friar was a liar. Hallenbeck here draws on his intimate first-hand knowledge of the country to prove beyond doubt that mendacious Marcos could not have traveled much farther north than the Arizona-Mexico border at a point four hundred miles from Cíbola. This first-rate amateur historian also uses his knowledge of Pueblo character and customs to argue convincingly that the Indians' slander of Estebanico must be heavily discounted. It becomes evident from Hallenbeck's closely reasoned argument that Estebanico was killed through no fault of his own except that he aroused the fears of the Háwikuh people by trying to run away when, as was their custom in dealing with all strangers, they had suspiciously detained him outside their pueblo walls. At any rate it is the slave and not the friar who must be given credit for the first exploration of Arizona—an adventure which has an important bearing on the history of Texas because it led directly to the explorations of Coronado, who commanded the first formal Spanish expedition into what is now Texas.

Francisco Vásquez de Coronado, who continued the quest for the Seven Cities with a large and well-armed expedition, was a man of thirty who had enjoyed a rapid rise in wealth and honors since coming to Mexico as the penniless younger son of a noble family five years before. Besides being gifted with great personal charm, he appears to have had a strong sense of justice, and although his conduct toward the Indians is not without blemish, he was happily lacking in the ferocity that distinguished Cortez, Pizarro and many others of the conquistadores.

The full story of Coronado's quest is too long and too remote from Texas to be more than suggested here. The expedition traveled north through Arizona, discovered the Grand Canyon, and then moved east to find the Seven (actually six) Cities of Cíbola, which proved to be the pueblos of Arizona and New Mexico—towns with a high state of Indian civilization, but without gold and jewels, and in no sense "greater than Mexico."

From the Tiguex pueblo, in central New Mexico, the army moved eastward in quest of Quivira, another country of which some Indians had told Coronado, where the pueblos were supposed to be much larger than those of New Mexico, where the people had lords who governed them (evidencing a high state of civilization!) and where golden vessels were in everyday use. Coronado meanwhile wrote to the king that he did not know whether to believe these tales, but thought them worthy of investigation—as indeed they were, considering how little the Spaniards really knew of the interior of North America.

The eastward trek from Tiguex began April 23, 1541. After some weeks of leisurely travel, the expedition reached a village of nomadic Querecho Indians, who camped in tents made of buffalo skins near the point where the Canadian River crosses the present Texas-New Mexico line, on the edge of the Panhandle. The Indians told Coronado in sign language that Quivira still lay to the east, so the army moved forward into what is now Texas.

At a second Querecho village the story was repeated with embellishments. The Indians said the first village of Quivira was now only one or two days distant, which would place it in the western part of the Texas Panhandle. Yet there was nothing to be seen but flat plains of short grass, so bare of landmarks that one buffalo-hunting soldier became lost and was never seen again, although the men in the camp lighted beacon fires and blew trumpets to help him find his way.

Coronado sent out a small advance party to investigate the story of the first Quiviran village, which was called Haxa. Setting their course by compass as if at sea on the featureless prairie, the party, under Captain Diego López, came upon a great herd of buffalo. The soldiers gave chase and inadvertently drove the herd into a *barranca* (gully), but so numerous was the herd that the gorge was soon filled and the rest of the buffalo crossed over on the backs of those that had fallen in. The hunters, unable to rein in their mounts quickly enough, also fell into the *barranca* and three horses were buried in buffalo, never to be recovered, although the riders seem to have come out alive.

When the advance party did not return within the allotted time, Coronado sent out searchers who by great good luck were able to find a

few hoof prints showing what direction the first party had taken. All this
took place in the heart of the great (but misnamed) "Staked Plains" region of
the Texas Panhandle, a vast prairie raised above the surrounding country by a
ring of fantastic escarpments. The terrain is graphically described by Pedro de
Castañeda, in his chronicle of the expedition: "The country is like a bowl, so
that when a man sits down, the horizon surrounds him all around at the
distance of a musket shot. There are no groves of trees except at the rivers,
which flow at the bottom of some ravines ... Who could believe that although a thousand horses, five hundred of our own cattle, more than five
thousand rams and ewes, and more than fifteen hundred persons, counting
allies and servants, marched over these plains, they left no more trace when
they got through than as if no one had passed over them, so that it became
necessary to stack up piles of bones and buffalo chips at various distances in
order that the rear guard might follow the army and not get lost? Although
the grass was short, after it was trampled upon it stood up again as clean and
straight as before."

Castañeda told also of white wolves and white-spotted deer
(antelope or pronghorn), with long hair. He noticed that the jackrabbits were
so used to running about among the four-legged buffalo that they paid no
attention to men mounted on horses, although they ran away from men on
foot.

Looking at the buffalo, said Castañeda, "One could see the sky
between their legs, so that at a distance they looked like trimmed pine-tree
trunks with the foliage joining at the top. When a bull stood alone he
resembled four such pines. And however close to them one might be, when
looking across their backs one could not see the ground on the other side,"
but only the everlasting sky.

The advance party finally returned, to report that they had
found no golden cities, nothing but "cattle and sky." The main army again
moved east, following the buffalo herds, for even the Indian guides had lost
their bearings. They found several small lakes, some fresh and some salt, near
which the grass grew higher than on the semi-arid plain. After three weeks an
advance party under Captain Rodrigo Maldonado threaded its way down into
what has been identified as Tule Canyon to the camp of an Indian tribe called
the Teyas—probably the same word, meaning friends or allies, which was
applied to many tribes in this whole region, was mistaken by the Spaniards
for a tribal name, and so eventually became the name of the whole province.
Even before this, some time prior to 1529, Don Nuño de Guzman had heard
tales of the Seven Cities from a young "Tejos" Indian who had come to

Mexico.

Both the Querechos and the Teyas followed the buffalo, from which they gained their whole livelihood. Later the Plains tribes were famous horsemen, but at this period, of course, they had only their dogs, which they either loaded with pack saddles like those used by the Moors in North Africa, or equipped with the travois, a sort of sled. Castañeda noted that when the pack load became disarranged the dogs would howl for someone to fix it.

This chronicler found the Plains Indians highly intelligent, kind-hearted, faithful friends and not inclined to cruelty, nor were they addicted to cannibalism. They were so adept at the sign language that interpreters were unnecessary. While hunting the buffalo they would eat the raw flesh and drink the blood, but they also dried the meat, "cutting it thin like a leaf, and when dry they grind it like meal and make a sort of sea soup of it to eat." A favorite delicacy was the juice left after mastication of grass in a cow's stomach. Their skill in skinning the buffalo with a flint knife was something to remember, Castañeda wrote twenty years later. So was their prowess with the bow, for at least one Teyas was seen to shoot a bull right through both shoulders with an arrow. This, said Castañeda, would be a good shot for a musket.

The chronicler fails to describe the dress of the Indian braves, but he says "The women are well made and modest, covering their whole body. They wear shoes and buskins made of tanned skin. The women wear cloaks over their small under petticoats, with sleeves gathered up at the shoulders, all of skin, and some wore something like little *sanbenitos* [serapes] with a fringe, which reached halfway down the thigh over the petticoat."

The "Teyas" Indians of the Panhandle were described by Coronado as "a large people of very fine appearance," with tattooed bodies and faces.

In the Tule canyon occurred a remarkable incident. The Indians set out a huge pile of tanned skins. Coronado, assuming that the skins were a present, began to distribute them among some of his men. But the soldiers who had been overlooked pitched into the pile unbidden, so did the Indians, and in a few minutes the hides had vanished. In the course of the argument it turned out that the Indians had not expected the Spaniards to take the skins at all, but merely to make the sign of the cross over them as Cabeza de Vaca and his party had done when they passed through Texas six years before.

It is nearly two hundred miles from Tule Canyon to Big

Spring, which was probably the nearest point touched by the Children of the Sun in their pilgrimage. But a blind old Indian told Juan de Jaramillo, one of the chroniclers of the Coronado expedition, that "many days before, he had met four others of our people near there but closer to New Spain." This account was of course given in sign language, hence is lacking in detail. The old man might well have been a resident of one village, described by Cabeza de Vaca, where most of the inhabitants had at least one eye clouded with some obscure disease, and many had gone blind.

By the time the expedition had reached Tule Canyon, Coronado had begun to lose confidence in the Indian guide, called "The Turk" because he looked like one, who for weeks had been telling him that Quivira was just over the horizon. The leader was now ready to listen to the Turk's rival, Sopete, who "threw himself on the ground and indicated by signs that he would rather have his head cut off than go that way because it was not the correct route to Quivira." The Teyas Indians knew about Quivira, too. They said the Quivirans did not live in great stone houses but only had simple huts of grass and hides, and far from being rich in gold and jewels, they did not even have enough corn.

Coronado still wanted to see Quivira for himself, however. Realizing that he had veered too far to the south, he sent an exploring party northward through a string of Teyas camps along an arroyo running into the main Tule Canyon. This country, the explorers found, produced abundantly of mesquite beans, grapes and plums. The waiting army, meanwhile, was assailed by hailstones "as big as bowls." Food and drinkable water were dangerously scarce. In view of these troubles, Coronado held a council and all agreed that the best plan would be for thirty picked and mounted men to press on in search of Quivira, while the main party returned to its base at Tiguex. Definite arrangements for the separation of forces were begun at what was probably Palo Duro Canyon on May 29, 1541, thirty-seven days and approximately 650 miles out of Tiguex. Palo Duro, the largest of the great *barrancas* which lead eastward out of the Staked Plains, is a great abyss, now a state park, sixty miles long, nearly a thousand feet deep and varying in width from a stone's throw to a spread of badlands fifteen miles across, through all of which runs the Prarie Dog fork of the Red River.

With Sopete as guide instead of the Turk, the chosen thirty pressed on, from a point near Canyon City, Texas, while the main party spent fifteen days killing five hundred buffalo to provide a supply of jerked beef for the journey back to Tiguex. The return trip was made with the help of Indian guides who set a course toward the west by shooting an arrow away from the rising sun, then shooting another over it where it lay. With the help of this new method of prairie navigation, the return trip was made in twenty-five days instead of thirty-seven.

Meanwhile Coronado and his little exploring party moved northward, guided by Sopete although the Turk, who might still be of some use, was taken along in chains. So, without any notable incident, they ascended the Texas Panhandle, crosses the narrow Oklahoma Panhandle, continued north through Kansas to the Arkansas River, and found Quivira in central Kansas, between the Arkansas and Smoky Hill Rivers. The country of Quivira was beautiful, but its twenty-five villages had neither the wealth nor the advanced civilization of which the Turk had told. For this and other reasons the Turk was sentenced to death and executed by garroting, secretly, so as not to arouse the other Indians.

Coronado, who had only reluctantly consented to the execution, feared revenge when the secret became known, as it soon must, so he ordered a hasty retreat, following buffalo trails on a different route from the one the party had taken in moving northward. The new route, a much more direct one to Cíbola than the outward trail which the Spaniards had taken under the unreliable guidance of the Turk, must have cut diagonally across the northwest corner of the Texas Panhandle, probably approximating the route of the Chicago, Rock Island and El Paso Railway, which runs through Texhoma, Stratford and Dalhart to cross the Texas-New Mexico line near Romero, Texas, according to Dr. Bolton. (It should be noted that all routes given for the early explorers are approximate at best and in most cases are merely probable. The present writer, after careful comparison of conflicting evidence, has in each case given what seems to him the most probable route, without going into a dry and profitless discussion of other possibilities.)

The return trip to Tiguex was made without incident. So, bitterly disappointed at his failure to find "another Mexico," glittering with gold and jewels, either in the Seven Cities of Cíbola or in the remoter land of Quivira, Coronado passed beyond the scope of Texas history.

He left behind him in Quivira a missionary priest, Fray Juan Padilla; a Portuguese soldier. Andrés do Campo, and two Mexican Indian *donados* (lay brothers). Padilla was killed by the Indians, thus becoming the first Christian martyr in what is now the United States. Do Campo fled with the *donados*, Lucas and Sebastian, and after several years of wandering through Oklahoma and Texas all three of them finally reached Mexico. Like Cabeza de Vaca, Do Campo "blessed people with a cross, to which they made generous offerings, and wherever he went they gave him arms, shelter and food." The story of Do Campo and the *donados*, if all were known, might be as fascinating as that of Cabeza de Vaca, but unfortunately none of the three ever wrote a book, so we have only fragmentary and contradictory second--hand reports of their travels.

Even while Coronado's army was exploring in and near the Panhandle, another party of Spaniards wandered into the Piney Woods of East Texas. This was the remnant of the expedition of Hernando de Soto, the man who had succeeded to the dead Narváez's commission as conqueror of Florida. Cabeza de Vaca, after returning to Spain, had petitioned for this privilege, but he was too late, since the concession had already been granted to De Soto. At this time Cabeza de Vaca had not decided to publish a full account of his travels; his secrecy and wise looks gave full scope to the imagination of the Spaniards he met, and inspired many of them to join the expedition of de Soto for the conquest of Florida, a term which then embraced an indefinitely large area and might even include the Seven Cities, which at that time had not yet been discovered by Coronado.

De Soto's ten vessels and six hundred men landed at Tampa Bay in May, 1539, about the same time that Fray Marcos de Niza turned back after hearing of the death of Estebanico. De Soto's expedition moved slowly, by a zigzag route, and it was not until May, 1541, while Coronado was traveling from Tiguex to Quivira, that De Soto stood on the banks of the Mississippi River near Memphis. He is known to every schoolboy as the discoverer of the Great River, but actually it had been seen at its mouth by many Spaniards before.

During the summer De Soto journeyed far into Arkansas, and at one time it is probable that he and Coronado were no more than three hundred miles apart. They of course had no definite knowledge of each other's activities, though Coronado heard rumors among the Indians that there were other white men in the East.

De Soto died on May 21, 1542, where the Red River runs into the Mississippi, after appointing as his successor, Don Luis de Moscoso. Like his master De Soto, Don Luis was a man of very different stamp from the gentle Cabeza de Vaca or the moderate Coronado. De Soto had cut a long swath through most of the later-to-be Confederate States, looting and taking slaves and killing and having his men killed in turn. It was therefore natural that when he knew death to be upon him, he chose as his successor a man of like temperament, and the choice of Moscoso was ratified by the *hidalgos* of the expedition.

De Soto was first buried secretly, then exhumed and cast into the river to conceal his death from the Indians, for although a common Spanish soldier might die, the absence of the great *adelantado* could be explained only by announcing that he had ascended into the heavens. The governor's property, consisting of five slaves, three horses and seven hundred swine, was sold by Moscoso's order at public auction, the horses and slaves bringing the same price of from 2,000 to 3,000 *cruzados,* or ten times the price of a hog, to be paid when gold was found, or, if none was found, then in a year's time. It was these De Soto hogs, driven along by the expedition to provide pork, that strayed to become the ancestors of the razorbacks of the whole South, from Florida to Texas.

With the advice of "the captains and principal men," Moscoso decided to beat his way to Mexico by land, rather than build barks and attempt a sea voyage. The little army set out in a generally westward direction and, after fighting an entirely unnecessary battle with the Indians, came to the town of Naguatex, which all students agree was somewhere just outside the border of what is now Texas, although they place it at various points from southeastern Oklahoma to southwestern Louisiana. This was on Sunday, July 23, 1542.

The Indians of this area, and of the entire section of Texas traversed by Moscoso, probably were members of what later came to be known as the Hasinai Confederation, misnamed the "Tejas" because of their frequent use of this, their word for "friends." They lived in a higher stage of civilization than the miserable Karankawa and Coahuiltecan Indians known to Cabeza de Vaca in the early stages of his wandering, for they cultivated corn and lived in comparatively stable village communities. Like Cabeza de Vaca's Indians, however, the people of Naguatex arrived weeping when they presented themselves to Moscoso.

Four days after Naguatex, Moscoso arrived at a river which was so full that the troops could not pass it, although there had been no rain in that part of the country for more than a month. This was either the Red River or the Sabine; but the high stage of water in the absence of rain favors the Red, which is by far the larger of the two. Within eight days, however, Moscoso was able to cross the river, and it was presumably then that he entered Texas.

On the farther bank, Moscoso found all the Indian huts deserted, for reasons not hard for us to guess. So the governor sent orders to the Indian chief to come to him, bringing a guide to lead him through the country *mas allá.* When after several days the chief had not reported, Moscoso naturally sent out two companies of soldiers to set fire to the towns and seize any people they might find. This method of persuasion proved so effective that the chief quickly provided Moscoso with not one guide but three, and the expedition thus went on to a province poor in corn, called Nissohone. Soon the alert Governor suspected the Indian guides of misleading him, so he ordered all three of them hanged and replaced them with a woman captured in Nissohone, who managed to save her life by leading the expedition back to the westward trail. (It should be noted that the "trackless wilderness" of fiction is fiction and nothing more. All accounts of early exploration in America show that the country was crisscrossed with trails which often followed the same lines of least resistance as modern highways and railways. Some of these trails were double, so that they resembled wagon roads.)

At another miserable village, called Lacane, an Indian was captured who told of a more prosperous town to the west, called Nondacao. There the weeping Indians came out with gifts of fish and provided a new guide, who was to lead the Spaniards to the "province" of Soacatino. First, however, the explorers had to pass through a region called Aays, whose inhabitants, according to our chronicler, the Gentleman of Elvas, "had never heard of the Christians." This may be doubted, however, for the Indians of Aays immediately came out in battle array and fell upon the Christians both front and rear, but without causing much damage.

Now Moscoso heard a rumor that the Indians farther on in Soacatino had seen other Christians. At this the Spaniards were delighted, thinking that the unknown white men might be able to show them the way to New Spain. But the guide who had brought in this rumor, like the three previous guides, was suspected of leading the expedition "out of the way." Put to torture, he confessed that the chief of Nondacao had ordered him to mislead the Spaniards—for what purpose does not appear, since neither the Spaniards nor their Indian guide had any idea how to reach their destination in Mexico. The guide, however, was thrown to the dogs, and another Indian led the expedition to Soacatino.

Here the natives said they had heard that "near there, toward the south," other white men were moving about. In all probability this was a delayed rumor of Cabeza de Vaca's party, for Coronado's nearest approach to this region had been in the Texas Panhandle, far to the northwest.

Moscoso soon reached two other "provinces," Guasco and Naquiscoca. In the latter place the Indians said they knew nothing of any Christians, but when put to torture they admitted that *mas allá*, in the land of Nácacahoz, the Christians had stopped briefly and then gone back to the west, from whence they had come. Two days later, in Nácacahoz, Moscoso's men captured a tattooed woman who said she had been in the hands of the Christians but had escaped them. She promised to take Moscoso's party where the other Christians had been, a few leagues off, but after guiding them three or four leagues she recanted and declared that all she had said was false. Moscoso then decided that all the other rumors of Christians roaming about had been false, too.

Here he was wrong, of course, for both Coronado's army and the castaways of the Narváez expedition had not long ago traveled through Texas, and there was enough communication among the Indians so that at least a vague rumor of the Spaniards' passing must have been heard in the region visited by Moscoso. Witness what the Indians had told Coronado about Cabeza de Vaca.

As for the Indian woman, a sequel is provided by Castañeda, the chronicler of the Coronado expedition, who says: "A painted Indian woman ran away from Juan de Saldibar and hid in the ravines about this time [Summer, 1541] because she recognized the country of Tiguex where she had been a slave. She fell into the hands of some Spaniards who had entered the country from Florida to explore it in this direction. After I got back to Spain I heard them say that the Indian told them she had run away from other men like them nine days before, and that she gave the names of some captains; from which we ought to believe that we were not far from the region they discovered, although they said they were more than two hundred leagues inland. I believe the land at that point is more than six hundred leagues across from sea to sea."

The "nine days," of course, is a mistake, for it was fully a year from the time when the woman escaped from Saldibar in the Panhandle until she was captured by Moscoso somewhere in East Texas. Why she retracted her story is a mystery, but the lack of clearness in the account is probably due to the fact that she conversed in sign language or at any rate in a tongue with which she was not very familiar. As for her "recognizing" the country of Tiguex while in the Panhandle, several hundred miles away, this must mean that she recognized from the conversation of the soldiers that they planned to return to the Tiguex Pueblo.

The Nácacahoz country was barren of both corn and information, so Moscoso returned to Guasco, asking every Indian he caught whether any other Christians had been seen or heard of. The natives said they had never been west of the Daycao River, ten days' journey to the west, where they sometimes went to hunt deer. They had occasionally seen people on the other side, they said, but could not tell who or what they were.

So the Spaniards went to the Daycao and crossed it, seeking for Christians, but found only an encampment of some of the most miserable Indians they had yet encountered, who wisely fled as soon as they saw the Spaniards. Moscoso captured two of these Indians, but was unable to question them because none of his interpreters understood their language—and evidently they were unversed in sign language, the *lingua franca* of the more advanced tribes. Moscoso guessed, however, that the country beyond the Daycao was that described by Cabeza de Vaca, where the Indians had not even food enough for themselves to say nothing of providing subsistence for the Spaniards. Then too, it was already the beginning of October, and freezing weather could not be far off. So, at a council of war, it was decided that the expedition should return by the way it had come, build vessels on the Mississippi and sail down the Gulf Coast to Mexico the following Spring.

So, says the Gentlemen of Elvas, "The Governor, who longed to be again where he could get his full measure of sleep, rather than govern and go conquering a country so beset for him with hardships, directly returned, getting back from whence he came."

On the Mississippi seven brigantines (small two-masted vessels) were built by a Genoese shipwright with the aid of four or five Basque carpenters, while another Genoese and a Sardinian closed the cracks with oakum obtained from the henequen plant, except that when henequen ran short they used native flax and the ravelings of Indian shawls. The complete shawls were sewn together to make sails. Cables were twisted out of mulberry bark; stirrups were fashioned into anchors, the horsemen using new stirrups carved out of wood. Spikes were forged from the chains and iron collars which all the Spaniards had brought along for their Indian slaves.

The best twenty-two horses were taken on board the brigantines; the rest were killed and their meat jerked, as was that of the swine. In this way the seven brigantines set sail down the Mississippi on July 2, 1543. Five hundred of the six hundred Indian slaves, gathered at various places through the South, were left on the Mississippi, presumably to be slaves of the resident Indians. "The most of them wept, which caused great compassion, as they were all Christians of their own free will, and were now to remain lost."

In the seven rickety vessels went 322 Spaniards, the remnant of the six hundred who had followed De Soto into Florida four years earlier. Through a series of running battles with the Indians along the bank, the brigantines finally reached open water. After a debate, the majority of the leaders agreed that it would be safer to sail along the coast toward Mexico rather than strike out across the Gulf. They set out on July 18, and sailed all day in the tremendous mass of fresh water which the great river poured into the sea. After various minor vicissitudes, including clouds of mosquitoes, the voyagers came together in a creek on the Texas coast, where they smeared the bottoms of their leaky vessels with "a scum the sea casts up, called copee, which is like pitch and is used instead on shipping, where that is not to be had." This "scum" was, of course crude petroleum which had seeped out under the shallow waters of the Gulf Coast and been carried to land by the surf. It was found in the form of dried slabs weighing ten or twelve pounds. The passage quoted is history's first mention of Texas Oil, the production of which had amounted to more than sixteen billion barrels by the 1960s.

Farther down the coast, but still in Texas, the brigantines took shelter from the heavy weather in a large bay, abounding with fish, where they remained two weeks. When fair weather returned they navigated for six days more, and apparently passed the mouth of the Rio Grande in the night, without seeing it, for one morning the mountains of Mexico loomed on the western horizon. After another sixty leagues of beating down the coast, they found Indians wearing European clothes who spoke Spanish and told them that "the town of the Christians" was fifteen leagues inland, up the Páuco River. At this news, says the Gentleman, "Many, leaping on shore, kissed the ground; and all, on bended knees, with hands raised above them, and their eyes to heaven, remained untiring in giving thanks to God."

All told, twenty Spanish expeditions are definitely known to have entered what is now the State of Texas or touched its coast before a burst of activity, resulting from the incursion of La Salle in 1685, led to the permanent occupation of the area by Spanish missionaires, soldiers and settlers. Thirteen other expeditions may possibly have entered the State during the pre-La Salle period, although the contemporary descriptions of their routes are too vague to be conclusive. Most of these early *entradas* were small affairs with no important results. However, the cumulative total disposes of the notion, propagated by some careless historians, that the Spaniards showed no interest in Texas until the Frenchmen threatened to take it from them. When we consider that Texas lay on the fringe of a vast but sparsely populated and largely undeveloped empire which extended from Patagonia to Oregon, it is not surprising that its settlement was deferred until a hundred and fifty years after the first explorations.

From Carvajal to La Salle

The conditions for the Spanish colonization of Texas first had to be established by the northward movement of the frontier in New Spain. This movement began immediately after the conquest of the Valley of Mexico, proceeded rapidly at first, then more slowly, and later began to suffer reverses, so that colonies bravely established lay in ruins before they had had time to develop into anything more than frontier posts.

The central plateau of Mexico, inhabited by "sedentary" Indians whose relatively civilized institutions had conditioned them to submit to government and carry on the everyday work of the colony, had become a New Spain in fact as well as in name before the death of its conqueror, Cortez. Farther north, in the deserts, mountains and open plains, lived wild Indians whose subjugation took a great while longer. Even if the natives had been more docile, the sparse population of those regions would have made it difficult to establish the kind of civilization that required the strong bodies of subject peoples to give effect (in the words of Aristotle) to the foresight of their lords and masters.

By 1575, however, little more than half a century after the Conquest, the gateway to Texas was guarded by a colony at Saltillo, in a mile-high mountain valley some two hundred miles south of the Rio Grande. At the end of the century this settlement was described as follows by the Bishop de La Mota y Escobar: "The Villa de Saltillo is a collection of Spaniards who at one time were soldiers and now are growers of wheat who, because of the plentiful and good land and water of the place, have created many good farms, large and small, all irrigated, where they harvest large quantities of very excellent wheat, which they carry to market in the city of Zacatecas."

This agricultural development, which also included cattle ranches, had been made possible through the good offices of a colony of peaceable Indians from Tlaxcala, on the central plateau, who had been settled in a *pueblo* called San Esteban de la Nueva Tlaxcala, adjoining the Villa de Saltillo, by Don Francisco de Urdiñola, a Basque who was noted as the "pacificator" of large areas of northern Mexico, and whose descendants still live in the region, where one of them, Luis de Urdiñola, was recently the editor of a Monterrey newspaper.

Meanwhile in 1579 a Portuguese gentleman, Don Luis de Carvajal y de la Cueva, obtained from King Philip II of Spain a royal grant to "discover and pacify" a vast stretch of territory which was to be known as the New Kingdom of León and was more than worthy of the name, for it was a great square, nearly six hundred miles in diameter, with its southern side cutting clear across Mexico from Tampico on the Atlantic to a point near Chametla on the Pacific, and its northeastern corner embracing a good part of Texas, including the site of San Antonio. This huge undeveloped area, half again as large as Spain, is called by Mexican historians the "tragic quadrate" of Carvajal, for reasons which will shortly appear.

Landing at Tampico, Carvajal set out to explore his "new kingdom." Moving to the north and east of Saltillo, he established a mining camp which he called the City of León (now Cerralvo), and then recruited some of the inhabitants of Saltillo to form a new colony which he named San Luis (later abandoned; reestablished in 1596 as Monterrey). Meanwhile he prepared trouble for himself by making his own laws and setting aside the orders of the Viceroy of Mexico.

In the next few years Carvajal founded Nuevo Almaden (later abandoned and reestablished as Monclova) and opened a number of mines in that portion of his grant which he had selected for early development. However, he ran into continual disputes with the Viceroy, the Conde de Coruña, over their respective jurisdictions, and finally became rash enough to file a suit against the noble lord before the royal *audiencia* (council), in Mexico City. He won the suit, but his victory spurred the Viceroy into making hostile researches into Carvajal's genealogy, which revealed the shocking fact that he was a descendant of Christianized Jews. It was also alleged that he had shown favoritism toward colonists of the same or worse character. The Inquisition, which had come to Mexico in 1571, was notified, and a judge went out with a company of soldiers to arrest the Governor of the New Kingdom of León.

It was now adduced against Carvajal that as he, then ignorant of his Jewish ancestry, was saying his prayers one day and pronouncing the words, *"Gloria, Patri et Filio et Spiritu Santo,"* his sister had whispered to him, "Don't say that, brother, for the Son has not come." Although he sharply rebuked his sister, his failure to report her to the authorities was one of several charges brought against him by the Inquisition. It was also charged that he had filled his colony with people who were either "New Christians" or "recalcitrant and obdurate" Jews.

On February 24, 1590, Don Luis de Carvajal was condemned to be exiled from the Indies for six years, and all his relatives were punished by confiscation of their property "for having kept and believed the dead law of Moses and followed the rites, celebrated Passover, fasts and Sabbaths and other ceremonies of the said law, waiting for the coming of the Messiah, who was to give them riches and raise them to glory, believing that our Lord Jesus Christ had not been that Messiah, and that his law was a falsehood and a thing of air."

Carvajal never lived to go into his exile, but died while still in prison—of a broken heart, it was said. His whole family, after apparently being let alone in their destitution for six years, were finally again haled before the Inquisition, and in the *Plaza Mayor* of Mexico City were first put to prolonged and ingenious tortures and then garroted to death, all in celebration of the Second Sunday in Advent, 1596, in the presence of the Viceroy and the judges of the *Audiencia*.

With Carvajal dead and his kingdom forfeit, the development which might soon have led to colonization in Texas slowed almost to a full stop, and the course of empire in the North turned toward New Mexico, to which Gaspar Castaño de Sosa, Carvajal's former lieutenant governor, made an unauthorized expedition in 1590-1592, and of which Juan de Onate in 1598 took formal possession from a base in the El Paso district.

Nuevo Almaden and Cerralvo were abandoned, to be re-founded many years later, but Monterrey and Saltillo remained as bases for further exploration across the Rio Grande into Texas, and various isolated missions were founded from which the priests looked with longing eyes toward the unconverted Indians beyond the great river. In 1674-1675, Father Juan Larios and Fernando del Bosque went on an expedition into Texas, where they found the Indians eager to be converted. Still nothing was done to establish missions or other settlements beyond the Rio Grande.

The Spanish authorities were startled into action when, on September 10, 1685, a pirate ship belonging to the notorious Grammont was captured by the Spanish Windward Squadron and taken to Vera Cruz with 120 buccaneers aboard. These Frenchmen were straitly questioned, and the story that they told overshadowed any concern over their piracy.

Among the prisoners was a young man named Denis Thomas, who deposed that he was a native of Longueville, near Dieppe, and a former page of the Marquis de Gréville; that he had sailed from France a year earlier on a frigate commanded by Captain Beaujeu; that in the same convoy there were three vessels which carried supplies for a new settlement at a place called "Micipipi"; that the settlers numbered some 250 persons, including soldiers, tradesmen, seven priests and several women; that the leader of the expedition was one whom the Spanish scribe at Thomas' interrogation recorded as "Munsuir de Salas"; that the said De Salas planned to conquer some rich mines, believed to be not far from the great river, which could only have been the mines of Mexico.

Thomas told his captors that these things had been revealed to him by a servant of La Salle's with whom he had become friendly while at sea. The truthfulness of his report was evidenced by many convincing details, as when he described La Salle's faithful Indian guide, Nika, who, he said, was rather corpulent, with black coarse hair, and accustomed to wearing red clothes in the French fashion, including a red bonnet, trimmed with gold, which La Salle had given him.

This report, confirmed in many particulars by Thomas' shipmates, was conveyed to the Viceroy, Don Antonio de la Cerda y Aragon, Conde de Paredes y Marqués de la Laguna, and it led to action with a speed almost unparalleled in Spanish history, for within two months a maritime expedition, headed by two experienced pilots, Juan Enríquez Barroto and Antonio Romero, set out from Havana to find the hostile colony, the location of which was known only with the utmost vagueness.

The expedition explored most of the Gulf Coast without finding anything significant to report, although it passed, without recognizing it, the mouth of the Mississippi, which was supposed to be (though it was not) the site of the La Salle colony. So Barroto and Romero sailed empty-handed into Vera Cruz in March, 1686.

Meanwhile the government of New Spain had acted to strengthen the northern frontier by enlarging the *villa* and *presidio* of Monclova in Coahuila. All together, the Spaniards sent out by sea and land a total of twelve expeditions, each one of which was ordered to find and destroy the La Salle colony, supposed to exist on the Bay of Espíritu Santo. The vagueness of the American geography of that period can be estimated from the fact that there was, of course, no "bay" at the mouth of the Mississippi—a hard fact which may have misled La Salle as it did the Spaniards, who sailed past the delta mouth four times without guessing that they had seen the Mississippi. Because La Salle's colony was later found to be near what is now called Matagorda Bay, the name "Espíritu Santo" was transferred to that location, without, at first, the faintest idea that a change had been made. To add to the confusion, the Mississippi was also called Río de la Palizada by the Spanish, and Colbert by the French, while Matagorda Bay was sometimes called the Bay of San Bernardo.

Of the twelve Spanish expeditions in search of La Salle, the most important were the last two of the five led by Alonso de León, Jr. De León's fifth expedition, which founded a mission in East Texas, caused the frontier of settlement in New Spain to leap the four hundred miles from the Rio Grande to the Neches at a single bound.

The first De León expedition started at a disadvantage. In a manner typical of the times, and not unheard of in the military operations of a later day, the instructions of the Viceroy to the Marqués de San Miguel de Aguayo, Governor of Nuevo León, did not reach the provincial capital until six months after they were issued, and then did not include any data as to the location of Espiritu Santo Bay. Aguayo called together all the veteran frontiersmen he could find, but none of them had ever heard of a bay by that name. Finally, however, they concluded that it must be somewhere to the north or northeast.

De León left Cadereita, a town near Monterrey, on June 27, 1686, with seventy-five men, including three Indian guides and a chaplain, Fray Diego de Orozco. The party took with them a good supply of flour, hard-tack, dried beef and chocolate, and rode or drove 468 horses, the point in this being that horses were cheap and it was easier to abandon those which became exhausted than to nurse them along.

Near the mouth of the Rio Grande, De León captured three stragglers from an Indian tribe which had fled at the Spaniards' approach.

These captives told him that there were "other Spaniards" living to the north or northeast, though they could not explain just where. De León went on, reached the gulf and explored the coast for a distance of some twelve leagues. Along the beach he found a few boards, pieces of masts, broken rudders, barrel heads, four artillery wheels, three smashed canoes, and a thick glass bottle, containing some soured wine. The wreckage was in various stages of decay, indicating that vessels had presumably met with disaster along this coast at various times. But the thing that most amazed De León was the great number of green cornstalks that appeared to have been washed up by the tide. "I concluded," he wrote, "that there must be a settlement in the neighborhood on a river whose flood waters had washed this corn to the sea."

The expedition returned to Cadereita on July 18, having failed to find the French settlement. Aguayo soon ordered another expedition to explore the coast north of the mouth of the Rio Grande, with Alonso de León again the leader. This second expedition also had no results, and encountered nothing worthy of note with the exception of numerous hostile Indians. This was in February and March, 1687, nearly two years after the Spaniards had learned of the invasion. Further searching was delayed by a revolt of the Toboso Indians, who were interfering with the establishment of De León's proposed new *presidio* and *villa* in Coahuila, the province of which he was now governor. The following year he became a general at the age of forty-seven, having risen from a private in twenty-seven years of service on the frontier.

We now come upon a conflict of personalities which is of considerable interest in itself, and further is a prime example of the innumerable conflicts which arose between military officers and missionary friars on the Spanish frontier. In these differences, the friars usually showed true Christian forbearance, but there was at least one important exception.

This was Father Damián Manzanet (sometimes called Masanet), who was living in the Mission Caldera, in Coahuila, during De León's earlier expeditions. This *padre,* although he showed a commendable spirit of devotion to his missionary calling, was nevertheless a sanctimonious, spiteful and self-willed man, never able to get along with any of the laymen who had the ill fortune to serve with him during his six years in North Mexico and Texas. It is unfortunate that a man who deviated to such a degree from the almost saintly character of the typical mission priest was destined to play a controlling part in the earliest attempts of the Spaniards to carry their civilization into Texas.

Manzanet first appeared in Northern Mexico in 1687, drawn

from Spain by the legend of "the woman in the blue dress," Mother María de Jesús de Agreda, who was alleged to have visited the Texas Indians five hundred times in a series of mystical trances while she was the mother superior of a convent in the Pyrenees some sixty years before. Except for his career in Texas, Manzanet's history is obscure, and what we know of him is almost entirely based on his own letters and diaries in the period from 1687 to 1693. Chief among these is a long and rambling letter to Don Carlos de Sigüenza y Góngora, filled with complaints over the conduct of De León and other soldiers, and with complacent boasting of Manzanet's own righteous and holy conduct. To an unbiased reader, this letter is likely to have the opposite effect from what was intended.

It is from this same letter that we learn Manzanet's version of the discovery of Jean Géry, the French King of the Indians—a version which differs in some important respects from that given by De León.

Manzanet tells us that, in his ardent desire to assist his Excellency, the Viceroy, he made an effort to learn from the Indians coming across the Rio Grande whether there were any white men in the interior of Texas. One of these Indians, whom Manzanet had converted some time before, and in whom he had "recognized a high degree of truthfulness," told him in a general way that there were indeed some white men in Texas. Manzanet asked him what he would do to prove this, and the Indian, whose name was Juan or Juanillo, offered to go and bring in a white man whom he knew to be living in a *ranchería* (Indian village) some sixty leagues distant. Manzanet gave him some clothing and horses as presents for the Indians, and Juanillo set out on his errand.

About the same time, Manzanet says, an Indian of the Quems nation arrived and told him that he had been "even in the very houses of the French." There were many French men and women, well armed and busy sowing maize and other crops. This Indian said he could take Manzanet to the place without any risk. This was in July, 1687, the same month that the Viceory in Mexico City received, three years late, his first news from the Spanish ambassador in Paris concerning La Salle's authorization to found a colony.

The converted chief of the Pacpuls, Juanillo, returned after a while, says Manzanet, to report that he had found the lone Frenchman in an assembly of many Indian nations at the sierra of Sacatsol ("Stone Nostrils") twenty leagues beyond the Rio Grande, a place which has been identified with the modern Anacacho Mountain, near Brackettville in Kinney County, well into West Texas. He escorted the Frenchman to another *ranchería*, told him that Manzanet was asking for him, and left word with the Indians that they should not be afraid, that the missionary father desired to visit them.

Manzanet says he notified De León, who went with twelve men and without difficulty brought the Frenchman back to Mexico. His name, according to Manzanet, was "Juan Francisco So-and-So," and he said that he was a native of "Cheblie" in New France. "And in all his testimony," adds the charitable father, "the said Frenchman always lied."

So much for the Manzanet version. De León tells a story which, though startlingly different from Manzanet's, is sufficiently similar to convince us, after some thought, that it must refer to the same sequence of events.

During the Tobosa revolt, says De León, he sent a Tlaxcaltecan Indian, named Agustin de la Cruz, into the North to find allies. When he returned, Agustin told an interesting story. Somewhere beyond the Rio Grande he had come to a large *rancheria* whose inhabitants took him to the chief's house to make obeisance. What was Agustín's surprise to find the chief a white man, though he did not speak Spanish. He sat naked, with his body painted in the Indian fashion, on a bench covered with buffalo skins, and on either side stood an Indian brave, fanning him in Oriental style. Through signs and with the help of interpreters, the great chief told Agustin that he was a Frenchman sent by God to establish *pueblos* among the natives and help them in their wars. When Agustin told him of Governor De León, the chief graciously replied that he would be pleased to grant the governor an audience. As evidence of the truth of his story, the white chief gave the emissary some pages from a French book.

Alarmed at this report, De León concluded that the "white chief" was certainly an agent sent out by the French to gain the friendship of the Indians and lay the ground for an invasion of New Spain. The only possible course of action, the governor decided, was to capture the Frenchman before he could do any harm. With thirteen trusted friends, De León hurried to what was apparently the same location described by Manzanet, where he found some Indians who said they were subjects of the white chief.

The little group of fourteen Spaniards rode boldly into the *rancheria* and reined up their horses squarely in front of the chief's house, which was guarded by numerous Indians with bows and arrows. Governor De León, Captain Martín de Mendiondo and Father Buenaventura Bonal pushed their way into the tent, where they found the Frenchman sitting on his buffalo-hide throne, just as Agustín—or Juanillo—had described him. The king knelt at his seat to kiss the hem of the friar's habit, then affably shook hands with the two other Spaniards, repeating over and over again what must have been the only Spanish words he knew—*"Yo Francés, yo Francés!"*

Disdaining further preliminaries, and ignoring the forty Indian guards, De León politely but firmly ordered the white chief to come with him to Mexico, promising that no harm would befall him, and that he could soon return. The Frenchman, who called himself Jean Géry and was about fifty years old, followed De León outside the tent, where he was placed on a horse and whisked away from the surprised Indian subjects.

Géry's interrogation at the presidio was conducted through an interpreter in the language of the tribe ruled by the errant Frenchman, for not one of the Spaniards on that frontier could speak French. Jean Géry deposed that he was a native of St. Jean d'Orléans, France; that he came from a large French settlement on a big river, from whence he had been set to win the friendship of the Indians, among whom he had lived for three years. He offered a detailed but fantastic description of the alleged settlement, and declared that in his exile among the Indians he had twice been visited by his countrymen.

The falsity or extreme distortion of Géry's statement is, in view of later knowledge, no less obvious than the fact that it fitted in neatly with the earlier suspicions of the Spaniards on the frontier, and their desire to persuade the Viceroy into authorizing a full-scale expedition against the French. Considering also Géry's probably disturbed mental condition and the difficulties of the examination in an obscure Indian tongue, it is not unreasonable to suspect that some of the Frenchman's more pat statements may have been put into his mouth by his Spanish interrogators. However, the mystery of Jean Géry has not to this day been completely solved. Some students believe that he never belonged to the La Salle colony in Texas at all, but wandered alone from the French settlements on the Illinois River, a thousand miles away.

De León sent the prisoner to Mexico City, together with a detailed report on his arrest and a strong recommendation for an immediate attack on the French by land and sea. Géry's replies to the interrogation in Mexico, we are told, were very different from the statements he made in Monclova. No definite information regarding the alleged French colony could be obtained, but at least it was evident that Jean Géry was a Frenchman in Spanish territory, far from any known French outpost.

At a *junta general* on July 23, 1688, it was unanimously decided to place De León, who was now a general, in charge of a new and larger expedition early in the following year. Meanwhile in January, 1689, another small expedition went out independently from Parral, in Nueva Vizcaya, under Captain Juan de Retana, but found nothing except a few torn sheets of paper which carried French writing, and a piece of parchment with a picture of a ship on whose sail was inscribed some French verse. These were recovered from some Indians who had taken part in the massacre of the French. The news of the massacre, however, did not reach De León.

A maritime expedition under Rivas and Pez had gone out in the summer of 1688. A landing party picked up a few shattered and rusty muskets but found no other traces of the colony, though they came within less than thirty miles of Fort St. Louis, where even yet a handful of Frenchmen were dragging out a half-starved existence.

As De León had hoped, it was a full-dress expedition that the Viceroy ordered after the interrogation of Jean Géry. The component parts of the *entrada,* assembled from different places, passed in review before General De León at the Sabinas River, in northern Mexico, on March 27, 1689. There were two priests, the *Bachiller* Toribio García de Sierra, curate and vicar of the province of Coahuila, and Padre Manzanet, now minister in charge of the Mission of Caldera. There was the supposedly half-crazed Jean Géry, who had been returned from Mexico City as a guide; twelve mule drivers, most of them well armed; thirteen servants, and the rest soldiers, making 115 in all. This is according to the official list compiled at the moment of the review by General De León. Manzanet, in his letter to Sigüenza, eighteen months later, says there were only eighty persons, a statement typical of his piddling insistence on belittling the military leaders with whom he was associated. In any case, the expedition took along a complement of 720 horses and mules, eighty-two pack loads of flour, biscuits and other provisions, and three pack loads of presents for the Indians.

Even before this cavalcade had crossed the Rio Grande, a troop of redskins, referred to in the chronicle as "the Indians of the Frenchmen," came out from their village to meet the arriving expedition, and installed their revered Jean Géry temporarily in a buffalo hide hut, where they again treated him as a king, with many demonstrations of affection, such as decorating the front yard of his hut with a stake, eleven feet high, on which were fastened the severed heads of sixteen freshly killed enemy Indians. This incident is carefully noted by De León in his "Itinerary," but Manzanet makes no mention of it in the long and detailed account which he gives of the expedition, although one might think that the good friar would be so shocked at such barbarity that he would be sure to speak of it. The explanation of his silence, of course, is that he was interested in emphasizing the good qualities

54

of the Indians and their aptitude for "reduction" by mere persuasion, as against De León, who wanted to establish a string of presidios to rule the Indians by force.

The expedition passed on after endowing the Indians with cotton garments, blankets, beads, rosaries, knives and arms. Five cattle also were killed for the 490 Indians in the village. At the Rio Grande, De León picked up Manzanet's faithful Quems Indian, who told them when they forded the stream that they were about six days' journey from the place of the Frenchmen.

De León and his men spent Palm Sunday, April 3, riding over a level prairie, spotted with mesquite thickets, near which there were pools of water around which thousands of crows gathered at nightfall. They crossed several dry arroyos, then stopped for the night at one that had water in it. On Monday they crossed a larger river, which they named the Nueces (nuts) because of the many pecan trees along its banks. Near the rivers the men had to unlimber their cutlasses and axes to chop their way through the dense growth of prickly pear and mesquite. Passing on, they came to the river which they called Hondo (deep), not because of the depth of the water but because the descent of its banks on either side was about forty feet. Near the river there were little motts of oak, low hills, and white rocks on which Indian pictographs had been carved, apparently a long time ago.

On Holy Saturday, De León ordered a cask of wine broken open and distributed among the men. The same night, by an odd coincidence, the horses stampeded, although fifteen soldiers were on guard; and 102 of the animals got away. Most of these horses were brought back in a roundup on Easter Sunday.

The expedition was now approaching what, on the basis of later and better information than De León had had on his earlier expeditions, was believed to be the site of the French colony. After crossing a river which De León named in honor of Our Lady of Guadalupe, whose statue was carried as protectress of the *entrada,* and whose picture was painted on the royal standard of the expedition, the general called a council of war to determine what should be done to ascertain the strength of the French before venturing into their fortress. "With regard to this," says Manzanet, "there were various opinions, mine being that, since we had with us the Quems Indian, who was well acquainted with the country, we should all have a mass sung in honor of the Blessed Virgin of Guadalupe."

De León accepted this suggestion, which no doubt was de-signed to provide inspiration for the difficult time ahead, but he also decided to lead an advance party of sixty men to spy out the land. Before long, this party found a friendly Indian who told them that, two or three moons past, the Indians of the coast had killed all the white men except a few boys, whom they had carried off. This Indian took the Spaniards to his village, from which all the people ran off when they saw the strangers approaching. The guide persuaded them to come back, however, and finally they embraced the Spaniards, saying "Techas! Techas!" (Friends! Friends!). This is another early appearance of the word which from its frequent repetition and its application to a confederation of Indian tribes more properly known as the Asinai or Cenis eventually came into use as the name of the Province, the Republic and the State of Texas.

And still De León had not found any Frenchmen, although one young Indian buck was wearing the habit of a Recollect friar, which the horrified Manzanet took from him in exchange for a blanket. Through "a poor interpreter," the expedition learned either that four Frenchmen had been at the Indian village two days ago, or that two Frenchmen had been there four days ago, traveling with a group of "Tejas" or Asinai Indians. All the rest of the Frenchmen were dead, said the Indians; those who had not died at the hands of the coast cannibals had succumbed to an epidemic of smallpox.

While searching for the surviving Frenchmen, De León and Manzanet found more Indians dressed in the red clothing of the French, and carrying French books which they hoped to exchange for "presents." Finally De León decided to have his *alférez* (sergeant major), who had served in Flanders, write a letter in French, inviting the fugitives to meet the expedition. De León expected, rightly as it turned out, that the Frenchmen would rather surrender to the Spaniards than continue to brave the terrors of the wilderness.

On Thursday, April 21, the expedition came to another large stream, and their Indian guide told them the French settlement was a little farther down. All this time Jean Géry, with perhaps more guile than the Spaniards gave him credit for, had been attempting to confuse De León by telling him that his Indian guides were misleading him and that the colony was not where they said it was. De León's insistence on allowing the Frenchman to speak led to arguments between the General and Manzanet, but when the priest grew angry, he tells us, De León said, "Father, we are going wherever you wish." When they had reached the river, however, Géry apparently saw that further attempts to lead the expedition away from his friends' colony were useless, and he said, "Sir, now I know very well, yea,

56

very well, that the houses are on this little river."

Three leagues farther on, at eleven o'clock in the morning, the Spaniards found what they had been so anxiously seeking for so many years. There, standing deserted on a flat plain near the edge of the river, were five small houses, built of poles plastered with mud and roofed over with buffalo hides; a hog-house of similar construction, and a wooden fort made from the hull of a wrecked vessel, with the date "1684" carved over the door. The fort had four rooms on the lower floor, one of which had evidently been used as a chapel. In the upper story, which served as a store-room, the discoverers found six pack-loads of iron bars; eight small guns, and three swivels, the largest being a six-pounder. There also were more than a hundred small arms—firelocks, carbines and cutlasses—which had been shattered by the Indians. Also about the area there were dead pigs, plantings of corn and beds of asparagus and endive.

Evidently the Indians who massacred the French settlers had pulled all the Frenchmen's possessions out of their chests, and what they had not carried away they had torn to pieces, so that the whole area was littered with rubbish, including the remains of many fine books in tooled-leather bindings. There also were three unburied bodies scattered over the plain, one of which, from a dress that still clung to the bones, appeared to be that of a woman. Father Manzanet said mass over the remains, and they were buried on the spot. The soldiers carefully searched for other bodies but could not find any, from which it was supposed that they had been thrown into the river and eaten by alligators.

De León, the experienced soldier, noted that the fort and the houses were of such flimsy construction that "All are quite useless for any defense." The "beautiful, level site," however, was "capable of defense in any event."

After being assured that there were no living Frenchmen in the immediate vicinity of the fort, De León went on to explore the mouth of the stream. Near the shore of the bay, which was too wide to see across (the shores being low and sandy with no prominent landmarks) he saw the wrecks of two ships, which we know were La Salle's *L'Aimable* and *La Belle*. In an abandoned Indian village they found a French book, a bottle-case, and, as De León says with chilling vagueness, "other things which gave us indications that the Indians of the village had taken part in the massacre of the French."

Returning to their base camp at the Indian village, the explorers found an answer, written in red ochre, to their letter to the wandering Frenchmen. It was signed by one Jean L'Archevéque de Bayonne, which led

Father García to surmise that the writer might be an archbishop, though actually, of course, "L'Archevéque" was merely a surname.

The letter said that the Frenchmen who had gone with the Tejas would join the Spaniards in two days, for they were tired of wandering among the barbarians. Still the Frenchmen did not come, so De León took a few men to search for them, and found them in an Indian village. L'Archevéque and the other, Jacques Grollet, were naked but for an antelope's skin, and were painted like the Indians. De León questioned them while Manzanet labored to convert the Indian chief and his followers. In this way the Spaniards received the most complete account which they had yet obtained of the disaster of La Salle's colony.

First, said L'Archevéque and Grollet, an epidemic of smallpox had killed more than a hundred persons. Those who remained, being on friendly terms with the Indians, had no suspicion when, one day, five tribesmen came to the outskirts of the settlement on the pretext of telling the colonists something of the highest importance. All the Frenchmen went unarmed to an outlying house to see the Indians, who embraced them while another party of Indians crept up from the neighboring river bottoms, armed with daggers and sticks, to stab and beat to death all of the colonists except a few who escaped or were absent at the time. They then sacked the fort and all the houses, destroying or befouling whatever they did not wish to carry away.

The two narrators and two other Frenchmen, all four of whom had been away among the Tejas Indians at the time of the massacre, returned to find fourteen dead bodies of their companions, to which they gave decent burial, they said, not mentioning the three bodies which De León had found lying in the open. They also exploded nearly a hundred barrels of powder, so that the Indians would not be able to carry it off, and then returned to their good friends the Tejas.

Having thus elicited an incomplete but definitive story of the destruction of La Salle's colony, De León and his party returned to Mexico. There the General was promptly subjected to criticism by the nervous grandees of New Spain because he had neglected to destroy the pitiful little fort and other buildings. L'Archevéque and Grollet were sent to Spain before the year was out. Later they were returned to Mexico—either as prisoners in the mines or at their own request as settlers, depending on which account we accept. L'Archevéque eventually settled in New Mexico and was killed while fighting Indians many years later.

La Salle in Texas

Leaving De León and Manzanet for the moment, we must now go gack in time and ascend to a higher point of vantage to view the train of events that produced the debris at Fort St. Louis. As early as the 1670's, the southwestward movement of French imperialism in America had been nudged into activity by Don Diego Dionisio de Peñalosa Briceño y Berdungo, who called himself the Count of Santa Fé and was in fact the exiled former governor of New Mexico, an irrepressible character who whiled away his time in London and Paris trying to interest the English and French governments consecutively in a project to regain what he considered to be his rights by an invastion of the northern frontiers of New Spain.

Peñalosa's activities in Paris finally became known to a high Spanish official in Flanders, who transmitted the information to the king, who conveyed it to the Council of the Indies. The Council was not greatly alarmed, but it made certain recommendations which induced the king to issue a *real cedula* directing the viceroy of New Spain to investigate the possibility of opening communication with New Mexico by Way of the Bay of Espíritu Santo. This *cedula,* dated December 10, 1678, was the first tangible evidence of a renewal of Spanish interest in the vast territory, larger than Spain itself, that lay within the triangle formed by the Rio Grande and the coast of the Gulf of Mexico.

Yet nothing actually was done, and when war broke out between France and Spain in 1683, the French ambassador in London openly threatened his Spanish colleague with an invasion of New Spain's undefended northern provinces. France, however, had as yet no suitable base for such an invasion, and even in time of peace the Spaniards had seized and imprisoned unwary Frenchmen who merely ventured to sail their ships into the Gulf. When war, based on other causes, gave France the opportunity of settling the question of free trade in the Gulf region forever, the king's minister, Seignelay, had renewed his father, Colbert's, earlier proposal to establish a French port on the Gulf coast of North America.

At this opportune time there arrived in Paris Robert Cavelier, Sieur de la Salle, a Norman who had recently won a great name for himself by his explorations in the interior of North America. There is hardly a personage in history, unless it be Coriolanus, whose qualities and defects are so readily apparent to a casual view, but these qualities and defects were not distinct elements in La Salle's character. Rather they were different aspects of the same traits. What appeared in one situation as a high sense of honor assumed, at another time and place, the look of priggishness. What appeared as noble resolution when directed against the dangers of the wilderness became wrong-headed stubbornness when opposed by human associates. The austere pride that won La Salle the respect of the Indians antagonized his French equals and subordinates. The wary alertness that protected him from the lurking perils of the frontier became in civilized society a morbid suspiciousness that isolated him from human friendship.

La Salle was forty-one years old in 1684. Born Robert Cavelier at Rouen, the son of a wealthy merchant, he had been connected with the Jesuits in his youth in some way which still remains vague because of his unwillingness to speak or write of it. He must have been a teacher at one time, for his enemies sneered that he "never commanded anybody but schoolboys." Be that as it may, he parted company with the Jesuits and forever after suspected that the whole Society of Jesus was plotting his ruin.

At the age of twenty-three he went out to Canada, and within three years undertook a tour of exploration in what was then the remote West, where he discovered the Ohio River. A year later he explored the upper Illinois River and the vicinity of Chicago. In recognition of these and other services he was granted a patent of nobility as the Sieur de la Salle. Later he established two trading posts, Forts Crévecoeur and St. Louis, on the Illinois River and through the neglect of his business in Canada lost most of his investments there. In 1682, although he was overwhelmed with debt and even his Illinois outposts were threatened with dissolution, La Salle, with his faithful friend, Tonty of the Iron Hand, led history's first expedition down the Mississippi to its mouth.

Despite his great discoveries, La Salle found his position in New France untenable, for the governor, La Barre, was openly his enemy. Consequently La Salle could do nothing but fly to the protection of the royal court at Paris. So, on the long voyage across the Atlantic, he matured his plans for the establishment of a French colony at the mouth of the great river which he had been the first to trace along a great part of its extent.

The plan was presented to Louis XIV at a private audience, after which the royal lips were so tightly sealed that the courtiers supposed La Salle's proposal had been rejected. But actually it was La Salle's scheme and not the far more practicable plan of Peñalosa that was accepted and put in motion.

For besides founding a colony at the mouth of the Mississippi, La Salle proposed to lead an army of fifteen thousand Indian recruits on an invation of the northern provinces of Mexico, rich with silver-mines and defended only by a few lazy Spaniards. To clinch the argument, La Salle declared ominously: "Should foreigners anticipate us, they will complete the ruin of New France, which they already hem in by their establishments of Virginia, Pennsylvania, New England and Hudson's Bay."

The grandiose plan to slice off a corner of the greatest empire in the world was to be carried out with one vessel of thirty tons, a few cannon, and two hundred armed Frenchmen. La Salle was given more than he asked, though still not enough for what he hoped to achieve. He was provided with four vessels, while agents of the king were sent to Rochelle and Roche-fort to gather recruits for his little army and his civil colony. Besides a sufficiency of mechanics and laborers, a hundred soldiers were picked up from the grog-shops and alleyways. A few "persons of quality" also joined the expedition, to say nothing of several complete families and a number of young girls bent on matrimony. The spiritual needs of the colonists and the Indians were to be served by at least six priests, including La Salle's elder brother, the Abbé Jean Cavelier of the Sulpician Order.

One thing was lacking, however. La Salle was denied the sole command of the expedition, and its management while at sea was entrusted to Captain Beaujeu of the royal navy, a matter-of-fact and unambitious sailor whose temperament was quite opposite to that of the compulsive and visionary La Salle.

Beaujeu, though he seems to have been amiable enough when not goaded, soon wrote to Seignelay, "You have ordered me, Monseigneur, to give all possible aid to this undertaking, and I shall do so to the best of my power; but permit me to take great credit to myself, for I find it very hard to submit to the orders of the Sieur de la Salle, whom I believe to be a man of merit, but who has no experience of war except with savages, and who has no rank, while I have been captain of a ship thirteen years, and have served thirty by sea and land." Rebuffed, Beaujeu wrote again, expressing his willingness to obey orders, but complaining, "He changes his mind every moment. He is a man so suspicious, and so afraid that one will penetrate his secrets, that I dare not ask him anything. . . . I am bound to an unknown country, to seek what is about as hard to find as the philosopher's stone. It vexes me, Monseigneur, that you should have been involved in a business the success of which is so very uncertain. M. de la Salle begins to doubt it himself."

Among those who observed the preparations at the port of Rochelle, a feeling grew that the expedition was doomed even before it started. Beaujeu and La Salle quarreled continually. Once the captain wrote, "He could hardly keep his temper, and used expressions which obliged me to tell him that I cared very little about his affairs, and the the king himself could not speak as he did. He retracted, made excuses, and we parted good friends. . . . I do not like his suspiciousness. I think him a good, honest Norman, but Normans are out of fashion. . . . His continual suspicion would drive anyone mad except a Norman like me; but I shall humor him, as I have always done, even to sailing my ship on dry land, if he likes."

Beaujeu's impression of La Salle's honest but self-isolated character is confirmed by all that we know of him. Even in his affectionate letter of farewell to his mother, La Salle spoke of his plans only negatively: "We are not going by way of Canada but by the Gulf of Mexico." He then added, "I hope to be successful against them [my enemies] as I have been thus far, and to embrace you a year hence with all the pleasure that the most grateful of children can feel with so good a mother as you have always been."

In speaking of his enemies it would seem that he included the entire human race, or at least the entire French population of North America, for in an earlier letter from Canada he had replied to a correspondent, "You write me that even my friends say I am not a man of popular manners. I do not know what friends they are. I know of none in this country. To all appearance, they are enemies, more subtle and secret than the rest. I make no exceptions; for I know that those who seem to give me support do not do it out of love for me, but because they are in some sort bound in honor, and that in their hearts they think that I have dealt ill with them.''

Naturally such a man had enemies on all sides, enemies of his own making. But whatever he may have thought, he also had a few fanatically loyal friends who were attracted and held by his honesty and his unswerving fortitude.

At the very time when La Salle was making his optimistic preparations for the establishment of a colony at the mouth of the Mississippi, his affairs were in a state which would have crushed a lesser man. One of his forts, Crévecoeur on the Illinois, had been destroyed by mutineers who had also plundered his caches of food and ammunition along the trail to Canada. His other two properties, Fort St. Louis on the Illinois and Fort Frontenac in Canada, were in a deplorable state. His debts exceeded 100,000 *livres*—nominally about $19,000 but many times that amount in purchasing power today—and he had no means of paying them. Yet he was hopeful that he could establish the new colony and return triumphantly to France within a year. As for the conquest of Northern Mexico, it is doubtful if even La Salle seriously thought that he could complete such a project before the end of the war, which already was visibly drawing to a close.

The four little vessels, overloaded with stores and with some 280 persons aboard, including the crews, set sail from Rochelle on July 26, 1684. The quarrels between La Salle and Beaujeu continued during the wretched two-months' voyage, and when the fleet touched port at Santo Domingo, the captain lost no time in writing to Seignelay: "I grant that he is a man of knowledge, that he has reading, and even some tincture of navigation; but there is so much difference between theory and practice, that a man who has only the former will always be at fault. There is also a great difference between conducting canoes on lakes and along a river, and navigating ships with troops on distant oceans.''

While Beaujeu merely complained, many of the rank-and-file deserted because of La Salle's strict discipline and the gloomy reports of the new land which they heard from French buccaneers at Petit Gouave. After three months of delays in the West Indies, during which one of the vessels was captured by the Spaniards, the remaining three ships sailed into the Gulf of Mexico, and in late December they approached the mouth of the Mississippi.

But the bad advice they had received concerning the supposed force of the easterly currents led both La Salle and the more experienced navigators to believe that they were far east of the great river. And when La Salle had come down the Mississippi to its mouth two years before, although he had taken the latitude, he had had no way of determining the longitude. So now the three ships moved westward along the strange coast with the eyes of all on board straining to detect some signs of the great flood of water emptying into the Gulf, not knowing that they already were west of the river's mouth. Soon they were coasting the shores of Texas, hundreds of miles beyond their real destination. They came close enough to land to see buffalo and deer grazing along the shore. A party of Indians breasted the surf and were taken aboard. But they spoke a language that was strange to La Salle, and he could learn nothing from them.

A landing party that went ashore somewhere between Matagorda Island and Corpus Christi Bay found nothing but barren plains, mud flats, oyster beds, and never a sign of fresh water. The coast tended southward, and La Salle, now 500 miles from the Mississippi, was at last convinced that he had passed its mouth. So his ship, the 300-ton flyboat *Aimable* (temporarily separated from the man-of-war *Joly* and the bark *La Belle*) sailed back along the coast. Naturally all this did not happen without further quarrels between La Salle and Beaujeu.

Finally the ships cast anchor just outside of Matagorda Bay, which La Salle announced was the "western mouth" of the Mississippi, though actually it was some 450 miles from the tip of the delta. Beaujeu, noticing the shallow water and swift currents, was unwilling to risk entering the bay, but La Salle insisted and the attempt was finally made after buoys had been set out to mark the channel, the heaviest stores had been unloaded, and the time of high tide had been carefully observed.

The first trip-hammer blow of disaster struck even before the three little ships came into the bay. La Salle had sent seven or eight workmen to cut down a huge tree for the making of a dugout canoe. Soon several of these workmen came running and panting to tell La Salle that their companions had been captured by Indians. So La Salle and a party of soldiers set out for the Indian village, nearly five miles away, to rescue the captured Frenchmen. As they marched, La Salle anxiously watched the flyboat *Aimable* steering toward the shoals, but there was no way to warn her without abandoning the rescue attempt. Soon La Salle heard a cannon shot from the *Aimable,* a signal it had run aground, and a moment later the flyboat, still visible in the distance, furled its sails.

At the Indian village, La Salle found that his men were not being mistreated. The Indians, whom La Salle's lieutenant, Joutel, described as "ugly and altogether naked, except for a skin wrapped about them which hung down to the knees," were in fact friendly enough to bring the Frenchmen some pieces of buffalo meat, both fresh and dried, and some porpoise meat which they slashed with a stone knife, daintily setting one foot on it and holding it with one hand while they cut with the other hand. In spite of such hospitality, La Salle was too uneasy over his ships to stay long with the Indians.

Before morning, the waves broke up the grounded ship and most of the cargo was washed away. The colonists camped on the beach within a rampart crudely fashioned from driftwood. The whole party fell sick with nausea and dysentery, and five or six died every day. Having no ovens to bake bread, they made a slimy porridge out of the flour saved from the wreck, mixed with brackish water. This was the beginning of the proposed conquest of New Spain—a beginning hardly less miserable than its end.

A small party led by La Salle's nephew, Moranget, returning from an Indian village where they had reclaimed some stolen goods, were overtaken by warriors while they slept. Two were killed, one was severely wounded, and Moranget received an arrow through his arm.

Meanwhile Beaujeu, having fulfilled his duty, was preparing to return to France, but offered first to go to Martinique and bring provisions for the colony. La Salle refused the offer, but wrote with unaccustomed mellowness: "I have done my part toward a perfect understanding between us, and have never been wanting in confidence; but even if I could be so, the offers you make are so obliging that they would inspire complete trust."

When Beaujeu finally set sail with the *Joly,* on March 12, 1685, several faint-hearted colonists went with him. Even La Salle's brother, the Abbé Cavelier, was only with difficulty persuaded to remain. The leaders among those who stayed included also another Cavelier, La Salle's nephew, a mere schoolboy, whose first name is not recorded; two Recollect friars, Zenobe Membre and Anastase Douay; Henri Joutel, a gardener's son who was a sort of Admirable Crichton, the most useful man on the expedition; the Marquis de La Sablonniére, a debauched and poverty-stricken nobleman, and four or five other people of some education. These were the chief persons of the expedition that was to establish the power of France on the Gulf of Mexico. The rest were floaters shanghaied from the waterfronts, a few miscellaneous families, and the young women who could not find husbands at home.

Within a few days the chronicles of the colony recorded one man dead from snake-bite; two deserters lost in the wilderness; one hanged for trying to desert. A plot to murder Joutel was discovered and crushed. Once a Spanish ship sailed down the coast, but passed without noticing the huddled interlopers on the beach. La Salle went out on a reconnaissance and finally became convinced that he was not at any of the mouths of the Mississippi.

It was necessary to find the river; but meanwhile the 180 colonists required shelter and defense, and gardens must be planted to provide fresh food. While thirty men remained with Joutel at the stockade on the bay, the rest of the people removed with La Salle a few miles up river. This was in March, 1685. When Joutel joined the main party in midsummer, he found them still lodged in tents and shanties. Drought and wild animals had almost totally destroyed the crops that had been planted. The graveyard near the settlement already had thirty occupants, and as many more lay helplessly ill.

The practical Joutel returned to the first "fort," made a raft and brought up the timber collected there, including the remains of the shattered *Aimable*. Soon a fairly large building was constructed which La Salle named Fort St. Louis, in honor of Louis XIV and the patron saint of the kings of France. The same name was given to the adjoining bay.

Thanks to Joutel's good work, La Salle was now free to continue his explorations. He took with him most of the men and left Joutel in charge of the fort with thirty-four persons, including an unspecified number of women and children. Characteristically, La Salle ordered those remaining to have no communication with the Indians, but to fire on them if they approached—either because he felt that the colonists were not wise enough in Indian ways to deal with them without causing trouble, or because he suspiciously imagined that they might form a league with the Indians against him. He also directed Joutel not to receive any men who might return singly from the expedition, unless they showed a written order from La Salle himself.

La Salle's comparative serenity at the time of the landing had again given way to a mood of fear and persecution. He, who had walked undefended into the very houses of hostile chiefs, now wore a coat of mail which he had pieced together from wooden laths. The strain showed itself in his bearing, and he often insulted his men with little reason, the faithful Joutel admitted.

La Salle left the fort in November, 1685, and nothing was heard from him for two months, until one Duhaut returned with a story of having been lost from the exploring party, and Jontel, after some hesitation, admitted him without the required document. Duhaut reported that La Salle had first returned to the bark *La Belle,* where it lay at anchor in the bay. Here six men were surprised and killed by the Indians, and La Salle found their bodies torn by wolves. Then, leaving most of the party on board the bark, La Salle chose twenty men to continue with him on his exploration. Duhaut, one of the twenty, said he had been left behind while stopping to mend his shoes and knapsack. Unable to pick up the trail, he had returned to the fort by a month of difficult marching, traveling only at night for fear of the Indians.

"Thus it pleased God," writes Jontel, "that he who was to be one of the murderers of M. de la Salle should come off safe and surmount almost infinite dangers."

It was now a full year since the landing, and still nothing much had been accomplished. At the end of March the explorers returned, all in rags and bowed down under loads of dried buffalo meat, for La Salle had feared that those left at the fort might not have had good hunting. "We met with great joy and many embraces," says Joutel. La Salle was first angered at seeing Duhaut, but he too was soon convinced by the man's excuses.

After several encounters with hostile Indians, the returning explorers reported, they had finally found a friendlier tribe who welcomed them as allies against the Spaniards. Farther on to the northeast, La Salle had come to a large river which he first supposed to be the Mississippi, though he had changed his mind later. Here he had built a stockade and left several men whose fate is not on record.

Unable to find the *La Belle* when he returned to the bay, La Salle was immediately convinced that the men left on the bark had abandoned the colony and sailed away to France or the West Indies. Worn down by the hardships of exploration and the mental strain generated by his settled conviction that he was alone against a hostile world, La Salle fell dangerously ill. While recovering he conceived a desperate plan to make his way overland to Canada and bring help to the colony.

Being the man he was, La Salle concealed the extent and difficulty of his plan from his followers, who were allowed to think that he was going only to the Illinois, from where messages might be sent back to Canada and France. So, after stripping the dead to provide clothes for the living, La Salle set out with twenty men, including his brother, his nephew Moranget, and Dominic Duhaut, a younger brother of the man who had returned alone from the previous expedition.

The party journeyed northeast across the buffalo plains, then east to a Cenis village where they were hospitably received. At another village the Indians, who feasted and embraced the Frenchmen by day, crept up to attack them by night, but were driven off by the deep-voiced maledictions of La Salle. At one point, attempting to cross a river on a raft, La Salle and several companions were swept away by the current, but after many hours succeeded in making land. Short of food, the travelers once had to make a supper of two young eagles which they knocked out of their nest. When they became entangled in a cane-brake, La Salle swung a hatchet in each hand and hewed out a path.

At a Cenis village on the Trinity River, the voyagers were met by warriors in shirts of embroidered deerskin, bearing the calumet, followed by the rest of the villagers with offerings of food. The huge beehive-shaped lodges, forty or fifty feet high, were full of loot gathered from the Spaniards and brought here by a party of Plains Indians, who were just now visiting the Cenis. There were silver spoons and lamps, arms, money, clothing, and a printed copy of a papal bull which dispensed the Spanish colonists in New Mexico from fasting in the summer—a dispensation which remained in effect until 1951. The French priests were delighted to find an Indian who pantomimed the ceremony of the Mass and sketched a picture he had seen in some church, which plainly showed the Virgin weeping at the foot of the cross. The visitors invited the Frenchmen to join them on a raid into New Mexico, but La Salle was in no situation to accept the offer.

Parkman says the visitors were Comanches, but it is more probable that they were Apaches, since the Comanches are not known to have reached Texas until well along in the 18th Century.

For two months the party was delayed by illness near what is now the Texas-Louisiana state line. By the end of this time the stock of ammunition was low, and the men who had not deserted were so depleted in strength, that there seemed to be no choice but to return to Fort St. Louis.

Meanwhile, the colonists at the fort, left in charge of Joutel, waited anxiously. Only a week after La Salle's departure, Joutel heard a shouted "Qui vive" down the river and went out to find a canoe bearing six of the people who had been left aboard the La Belle—four men, a girl and a little boy. The Belle was aground on the other side of the bay, and presumably broken up by now. The rest of the people on board had been drowned or had died of thirst and exposure. Of the valuable stores on the bark, nothing had been saved but some of La Salle's personal baggage and papers.

Joutel attempted to assuage the growing uneasiness of the doomed colony by keeping his people busy with various projects for the improvement of their little fortress. The nights, at his command, were taken up with the forced gayety of singing and dancing. One couple were given leave to marry when Joutel and the priests feared that they had "anticipated matrimony," but the ne'er-do-well Marquis de la Sablonniére was refused permission to marry a girl of less exalted lineage than himself. Father Anastase Douay, hampered by his clerical robes, was attacked by a wounded buffalo and lay ill for months. Father Maxime Le Clerc, less innocently employed in writing some "memoirs" which condemned La Salle, had his manuscript thrown into the fire by the loyal Joutel. Before La Salle had been away two months, the men began to mutter over his failure to return, although even a journey to and from the Illinois, to say nothing of Canada, would take much longer than that under the best of conditions.

The elder Duhaut, who had long been disaffected, contended with Joutel for leadership, and attempted, according to Joutel, to bribe the men with a quantity of supplies which were his own property. Many years later Joutel wrote, "It was not long before I had intimation of the whole affair, and I should have done M. de la Salle a singular piece of service, had I then put to death the person who was to be his murderer; but I rested satisfied with giving him a severe reprimand, and threatening to cause him to be secured if he persisted, being able to do no other under my present circumstances. However, I talked to all concerned, and put them in such hopes of M. de la Salle's return, and that things would soon change to their satisfaction, that they were all pacified."

Of the twenty who had gone out with La Salle, eight returned with him. Four had deserted, one had been lost, one had been eaten by an alligator. Six others, given permission to return when they seemed too weak to continue the exploration, had presumably perished in attempting to regain the fort. One of these lost ones—a matter of grave significance for La Salle's destiny—was the younger Duhaut, brother of the man who had already been muttering mutiny.

The End of the Tragedy

It would seem that the outlook was even more dismal now than at the time of La Salle's departure. Since the latest losses, less than forty-five remained out of the hundred and eighty colonists who had bravely landed in Texas two years before. Most of their stores had been destroyed and their way of retreat was cut off by the loss of the ships. The Mississippi had not been found, and the conquest of northern Mexico was seen to be as impracticable as an invasion of the moon. The colonists were hard put to it even to defend themselves from the miserable Indians of the coast. Yet, though La Salle frowned on the singing and dancing which Joutel had instituted, the leader's indomitable courage and his fertility in producing new expedients revived the flagging spirits of the little colony.

La Salle set the men to work building a storehouse, and at the same time prepared for a new expedition to Canada. When he began to suffer from a hernia, Joutel offered to go in his place, but La Salle refused the offer—a refusal which meant his death.

Meanwhile the Barbiers, the couple who had recently been

married, claimed for their expected child the privileges which the king granted to the first-born child in a new colony. This claim was disputed by the Widow Talon, who had a child born on the voyage from France. The dispute became moot when Mme. Barbier suffered a miscarriage.

La Salle's departure was delayed during a mournful celebration of Christmas (1686) and on Twelfth Night the colonists drank a toast according to the old French custom—"The King drinks!"—although the drink was only water. La Salle then took most of the able-bodied men, seventeen in all, and five horses which he had brought back from his last expedition, leaving thirteen men and seven women at the fort under charge of the Sieur Barbier. For provisions the colonists had seventy or seventy-five hogs, eighteen or twenty chickens and a few casks of meal which were reserved for the sick. There was a small supply of powder and shot, but no ammunition for the eight little cannon.

Up to a certain point, La Salle's third exploring expedition was much like all other journeys made by early explorers through the wilds of Texas. The party saw many Indians, whom La Salle approached in a conciliatory manner; as Joutel says, "An infallible maxim, the practice of which might have been fortunate to him, had he followed it sooner."

For the most part the expedition followed the tracks of the buffalo, who instinctively traveled on the lines of least resistance. In one place the Indians told them of "men like themselves" who were no more than ten days' journey away. This was either a delayed rumor of the first De León expedition the previous summer or an inaccurate reference to Mexico itself, where some of the Indians said they had been, although it was much more than ten days' journey. With the infallible Indian instinct for saying what would please the hearer, the Cenis told La Salle that a hundred Spaniards were to have joined them in war against another tribe, but retreated when they heard of the Frenchmen's arrival.

In private matters, as well as in the affairs of nations, a settled attitude of hostility may bring about a fatal quarrel over the most trivial causes. On March 15, 1687, ten weeks after the departure from Fort St. Louis, the expedition was encamped at a place believed to have been near the present town of Navosota, 125 miles from Fort St. Louis. Two or three leagues away was a cache of corn and beans which La Salle had hidden on his former journey; so, with provisions running short, La Salle sent five men to open the cache and bring the foodstuffs to camp.

These men were the Sieur Duhaut, the same who had lost his younger brother and who had long been muttering against La Salle; the surgeon Liotot, who had lost either a brother or a nephew during the Texas venture; "English Jem" Hiens, a German buccaneer who had won his nickname by serving on a British pirate ship; La Salle's faithful Shawano hunter, Nika, and La Salle's personal servant, Saget.

The corn and beans were found utterly spoiled, but on the return trip Nika killed two bufallo and Saget went to notify La Salle, who dispatched his nephew, Moranget, the Sieur de Marle and the latter's servant with horses, directing them to send back a horse-load immediately and leave the rest until it was dried sufficiently for smoking. But it turned out that the hunters had already smoked both of the buffalo and laid aside the marrow-bones, with the meat that remained attached to them, for their own use, according to the frontier custom.

Flying into a rage, Moranget used his delegated authority to seize bones and all, without leaving a crumb for the hunters. It was not the first quarrel between Moranget and the three other *sieurs*. La Salle's servants naturally stood with Moranget, but Duhaut, Hiens and Liotot went off by themselves and began to plot a horrible revenge.

It was soon decided that the trio would murder Moranget, Saget and Nika, but they thought it best to wait until night when the victims were asleep. Meanwhile two friends of the conspirators had arrived on the scene. These were Teissier, who had been a pilot on one of the ships, and L'Archevéque, Duhaut's servant, whom De León later found living among the Indians.

Keeping their own counsel, the conspirators shared in the arrangement of the guard roster for the night. Moranget, Saget and Nika, the first three, took their turns, wrapped themselves in their blankets and went trustingly to sleep, guarded by the murderers, who doubtless had only pretended to rest. It was necessary to do the thing quietly to avoid stirring up the nearby Indians, and on this still night a shot might even be heard by La Salle at the main camp, some six miles away. But Duhaut, Hiens, Teissier and L'Archevéque stood guard with their muskets in hand, ready to fire if there was any resistance, while Liotot, appropriately enough for a surgeon, stepped forward with an axe and gave each of the sleeping men several blows on the head, splitting their skulls. The Indian and the footman died without stirring, but Moranget rose to a sitting position, though unable to cry out, whereupon the conspirators compelled De Marle, who had been sleeping with the victims, to implicate himself by dealing the death blow.

The murderers immediately resolved to go on and destroy La Salle, both because of their long-standing animosity and because he was

72

certain to retaliate for the murder of the others. But the swollen river, difficult of passage, made them put off their murderous journey. Meanwhile La Salle became uneasy over his men's long absence, and inquired of Joutel and others whether Liotot, Hiens and Duhaut had ever expressed any discontent. "That evening," says Joutel, "while we were talking about what could have happened to the absent men, he seemed to have a presentiment of what was to take place. He asked me if I had heard of any machinations against them, or if I had noticed any bad design on the part of Duhaut and the rest. I answered that I had heard nothing, except that they sometimes complained of being found fault with so often . . . . We were very uneasy all the rest of the evening."

Parkman, who spent much time on a later but similar frontier, gives an imaginative but probably correct description of the scene in La Salle's camp during these ominous days: ". . . . The sheds of bark and branches, beneath which, among blankets and buffalo robes, camp utensils, pack saddles, rude harness, guns, powder horns and bullet pouches, the men lounged away the hours, sleeping or smoking or talking among themselves; the blackened kettles that hung from tripods of poles over the fires; the Indians strolling about the place or lying, like dogs in the sun, with eyes half-shut, yet all-observant; and, in the neighboring meadow, the horses grazing under the eye of a watchman."

Thus the time passed from March 17, the day of the triple murder, until the 20th, when La Salle, not minding the swollen stream (for his conscience was clear) set out with Father Anastase Douay and an Indian guide as his only companions, after directing Joutel to send up a smoke signal in case of any trouble with the Indians. He borrowed Joutel's gun, which was the best in the party, as well as his pistol.

"All the way," the good friar wrote later, "he spoke to me of nothing but matters of piety, grace and predestination; enlarging on the debt he owed to God, who had saved him from so many perils during more than twenty years of travel in America. Suddenly I saw him overwhelmed with a profound sadness, for which he himself could not account. He was so much moved that I scarcely knew him," says the friar, giving by implication a glimpse of the iron front that La Salle usually presented to the world, and the turmoil behind it.

Near the little river, La Salle saw two eagles circling in the sky, a sign which the experienced frontiersman interpreted as meaning that his hunters had left the offal of their quarry not far away. So La Salle fired two shots, one from the gun and one from the pistol, as a signal to any of his men who might be in the vicinity. But although his signal was heard, the response was not the answering shot fired in the air that La Salle expected. Duhaut, Liotot and L'Archevéque picked up their guns and crossed the river, with Duhaut some distance in the lead. While the *sieur* and the surgeon kept themselves screened by weeds and brush, L'Archevéque came into the open near the banks of the creek, and La Salle, seeing him, called out, "Where is Moranget?"

L'Archevéque stared at La Salle, evidently recognizing him, but without the customary lifting of the hat or any other show of respect, and answered in a tone which somehow combined studied insolence with involuntary agitation, "Oh, he's somewhere along the river."

La Salle shouted to the fellow to mend his manners and moved toward him, perhaps intending to box his ears, while L'Archevéque drew back, luring his master to the edge of the canebrake where the assassins lay hidden. La Salle had not even reloaded his weapons since firing the signal shots.

Suddenly, as La Salle stalked angrily toward L'Archevéque, Duhaut rose up and fired his gun, shooting La Salle through the head, so that he died instantly without a word.

Father Anastase stood trembling in his cassock, so terrified that he was unable to move, while Duhaut came forward and assured the priest that he had nothing to fear. It was only because of growing desperation, he said, that he had killed Moranget and La Salle. He accused the nephew of having conspired to ruin him, Duhaut, and blamed Moranget as "partly the occasion" of his uncle's death.

Drawn by the sound of the shot, the rest of the assassins gathered to hurl profane epithets at the bleeding corpse and to strip off its outer clothing, including a fine red coat, trimmed with gold lace, which Joutel soon afterward was disgusted to see the buccaneer Hiens wearing on ceremonial visits to the Indians. The surgeon Liotot pointed derisively at La Salle's dead body, with the eagles wheeling overhead, and several times repeated, "There thou liest, great Pasha, there thou liest!" ("Te voila, grand Bacha, te voila!") using the familiar *te* which he would never have dared to employ when his leader was alive. Finally they dragged the body away and hid it in the bushes. Douay, still terrified and confused, forgot his priestly duty of seeing to it that La Salle and the other murdered men received Christian burial. Meanwhile some of the Indians who had been present at the shooting were loud in their astonished contempt for men who murdered their own chiefs.

74

Douay, first to return to the main camp, wore such a look of grief and terror that Cavelier read the tragedy on his face and immediately cried out, "My poor brother is dead!" The murderers rushed close behind, and the two Caveliers fell on their knees, expecting instant death and begging a quarter of an hour to prepare themselves for eternity; but no more blood was shed. The conspirators told the Caveliers, as they had told Douay, that they had acted only out of despair and revenge for their injuries.

The conspirators, of course, were now in control of the camp. L'Archevêque, who had some friendliness toward Joutel, went and found him on a hillock, piling dried grass to burn for smoke signals to guide La Salle back to camp, and at the same time watching the horses as they grazed.

"When he came up to me," says Joutel, "he seemed all in confusion, or rather, out of his wits. He began with saying that there was very bad news. I asked what it was. He answered that the Sieur de la Salle was dead, and also his nephew the Sieur de Moranget, the Indian hunter, and his servant. I was petrified, and did not know what to say, for I saw that they had been murdered. The man added that, at first, the murderers had sworn to kill me, too. I easily believed it, for I had always been in the interest of M. de la Salle, and had commanded in his place; and it is hard to please everybody, or prevent some from being dissatisfied . . . . Having neither arms nor powder, I abandoned myself to Providence and went back to the camp, where I found that these wretched murderers had seized everything belonging to M. de la Salle, and even my personal effects. They had also taken possession of all the arms. The first words that Duhaut said to me were, that each should command in turn, to which I made no answer. I saw M. Cavelier praying in one corner, and Father Anastase in another. He did not dare to speak to me, nor did I dare go towards him until I had seen the designs of the assassins. They were in furious excitement, but nevertheless very uneasy and embarrassed. I was some time without speaking and, as it were, without moving, for fear of giving umbrage to our enemies.

"They had cooked some meat, and when it was supper time they distributed it as they saw fit, saying that formerly their share had been served out to them, but that it was they who would serve it out in future. They no doubt wanted me to say something that would give them a chance to make a noise, but I managed always to keep my mouth closed. When night came and it was time to stand guard, they were in perplexity, as they could not do it alone; therefore they said to M. Cavelier, Father Anastase, me and the others who were not in the plot with them that all we had to do was to stand guard as usual; that there was no use in thinking about what had happened, that what was done was done; that they had been driven to it by despair, and that they were sorry for it, and meant no more harm to anybody. M. Cavelier took up the word, and told them that when they killed M. de la Salle they killed themselves, for there was nobody but him who could get us out of this country. At last, after a good deal of talk on both sides, they gave us our arms. So we stood guard; during which M. Cavelier told me how they had come to the camp, entered his hut like so many madmen, and seized everything in it."

The six loyal ones also discussed the possibility of performing execution on the murderers, but were finally convinced by Father Cavelier's arguments that "we ought to leave vengeance to God," an adjuration that was presumably reinforced by his authority both as a priest and as the brother of the murdered leader.

The next day after the murder the ill-assorted party moved off, through a pouring rain, in the general direction of the Mississippi River. Several days out, they described two Indian horsemen and one man dressed in the Spanish fashion in a blue doublet with embroidered sleeves of white fustian, straight breeches, white worsted stocking, woolen garters, a broad-brimmed, flat-crowned hat, and with long hair. They approached him warily, with visions of arrest and transportation to the mines of Mexico, but he turned out to be an Indian who had appropriated the clothing of a slain enemy.

The following day, at an Indian village where the elders greeted them with such ludicrous howls that the Frenchmen, hard pressed as they were, could hardly keep from laughing, they found a fellow-countryman, a Provençal named Meunier, who had deserted La Salle on his first exploration and who now lived like one of the Indians. Here they heard of two other deserters who were supposed to be living among the Cenis. One of these, a sailor named Ruter, soon appeared and told Joutel of the other, Grollet. Both of these men were naked and painted like the Indians. They had each taken several wives and had fought in the Indian wars, in which they gained great fame as long as their powder and shot lasted.

From these men Joutel heard that there was a great river about forty leagues away to the northeast, with white men living on its banks. Assuming that this was the Mississippi, Joutel and his friends determined to go there, but their plans reached the ears of Duhaut, and he insisted on going along.

The friends of La Salle did not feel safe in Duhaut's company, yet feared to refuse, but their problem was solved in a startling manner.

Hiens, hearing of Duhaut's plan, demanded his share of the stores, declaring that he, at least, did not propose to go to a country where he might be put on trial for his crimes. Duhaut refused to give up the property, so Hiens drew his pistol and fired on Duhaut, who fell dead after staggering four paces. At the same instant Ruter, who had become allied with Hiens, shot Liotot through the body with three balls from his pistol.

Joutel, fearing for his own life, seized his firelock, but Hiens reassured him, saying that he had only avenged his master's death—a strange protestation from a man who had actively assisted at the murder of Moranget and remained hand in glove with the murderers of La Salle. Hiens insisted, however, that he would have prevented the killing of La Salle if he had been present at the time, and he further satisfied the Fathers Cavelier and Douay that he meant them no harm.

Liotot was permitted to live long enough to make his confession to one of the priests, after which Ruter delivered the *coup de grace* with a pistol, and Liotot and Duhaut were buried in a single grave. As in the case of La Salle's murder, the Indian witnesses were shocked and began to throw hostile glances toward the Frenchmen, so Joutel thought it his duty to explain, with all the eloquence at his command, that the dead men had been justly punished, according to the white man's law, because they had appropriated all the powder and ball and refused to give any to the others. This specious explanation convinced the Indians, and all was peaceful once more.

The Frenchmen—conspirators and innocents together—debated what to do next. Teissier and L'Archevéque, both accomplices in the murders, agreed to go along toward Canada after Cavelier gave them his pardon, for whatever it was worth. Hiens argued the difficulties of the journey and tried to persuade everyone to stay here among the Indians. For his own part, he said, "He would not hazard his life to return to France, only to have his head chopped off."

Late in May, 1687, seven men struck out for Canada. They were Joutel, the two Caveliers, Douay, De Marle, Teissier and a youth named Barthelemy. This was the melancholy outcome of La Salle's hopeful expedition of less than three years before—six men and a boy struggling through the forests; five renegades and another boy (Talon) living among the Cenis, and twenty people or less remaining at Fort St. Louis, nearly all of them soon to be massacred.

The seven refugees, with three horses and three Indian guides, made their way through the June weather among friendly Indians during three weeks when their most serious difficulties were occasional hunger, rain, and the oppressive hospitality of the various tribes along the way. Then the party was reduced to six when De Marle, who could not swim, drowned in a river while bathing.

Near the mouth of the Arkansas River, some seven weeks and three hundred miles from their starting point in East Texas, the voyageurs saw the first evidence of civilization that had met their eyes in three long and tragic years—a tall wooden cross and a small house of obviously European construction, from which in a moment two men came out and fired their guns in greeting. These were Couture and De Launay, who had volunteered to remain from a fruitless searching party which La Salle's faithful friend, Tonty, had led down the Mississippi the previous year.

After wintering at Fort St. Louis on the Illinois, Joutel's party finally reached Montreal on July 17, 1688, more than a year after they had left Texas, and early in October they reached France. But the arduous journey brought no result except their own safety. Joutel had strained every nerve to reach France as quickly as possible, trusting that the news he brought would induce King Louis to send help to the tiny band left at Fort St. Louis. But his majesty was not so disposed, and the colonists were left to the fate which overtook them as we have seen, for the meager information gained by De León's expedition is all that we know of the last days of the colony and its final destruction in an Indian massacre.

As for La Salle, his bones have long since crumbled away after being picked clean by the eagles of Texas. If there were any stone to his memory, a fitting epitaph might be inscribed in the words of his faithful lieutenant, Joutel, who knew him as well as anyone, and who admired his virtues without being blind to his faults:

"His firmness, his courage, his great knowledge of the arts and sciences, which made him equal to every undertaking, and his untiring energy, which enabled him to surmount every obstacle, would have won at least a glorious success for his grand enterprise, had not all his fine qualities been counterbalanced by a haughtiness of manner which often made him insupportable, and by a harshness toward those under his command, which drew upon him an implacable hatred and was at last the cause of his death."

The one lasting effect of La Salle's ill-starred attempt at colonization was the slight substance it gave to France's claim that Louisiana extended to the Rio Grande, as La Salle himself had affirmed when he planted the *fleur-de-lis* flag at the mouth of the Mississippi in 1682. This shadowy pretension endured long enough to be transferred to the United

78

States by the Louisiana Purchase in 1803, and the dispute was not finally settled in Spain's favor—except by adverse possession!—until the Florida Treaty of 1819. La Salle's legacy to Texas is her boast that the present state has endured under six flags—Spanish, French, Mexican, Texan, United States and Confederate States—rather than only five; and it is because of him that the Texas Cavaliers, a social fraternity in San Antonio, wear the uniform of the French Foreign Legion, which did not exist in La Salle's time.

7

Texas Established and Abandoned

Soon after De León had reported the destruction of Fort St. Louis, the Viceroy decided that, since there were rumors of Frenchmen still living among the Tejas, and there was at least the possibility of another French attempt at colonization, a new entrada should be sent into Texas to establish missions which, in addition to converting the Indians and helping to secure their friendship, would serve as listening posts in the far interior. Against the advice of De León, the Viceroy's fiscal decided that no presidios would be established, and that no more than twenty-five soldiers would be sent to protect the missionaries.

This decision was changed before it could be effectuated, when an Indian, Joseph, arrived opportunely and told a startling story which De León immediately transmitted by fast courier to the Viceroy. This Indian, according to De León, gave a circumstantial account of how eighteen Frenchmen had come from a great river and had already built three houses near the spot where L'Archevéque and Grollet had surrendered. News also arrived about this time (August, 1689) that war between France and Spain had been renewed after the Truce of Ratisbon.

Although Manzanet challenged De León's report, saying the same Indian had told *him* there were six Frenchmen wandering lost among the Tejas, and not eighteen building houses, the Viceroy asked De León for a detailed estimate of the number of men and the amount of supplies needed for a genuine military expedition. Governor De León's advice was, in the main, accepted, and he was able to start from Coahuila in March, 1690, with 110 soldiers, 150 loads of flour, two hundred cows, four hundred horses, fifty long firelocks, twelve hundredweight of powder, and three hundred-weight of shot, as well as the usual gifts for the Indians. With De León and the soldiers were six priests, two of whom were to be dropped off at the new Mission San Salvador, before the expedition entered Texas. Manzanet, of course, was one of the four priests who were to found the Texas mission. Jean Géry did not go on this trip. He had dropped out of sight since the preceding *entrada,* and his ultimate fate is not of record. Forty of the soldiers came from Zacatecas, and these, Manzanet says, were mostly tailors, shoe-makers, masons and miners, who could not even catch the horses they were to ride.

When the expedition reached the Guadalupe River, a party of twenty, led by De León and Manzanet, turned aside to visit the French fort. There they found all as before, except, as Manzanet says delicately, "Certainly there were signs that the Indians had dwelt there."

De León says in his report of the expedition, "We burned the French fort," while Manzanet, in his letter to Sigüenza, states emphatically, in his anxiety to minimize the accomplishments of De León, "I myself set fire to the fort." Whoever set it afire, the fort burned to the ground in half an hour. Afterward, some of the soldiers from the interior of Mexico asked permission to bathe in the sea, an experience which they considered so remarkable that they carried away flasks of sea-water, which later, in Monterrey, was examined and tasted by their friends with much marveling.

De León and Manzanet observed two objects far out in the bay which, they speculated, might be buoys set out by the Frenchmen to mark the entrance to the harbor. Nothing was done, however, because the expedition had no boats with which to go out to the harbor's mouth. Later, however, Manzanet joined in the criticism of De León for his failure to remove these "buoys". A full-fledged maritime expedition was sent out to take them up, but they proved to be logs which had become lodged, up-ended in the shallow bottom of the bay.

The De León expedition moved on toward the country of the Tejas, its course being partially determined by further reports of Frenchmen living among the Indians. At a *ranchería* near the Colorado River (not to be confused with the Far Western river of that name) they found and "captured," without difficulty, one "Pedro Talo" (Pierre Talon), aged twenty, and one "Pedro Muñi" (Pierre Meunier), aged twelve. These boys still had firelocks, a sack of powder and some shot, as well as twenty silver *reales* and eighty French gold doubloons, each worth eight Spanish dollars. After the doubloons had been passed from hand to hand among the eight soldiers in the party, Manzanet observed, there were only thirty-nine left.

Later in the expedition, De León found Pierre Talon's brother and sister, Robert and Madeleine, and an unnamed French boy, probably the Eustace Breman or de Bremont mentioned in other records. Of the striking adventures which these young people must have gone through since they escaped from the Fort St. Louis massacre more than a year before, the archives unfortunately have nothing to say.

De León also narrowly missed meeting the iron-handed Tonty on his generous, almost solitary, and foredoomed expedition to succor what might remain of the La Salle colony. Other than those just mentioned, and two boys rescued by the Terán expedition in 1691, there were no Frenchmen left in Texas, unless there were some who survived until this time only to perish in the wilderness unknown.

Late in May, 1690, the De León expedition arrived at a village of the Tejas. It had been raining for days. Manzanet characteristically decided that the best way to impress the chief with the holiness of the Spaniards was for him and the three other priests to march into the village through mud and water up to their knees, carrying the Virgin of Guadalupe and singing a litany. This pious conduct, he said proudly, endowed the priests with such fervor that they paid no attention to the water. But Manzanet was alert enough to notice that General De León and twenty of his soldiers remained on horseback—"we who walked were in their midst."

The priests and the officers were invited into the chief's house, a round, windowless building of stakes thatched with grass, fifty feet high. In the middle of the house a fire burned day and night. One half of the house was filled with ten beds, each made of a sort of reed rug, set on four forked sticks and covered with buffalo hides. In the other half of the house there were shelves holding baskets of corn, nuts, acorns and beans, earthen pots, and wooden mortars for grinding corn. The visitors were served a lunch consisting of tamales, nuts, *pinole* of corn, ground-nuts, and more corn, cooked with *frijoles.*

Near a place which some unidentified Frenchmen were supposed to have chosen for a settlement, the Spaniards were shown the graves of two Frenchmen who were said to have shot each other with carbines—presumably Liotot and Duhaut.

When Manzanet had chosen an auspicious site, his first mission chapel, a rude hut of logs, was finished in four days. It was dedicated on June 1, 1690, with a mass, a Te Deum Laudamus, and a royal salute fired by the soldiers. This was the Mission San Francisco de los Tejas, the first Spanish settlement in the future Province. Shortly afterward the missionaries left by the expedition broadened their activities to establish the Mission Santísimo Nombre de María a few miles away. No trace remains of these establishments today, but Dr. Bolton has established the location of the first mission as a point from one to two miles northwest of the modern village of Weches, in Houston County. The second mission was also in Houston County. The locations are in what is now called East Texas, not many miles due east of the midpoint on a line drawn from Dallas to Houston.

At the time of the establishment of San Francisco, De León raised the flag in the name of His Majesty, "whom God protects," accepted the homage of the Indians in the King's name, and appointed the Tejas chief as the governor of his people. This was Spain's first formal possession of the country which, at first called by various names, eventually came to be known as the Province of Tejas or Texas, the *j* and *x* being interchangeable in old Spanish (and both pronounced like an English *h*).

Now arose a characteristic argument between De León and the strong-minded priest, Manzanet. The general wished to leave a garrison of from twenty to fifty men to protect the mission, but the Tejas chief objected that so many unmarried soliders would raise hob among the virgins of the tribe, and Manzanet took his part. It was finally decided that three soldiers would be enough. Fortunately for Manzanet's side of the argument, the orders for the expedition had specified that he was to have the last word regarding the number of soldiers to be retained.

Manzanet had many complaints regarding the conduct of the soldiers on the expedition. Once he complained to De León that someone had tried to rape a chief's wife. "León did not say a word—perhaps because he feared exposure." Manzanet then gives a long list of "points of which I took special note," all unfavorable to De León, of which the tone may be savored from this extract: "Fourthly, Captain De León had a *compadre* along. Captain So-and-So, so honorable that he never failed to play the talebearer and excite quarrels. . . ." And so on at great length.

Hardly a day passed, Manzanet told Sigüenza, without some fighting among the soldiers, or else the officers stabbed the soldiers, so that a lay brother was kept busy treating the wounds with tepid wine, "an excellent remedy for stab wounds."

The expedition of Don Domingo Terán de los Rios, in 1691, was more ambitious in scope than those of De León, but it was a complete failure. Terán was instructed to establish eight new missions among the Indian tribes of East Texas. He was also to seek out any Frenchmen who might remain in the wilderness, for there was a lingering suspicion that another colony of the Grand Monarch, Louis XIV, had been planted in the Piney Woods. If any Frenchmen were found, the Viceroy told Terán, he was to take them prisoner and bring them to Mexico, but he was not to treat them very harshly. And if any French missionary priests were encountered, Terán was to deal with them kindly, reason with them, and try to induce them to cooperate with the Spanish padres. There was no war between France and Spain just at this time, though the old, cold war of imperialistic rivalry continued, complete with its iron curtain.

The fatal flaw in the carefully laid plans for the Terán expedition was the independent status of Fray Manzanet, now the leader of the twenty-one Franciscan missionaries who traveled with Terán's fifty soldiers. While Terán was nominally in command of the *entrada,* and presumably would be held to answer for its success or failure, it was Manzanet who controlled all the supplies. From what we know of Manzanet's character, it seems probable that he exacted this large portion of authority before he would consent to be a party to the expedition, even though he was eager to be in at the founding of the additional missions. It is certain that the entire plan of the expedition, with one insignificant exception, was based on the recommendations of Manzanet.

As for General Alonso de León, after leading the five expeditions which gave the Spaniards their first real knowledge of the interior of Texas, he was denied the honor of leading the new expedition and becoming the first royal governor of the new province. The *junta* in Mexico City declared that his "diligence and care" were needed in defending Coahuila against the Indians, but the truth was that, as a result of continual sniping by Manzanet and others, De León had fallen into disfavor.

It cannot be stated with any degree of assurance that De León died of a broken heart at his failure to become the first representative of the

King in this rich new land, greater than Spain, but the juxtaposition of dates is suspicious. Terán was named Governor of Tejas and the adjacent regions on January 23, 1691, and it must have taken several weeks for the news to reach Coahuila. De León died in March, 1691, at the age of fifty-one.

The Terán *entrada* departed from Coahuila on May 16, 1691, and drew near the site of what is now the city of San Antonio by June 12. Now occurs the first authenticated visit by white men to the site of what was to become the first city, the metropolis and the capital of Spanish Texas, as well as the most populous city of American Texas in most of the census years from 1850 to 1920.

Terán and Manzanet, in their diaries, both commented upon the large numbers of buffalo which they found on the level plains near the Medina River, a few miles southwest of San Antonio. Manzanet also noticed some deer, and Terán, who had served the King for twenty years in South America, compared the plain to that along the Rio de la Plata. From the Medina, Terán reports, they marched five leagues (thirteen miles) "over a fine country with broad plains, the most beautiful in New Spain." Then, he says, they camped on the banks of an *arroyo*, "adorned by a great number of trees, cedars, willows, cypresses, osiers, oaks and many other kinds." Manzanet lists only cottonwoods, oaks, cedar, mulberries and "many vines."

"This I called San Antonio de Padua, because we had reached it on his day," says Terán. The wording is ambiguous and does not make it clear whether the name referred to the place or the river. In accordance with his instructions, Terán regularly gave names to features of the landscape which had not been labeled by previous explorers. He went even farther, in fact, for he frequently reports giving new designations to features which earlier travelers had named to their own satisfaction. It was Terán who tried unsuccessfully to saddle Texas with the dignified but unwieldy name of *El Nuevo Reyno de La Nueva Montaña de Santander y Santillana*. This mouth-filler would at least have been in keeping with Texas' now outdated reputation for having the biggest of everything.

Terán's naming was not limited to rivers and mountains—or provinces—but extended to all sorts of identifiable locations. If he meant to name the San Antonio River, however, his ambiguity was fatal, for this baptismal honor was claimed by a much later expedition. Manzanet, in any case, flatly contradicts Terán when he writes, "I called this place San Antonio de Padua, because it was his day." He adds, "In the language of the Indians it is called Yanaguana."

This account seems to place the Indian village on the river.

though later accounts have it at San Pedro Springs, some distance away. This may be mere vagueness, but neither Terán nor Manzanet mentions the Springs. Probably the truth is that the village had no settled location. In any case it must have been a miserable affair of woven branches, daubed with mud. That was the usual type of Indian construction in this area, though our diarists do not describe Yanaguana.

Terán and Manzanet again disagree, though only slightly, on the name of the tribe inhabiting this village. To the soldier it sounded like *Peyaye,* while to the priest it was *Payaya.* Would it be too imaginative to suppose that the greater sonority of the priest's version was due to his familiarity with the Latin language, which modified his apperception of the sound that reached his ears? Terán's *Peyaye* is more convincing precisely because it seems more improbable from the point of view of one accustomed to the European languages.

Manzanet adds, "This is a very large nation and the country where they live is very fine." Terán goes on to say, "We observed their actions and I discovered that they were docile and affectionate, were naturally friendly, and were decidedly agreeable toward us. I saw the possibility of using them to form *reducciónes*—the first on the Rio Grande, at the Presidio, and another at this point. Different nations in between could be thereby influenced."

Reducción is a South American synonym for *mission,* and the manner in which it is used here implies that these friendly Indians would be employed as an influence and an example to *reduce* other and more refractory tribes to civilization. Terán thus gains the credit for being the first to envision the establishment of a mission at San Antonio, though there is some evidence that Manzanet, during the De León expeditions, had proposed such a project on the San Antonio River, if not at this precise location. In any event, the dream was not to be realized until the Mission San Antonio de Valero (the Alamo) was established in 1718.

Terán concludes his account of Yanaguana with the routine notation, "We did not travel on the 14th because it was Corpus Christi Day." Manzanet, of course, also notes the holy day, but says, "We did not continue our journey because of the presence of the said Indians." He then goes on to recount, with a liberal use of the first person singular, how he ordered the building of an arbor of cottonwood trees, where an altar was placed under a large cross. All of the priests then said mass in the presence of a crowd of Indians, and the soldiers fired a great many salutes, including a special salvo when the Host was elevated.

"After Mass the Indians were given to understand, through the captain of the Pacpul nation [Juanillo] that the Mass and the salutes fired by the Spaniards were all for the honor, worship and adoration we owed to God, our Lord, in acknowledgment of the benefits and great blessing that His Divine Majesty bestows upon us; that it was to Him that we had just offered sacrifice in the form of bread and wine which had just been elevated in the Mass.

"Then," says this strategist of salvation, "I distributed among them rosaries, pocket knives, cutlery, beads and tabacco. I gave a horse to the captain." For this generous distribution of the supplies under Manzanet's control, the "captain" was so grateful, we are carefully told, that he offered to guide the party to the next village, and also detailed four Indians to round up the expedition's livestock. Before this, forty head of horses had stampeded when they were frightened at the large number of buffalo in the vicinity, but they were finally reassembled.

Manzanet noted that in the midst of the Indian village there was a tall wooden cross. The Indians told him that "they knew that the Christians put crosses on their houses and settlements and had great reverence for them, because it was a thing that was very pleasant to him who was God and Lord of all."

The next day, June 15, the expedition moved eastward from San Antonio de Padua over a level country without woods, where Manzanet noticed alligators in an intermittent *arroyo* at a place five leagues east of San Antonio, which the Indians called by the interesting name of Ymatiniguiapacmicen, according to Manzanet, or Smatiniguiapacomlsem, according to other authorities, the name in either case meaning "River Where There Are Colors for Painting Shields." Manzanet and Terán, however, could not agree on a proper Spanish name for the locality. Terán says, "This I named San Ignacio de Loyola." Manzanet says, "I named this spot Santa Crescencia because it was her day." These numerous disagreements over questions of fact can hardly be blamed on faulty memory, for Terán was under orders to record the events of each day immediately upon stopping for the night, and Manzanet apparently did likewise.

More serious differences were in the offing. After learning from a messenger that the padres of San Francisco de los Tejas were in distress from pestilence, Manzanet would not agree to turn aside to the coast, as Terán wished, to make contact with a sea party which was being sent to Espíritu Santo Bay. His persuasive arguments, reenforced by his control of the supplies, won the day for the priest, and the expedition moved on. After reaching East Texas, Terán turned back to meet the sea party. When he returned two months later, Manzanet had done nothing about founding any of the eight new missions ordered by the Viceroy, but Terán had his orders and insisted on leading a party to establish missions in the land of the Cadodachos on the Red River. Nothing came of this sortie, however, and the party returned to San Francisco de los Tejas through severe winter weather, with the horses dying for lack of food and the men half starved.

Relations between Terán and Manzanet were becoming more and more strained. Terán decided to set out for Espíritu Santo, board the ship anchored there, and return to Mexico by sea. To reach the Bay, he needed horses for his men to ride, and cattle to be slaughtered for food along the way. Manzanet refused to yield either cattle or horses from the mission herds, and there was a long deadlock. Finally Terán, in desperation, ordered his men to take what they needed.

"It is to be understood," he explained later, "that I decided upon this measure because it was then that I ran out of military supplies. It is demanding too abject an obedience to expect us to risk such a long journey in the middle of winter, naked and without food."

After many difficulties, Terán and his men reached Vera Cruz eleven months after they had started from Coajhuila, the expedition having accomplished exactly nothing.

Sickness and crop failures beset the two lonely missions. The priests bickered with the soldiers, whom they accused of arousing the enmity of the Indians with their bad conduct—a charge that runs like a refrain through much of the early history of Texas, and which is not hard to believe. As for the Indians, they had lost all respect for the priests, and often threatened to kill them, Manzanet admitted. What was even worse, they refused to believe that there was only one God, but said there were two gods, one who gave the Spaniards clothing, knives, hatchets and the other gifts which they brought to the Indians, and another, the old reliable god who gave the Indians corn, beans, nuts, acorns and rain for their harvests.

In a report to the Viceroy, Manzanet advised that either the missions should be abandoned or a new policy should be adopted, providing for the establishment of a presidio (as had long since been sought by General De León) with a sufficient number of soldiers to compel the Indians to respect the missionaries. A relief expedition under General Gregorio de Salinas Varona, in 1693, had been little help.

The *fiscal* in Mexico City was astounded at Manzanet's *volte face*. "The *fiscal* marvels," he wrote, "at the proposal of violence and the use of force of arms in the conversion of these savages to our holy faith, these means being contrary to sound theology and the dispositions of the sacred councils."

Under the circumstances, however, it was necessary to consider the abandonment of the missions. A *junta general* on August 31, 1693, ordered the withdrawal on the ground that there was no longer any danger from the French, and that exploration of the country had proved beyond question its unsuitability for settlement—a finding which will surprise the present-day inhabitants of Dallas, Houston, and many other thriving communities not far from the sites of the abandoned missions.

An expedition was ordered to escort the missionaries back to Mexico the following Spring. But events moved faster than the Viceroy's messengers. Fearing for their lives as the Indians became more hostile, the missionaries buried their bells and such other property as could not be moved, and departed with the soldiers under cover of darkness for Coahuila. Four of the soldiers, including a fifteen-year-old boy named Joseph Urrutia (whom we will meet again in later chapters) promptly deserted, and Manzanet was told that they returned to show the Indians where the mission supplies were buried.

So ended, in October, 1693, the Province of El Nuevo Reyno de la Nueva Montaña de Santander y Santillana, so hopefully dedicated by Terán de los Rios two years before. The mission Indians ran back to their *mitotes* in the forest, the Texas frontier was formally abandoned by the Viceroy in a *cedula* of March 11, 1694, and for the next twenty-two years none but Indians, a few traders, and a rare exploring expedition disturbed the prairies and the woods between the Rio Grande and the Rio Hondo. Yet it was the experience of working in these first missions among the Tejas that lighted in Father Francisco Hidalgo, the companion of Manzanet, an unquenchable determination which was to lead, by a direct sequence of cause and effect, to the beginnings of permanent settlements in the province almost a generation later.

Meanwhile the general relations between France and Spain, which are of crucial importance to the early history of Texas, were undergoing a somewhat ambiguous development. Spanish power already had long since begun the decline which culminated catastrophically in the revolutions more than a century later. Before 1700, when Carlos II died, the autumn of Spanish power and glory had been signalized by the loss of much of the Netherlands, the island of Jamaica, parts of Alsace and Lorraine, and by concessions here and there to France and the Italian states. When Carlos left as his heir a 17-year-old grandson of Louis XIV, it was another opportunity for the Grand Monarch, in the friendliest way, to draw the Spanish Empire closer under his wing. But England, Austria and some other states disapproved of this threat to the balance of power, and so began the eleven years' War of the Spanish Succession (1702-1713) in which Spain and France were ranged as uneasy allies against most of the rest of Europe.

Around the Gulf of Mexico, however, the colonial officials of both countries continued in competition as before, though Spain seems to have remained largely negative while the Frenchmen busily went about consolidating their control over the mouth of the Mississippi. The whole relationship, like that of the U.S.S.R. and the Western Allies in World War II, seems to have contained a high degree of ambivalence. In the earlier case, this was probably due to two factors: The ministers and generals of Philip V seem not to have been wholly in accord with the King's filial feelings toward his grandfather; and the colonial officials were so far from the Pyrenees (which Louis said had "ceased to exist") that they may have found it difficult to participate in the new spirit of cooperation. Whatever his reasons may have been, the Viceroy of Mexico turned a cold and fishy eye on French efforts to establish trade with the Spaniards in Mexico and with the Indians along the border between Texas and Louisiana.

This Viceregal policy would logically have dictated the establishment of new missions and presidios beyond the Rio Grande. Such establishments, however, though solicited by the friars of the Mission College of Queretaro, were opposed by the clergy of the rival College of Coahuila on the ground that over-extension would be detrimental to the interests of their missions on and below the Rio Grande. These objections served as an excuse, if any were needed, for the indolence of the officials and their indifference to the spiritual welfare of the Tejas.

Once Padre Antonio de Olivares swam the Rio Grande with two soldiers and spent some time teaching prayers to the Indians along the Frio River in Southwest Texas. Returning, he proposed to the Bishop of Guadalajara that a mission be established beyond the Rio Grande. Later Olivares went to Mexico City and presented the case to the Viceroy with somewhat better success, but the new Mission San Francisco Solano, founded in December, 1699, in compliance with Olivares' plea, was on the Rio Grande, where other missions already existed.

It was fourteen years before the next *entrada*, after Salinas Varona's relief expedition to the East Texas missions in 1693, was sent into Texas. In 1707 the *Alferez* Diego Ramón, with twenty-three soldiers, set out to investigate a report that enemy Indians were encamped on the San Marcos River. The details of this expedition are not on record. It was in 1709 that an *entrada* with a similar objective, led by Padre Olivares, Padre Isidro Felix Espinosa and Captain Pedro de Aguirre, visited the San Pedro Springs and gave the San Antonio River its name.

The visit to San Antonio, the high point of this expedition, is described in Espinosa's diary for April 13, 1709, as translated by Gabriel Tous: "We continued our course towards the east through some ravines filled with holm oaks [live oaks], mesquites and some white oaks, until we arrived at the Arroyo of Leon [Medina River] and we crossed it about a gunshot from where General Gregorio Salinas crossed it some years before. We crossed a large plain in the same direction, and after going through a mesquite flat and some holm-oak groves we came to an irrigation ditch [!] bordered by many trees and with water enough to supply a town. It was full of taps or sluices of water, the earth being terraced. We named it *Agua de San Pedro* and at a short distance we came to a luxuriant growth of trees—high walnuts, poplars, elms and mulberries—watered by a copious spring which rises near a populous *ranchería* of Indians of the tribes Sipuan, Chaulaames and some of the Sijames, numbering in all about five hundred persons, young and old. The river which is formed by this spring could supply not only a village but a city, which could easily be founded here because of the good ground and the many conveniences, and because of the shallowness of the said river. This river not having been named by the Spaniards, we called it the River of San Antonio de Padua. Having distributed tobacco among all of them, we took four Indians to guide us from this *ranchería,* and after passing a forest of mesquite trees we came to an *arroyo* of briny water [Salado Creek] and stopped on the opposite bank."

Like too many of the old Spanish documents, this account is annoyingly vague, and the widely copied Tous translation enfolds it in even greater obscurity than that of the original archaic Spanish. First as to the "irrigation ditch." From all other accounts, it is obvious that the Indians of this region, even if they had learned about irrigation from the Spaniards, were not likely to make use of the knowledge, for they were not industriously inclined and, even if they had been minded to drive their women out to work, they did not stay long enough in one place to make such an effort worthwhile. The Spanish language has several terms, like the word used here, *acequia,* which can be used indifferently for a natural or an artificial watercourse, and it is certain that a natural one was meant in this instance, especially as the name *Agua de San Pedro* was forever afterward applied to San

Pedro Creek, a natural stream. Similarly the "taps or sluices" (*tomas*) must be the "seven streams" mentioned by this same Espinosa on a later expedition. The "terracing" of the ground is impossible, if an artificial improvement is meant, and the term, *colgada*, must refer to a natural terrace.

Difficulties also arise over the naming of the river. It is not even clear whether the explorers visited San Pedro Springs or the unnamed springs in present-day Brackenridge Park which are the source of the San Antonio River, though probably the former was meant. The creek and the river run parallel for some three miles before they come together in the southern part of the present city of San Antonio. It is also worthy of note that the river, in the lower part of its course, had been known to earlier explorers, but it was called by different names because the travelers, not being competent map-makers, confused it with other streams that ran in the same general direction.

Salado Creek was an intermittent steam until comparatively recent years, when it came to be fed by artesian wells. Probably it was never salty or briny, and the term used, *salobre*, may be a mistake for *salubre* (wholesome), a favorite word with the Franciscans, who were always intent in praising the country where they hoped to establish missions. However, the modern name *Salado* means *salty*, strangely enough.

Two years after the Espinosa-Olivares-Aguirre expedition, there were still no missions, no presidios and no colonists in Texas. Father Hidalgo, who had been with Manzanet in East Texas, had kept up an unwearying one-man campaign to induce the Viceroy to establish more missions so that he, Hidalgo, might return to his beloved Tejas Indians, from which we may conclude that he had not noticed or minded the lack of "respect" which had impelled Manzanet to abandon the missions.

There is even an unconfirmed story that Hidalgo, single-handed, spent several years working among the heathen in Texas, but this idea is apparently based on a misunderstood phrase in one of his letters.

In 1711, while Spain and France were still allies, Hidalgo despaired of his eighteen-year effort to persuade the Spanish authorities. From the Rio Grande, where he was stationed, he wrote two identical letters to Antoine de la Mothe, Sieur de Cadillac, the French governor of Louisiana, adroitly describing the combined opportunities for trade and salvation in the Piney Woods, and suggesting that the French establish one or more missions in the region.

One of the letters, passing from hand to hand among the Indians for two years, finally reached Cadillac at his headquarters on Mobile

Bay. The governor immediately dispatched Louis Juchereau de St. Denis to find Hidalgo and discuss the proposition with him. This St. Denis, a fascinating character, was a Canadian-born trader and soldier, then in his late thirties, who spoke Spanish and several Indian dialects and had made at least one previous journey through Texas. Although he was not quite scrupulous in his methods, he never did harm to anyone, and he was liked and admired—though not necessarily trusted—by all who knew him.

Carrying 10,000 francs worth of trade goods, St. Denis set out from Biloxi in September, 1713, on a leisurely expedition with the combined objects of trading with the Indians, establishing a small colony at Natchitoches in western Louisiana (the first settlement in the future Louisiana Purchase), and attempting through Hidalgo to establish trade with the jealous and suspicious Spaniards in Mexico. After leaving some of his party to build houses at Natchitoches, he set out to the Southwest with twelve Frenchmen and a few Indians in the spring of 1714.

After twenty days, in which time five of the Frenchmen had deserted, St. Denis arrived in the country of the Tejas (or Cenis, as the French called them). He found the chief, Bernardino, eager to accompany him in order to ask the Spaniards to send them missionaries, for it appeared that since 1693, when they drove out the first Spaniards, the Tejas had missed the gifts and other benefits brought to them by the *padres*. They were especially anxious to see their old friends, Father Hidalgo and Captain Urrutia, the latter of whom had spent seven years among the Tejas and led them in many expeditions against their enemies.

St. Denis left four of his companions with the Tejas and continued his march with three Frenchmen, Bernardino and twenty-four of the Tejas Indians. The Indians he had brought from Louisiana apparently had dropped out and returned to their homes.

Thanks to their four good French rifles, the party of twenty-nine persons was able to resist two hundred Apaches, armed only with bows and arrows, in an attack at the banks of the San Marcos River. After a pow-wow with the Apaches, however, it was deemed expedient for Bernardino and all but four of his Indians to return home, while St. Denis continued his journey with the four remaining Indians and three Frenchmen, two of whom are named as Medard Jalot, St. Denis' "valet," who seems to have been a barber-surgeon, and André Pénicault, a frontiersman who later wrote a "Relation" which is a valuable source for the history of this period, though it covers St. Denis' expedition only up to the time of his departure from the Tejas country. The third Frenchman presumably was Pierre L'Argent, who certainly was with St. Denis on his return trip through Texas two years later.

Without further incident, St. Denis and his little retinue arrived at the Presidio of San Juan Bautista, on the Rio Grande, in August, 1714. The journey from Mobile Bay had taken him twenty-one months. He arrived almost four years from the day when Hidalgo had written his eager letters, and two years after the wartime alliance between France and Spain had ended.

The commander at San Juan when St. Denis arrived was Captain Diego Ramón, a soldier of long service on the frontier, who had been Governor *ad interim* of Coahuila between León and Terán. Of his five grown children, only two need concern us. These are Diego, Jr.,*alférez* or sergeant major at San Juan, whose expedition into Texas in 1707 we have already noticed, and who had a marriageable daughter, Manuela Sánchez Ramón; and José Domingo Ramón, usually called Domingo, of whom more later. Old Diego had also a number of cousins, nephews and other relatives in northern Coahuila and apparently the clan ran things in this part of the country pretty much to suit themselves. Even today the name Ramón is both a common and a prominent one in the region, where it is borne by, among others, a recent mayor of Ciudad Acuna, the Mexican town across the Rio Grande from Del Rio, Texas. Old Captain Diego, by the way, was also a forebear of the Callagham family, prominent in San Antonio politics from 1846 to 1949, during which time it gave the city three mayors.

St. Denis bowed to the captain of the presidio with debonair French courtesy, presented his credentials, and explained that he had set out from Louisiana with orders from the Governor to purchase grain and cattle, greatly needed in Mobile, from the missions which (so he said) the French had believed were still functioning in the land of the Tejas. Having found the missions abandoned, St. Denis said, he had continued his march to the Rio Grande. Evidently no mention was made of Hidalgo's letter, and the chevalier said nothing about that part of his orders which instructed him to spy on Spanish activities on their northern frontier.

Captain Diego explained, quite truthfully, that his authority was so limited that he could not grant the desired trading privileges, but that he would promptly submit the question to the Viceroy. His message, when it arrived in Mexico City, threw the Viceroy and his aides into consternation over the suddenly revealed fact that a Frenchman could openly travel through Texas to the Rio Grande without any let or hindrance from the Spanish.

The Viceroy ordered that St. Denis be sent to Mexico City

under guard, though he was to be treated with the utmost courtesy, as befitted the son of a man who had been ennobled for his services to *le roi soleil*. While they waited for St. Denis to arrive, the Viceroy's officers studied the situation with what for them was unaccustomed diligence, so that in less than a year they had arrived at certain conclusions and two decisions.

The conclusions were that Spanish commerce in the North was on the brink of destruction; that the precious mines of Mexico were open to invasion, and that Texas was in imminent danger of becoming a French province. These findings were not as exaggerated as they may seem to us. It was only a few years since the Spaniards had lost their shadowy claim to the mouth of the Mississippi and the central Gulf Coast through their lassitude and cowardice in the face of French incursions only a little more forceful than St. Denis' expedition through Texas. The Viceroy also well remembered that La Salle, thirty years before, had claimed for the French King all the territory east of the Rio Grande.

The decisions which followed logically, according to the Spanish way of thinking, from these conclusions, were that the governors of the northern provinces must be ordered to "prohibit" the further entrance of Frenchmen into Spanish territory, and that an expedition must be sent to reestablish the missions on the eastern frontier, so that they might bring salvation to the Indians and news of French maneuverings to the Viceroy.

It was a year before St. Denis reached Mexico City, which he entered in June, 1715. It must have been an exhilarating experience for this backwoodsman to ride into what was then the greatest city of the Western Hemisphere, knowing that he was to meet the King's own deputy in the capital of New Spain. He enjoyed a pleasant afternoon with the Viceroy, during which he showed a map of Texas that he had drawn while on his journey, and he told the Viceroy things which no Spaniard yet knew about the interior of the Province. He offered his services for a Spanish expedition into Texas, and with all the assurance of a plenipotentiary (which he was not) he advanced the interesting proposal that the Mississippi should be designated as the boundary between French and Spanish possessions in North America. This last is all the more interesting if we remember that St. Denis had just come from establishing a new French post at Natchitoches, some 100 miles west of the Mississippi.

There can be no doubt that this charming Frenchman was somewhat disingenuous in his dealings with the Viceroy, but there is no reason to believe either that he was disloyal to the French Crown or that he was guilty of any heinous imposition on the Spaniards. His main purpose was to establish a trade which would be beneficial to the new French colonies near the mouth of the Mississippi and profitable to himself. To obtain official approval for this trade, he had to ingratiate himself with the Viceroy. and it was by no means inconsistent for him to aid in the reestablishment of Spanish missions or colonies in East Texas, for such a movement would facilitate commerce by bringing the frontiers of the two nations so much closer together. Further, the Spanish missions would aid in regulating, and keeping congregated in one place, the Indians with whom St. Denis also hoped to maintain commercial relations. Even though his methods were somewhat strange, he must have felt that his intentions were of the purest, for his later reaction of rage and hurt, when the Spaniards turned against him (as we shall see) had all the earmarks of injured innocence. Father Morfi, the 18th-Century Spanish historian, who carefully studied all the available records in the case of St. Denis, concluded that "during the time he was among us, he served with great honor, and the most scrupulous investigation has failed to reveal in his conduct the least reprehensible act on his part."

And yet, at the same time that St. Denis accepted a year's pay in advance to serve the Spanish government, he wrote to advise Cadillac that the Viceroy was about to send a party to establish a mission among the Tejas, asked that a French brigantine be sent to Espíritu Santo Bay, and declared it would be necessary for the King of France to require that the boundary of Louisiana be fixed at the Rio Grande. Also, during St. Denis' stay at San Juan Bautista, rumors were rife that the hills back of the presidio were full of "Ramonistas"—followers of the Ramon family—who were engaged with St. Denis in contraband trade.

Not only intrigue, but romance also was in the air. During the year that St. Denis spent at San Juan Bautista, virtually under arrest, he met the captain's granddaughter, Manuela Sánchez Ramón, daughter of the *alférez.* Love bloomed in the dusty patios of San Juan Bautista, and the result, as often happens, was marriage. Many adventures and a long separation, however, took place before the couple came to "live happily ever after" at the post of Natchitoches.

By this time the death of the Spanish King's beloved grandfather, Louis XIV, had left Spain free to purchase a more aggressive policy on the frontier of Louisiana. Besides St. Denis' operations, the Viceroy had as a spur to action a rumor that the French were planning to establish a new colony on the site of La Salle's ill-fated settlement at Matagorda Bay. This rumor had some foundation; but the colony actually established three years later was 400 miles farther east, near the mouth of the Mississippi, and its name was New Orleans.

The Texas Missions Reborn

P ursuant to the new Spanish policy, an expedition was organized in northern Mexico, early in 1716, under the nominal leadership of Captain Domingo Ramón, son of Captain Diego Ramón. But the real head of the *entrada,* bearing the titles of *cabo comboyador,* or chief guide, and *conductor de viveres,* or commissary, was none other than Louis Juchereau de St. Denis, who by this time had been adopted by the Spaniards to the extent that they called him "Don Luis de San Dionisio," or "Sandenis," or even, with an affectionate informality that was rare in those days, simply "Don Luis."

With St. Denis and Ramón went twenty-five soldiers, many of whose family names are found in present-day San Antonio; nine priests and lay brothers, including Father Hidalgo and Father Espiñosa; Médard and L'Argent; fourteen mule drivers, including a Negro named Juan de la Concepción; eight women; a boy of six and a girl of four; two "families" of unspecified components; two Indian guides and "three Indians with the goats." The presence of the women and children, it was said, convinced the

Indians that the Spaniards had come to stay.

The Venerable Father Fray Antonio Margil de Jesús, president of the College of Zacatecas, was to have gone with the expedition but was detained by illness. We shall hear more later of this priest, who today is said to be nearer canonization than any other man who ever lived in Texas. Another man who missed the expedition was Captain Joseph de Urrutia, who was much in demand for his knowledge of the Indians, having lived seven years with them after his separation from the Manzanet party in 1693—a separation which he now attributed to his having been left wounded on the banks of the Colorado. Of him Father Margil said, "If Urrutia goes, nothing can be done or planned either by the French or the Indians which the Tejas will not communicate to him. If the French, because of their following, can raise a thousand men, Urrutia can raise ten thousand." These words sound like an echo of remarks elsewhere attributed to Urrutia himself, who was by no means modest. It is true, however, that the Tejas Indians had begged for his and Father Hidalgo's return. Being engaged in the delicate task of pacifying the Indians of Nuevo León, however, Urrutia could not be spared for the Texas expedition. Of him, too, we shall hear more later.

The Ramón-St. Denis expedition crossed the Rio Grande on April 27, 1716, and had made the 150 miles to the Medina River near San Antonio by May 13. On the 14th, approaching the site of the future city, the party set out north-northeast through hills and dales covered with green grama grass. Espinosa noted in his diary that in Leon Creek "there are pools of water" and went on to describe the progress of the march: "From thence by northeast we entered the plain at the San Antonio River. At the end of the plain there is a small forest of sparse mesquites and some oaks. To it succeeds the *Agua de San Pedro;* sufficient for a mission. Along the bank of the latter, which has a thicket of all kinds of wood, and by an open path we arrived at the San Antonio River. This river is very desirable (for settlement) and favorable for its pleasantness, location, abundance of water and multitude of fish. It is surrounded by very tall *nopals,* poplars, elms, grape vines, black mulberry trees, laurels, strawberry vines and genuine fan palms. There is a great deal of flax and wild hemp, an abundance of maidenhair fern and many medicinal herbs. Merely in that part of the density of its grove which we penetrated, seven streams of water meet. Those, together with others concealed by the brushwood, form at a little distance its copious waters, which are clear, crystalline and sweet. In these are found catfish, sea fish, *piltonte, catan* and alligators. Undoubtedly there are also various other kinds of fish that are most savory. This place mellowed the dismal remembrance of the preceding one. Its luxuriance is enticing for the foundation of missions and villages, for both its plains and its waters encourage settlement."

Ramón, who also kept a diary, was more matter-of-fact. "On this day," he wrote, "I marched to the northeast seven leagues through mesquite brush with plenty of pasturage. Crossing two dry creeks we reached a water spring on level land, which we named San Pedro. There was sufficient water here for a city of one-quarter league, and the scenery along the San Antonio River is very beautiful, for there are pecan trees, grape vines, willows, elms and other timbers. We crossed said stream; the water, which was not very deep [i.e., the banks were not very high], reached to our stirrups. We went up the river looking for a camping place and found a very fine location. There were beautiful shade trees and good pasturage as we explored the head of the river. Here we found . . . hemp nine feet high and flax two feet high. Fish was caught in abundance for everyone, and nets were used in the river with ease. The day was spent at this place because it was very desirable to rest the horses and to celebrate the Feast of San Isidro." This last has the sound of a sly dig at Father Espinosa, whose name-day it was.

St. Denis kept no diary, but in a formal statement at Mexico City a year later he declared that "If the San Antonio River should be occupied with 500 veterans and the Bay of Espíritu Santo with 100, the dominion of the King our Lord will rest secured and many should be converted to the Faith, because from the Day it will be possible to control the Tejas, the San Antonio River and the Rio del Norte." The reference to the King of Spain as "our Lord" does not mean that St. Denis had completely turned his coat, since his testimony is quoted only indirectly in the archives.

Apparently no Indians as were encountered by the Ramón-St. Denis expedition at San Antonio—a blow to the theory held by some local enthusiasts that the Yanaguana described by Manzanet and supposedly visited by Cabeza de Vaca was a permanent settlement. From the San Antonio River the expedition continued across mesquite-studded prairies, rolling hills and dense woods, crossing many rivers and discovering the remarkable Comal Springs at the source of the little Comal River in what is now Landa Park at New Braunfels. In many places the expeditionaries were molested by ticks and mosquitoes, and the heat in the afternoons became oppressive, though it was still only May.

On Ascension Day, May 21, seven masses were said, one by each of the seven priests in the party. Many persons received communion, and a sermon was preached in the evening, as had been done every third day since the setting out of the expedition. In the late afternoon an atmospheric phenomenon appeared in the form of a white and dark-gray semicircle crossing the entire sky. "Let the critic draw conclusions," the Padre wrote cautiously. "I am just stating the incident. . . . To some, it seemed a presage of joy; but to others a foreboding of sadness and melancholy."

They found ample water all the way, testifying to an unusually wet season in this part of Texas, and on May 23 they found the Colorado River, just below Austin, so swollen that they had to pitch camp and wait a favorable opportunity to cross. In spite of a thunderstorm, the river fell three feet during the night, and the leaders decided to cross, after preparations which included the sayings of seven more masses by the seven missionaries, each invoking divine assistance through his own patron saint.

In spite of these precautions, it took two days for the expedition, with all of its animals, to cross over against the strong current, and one priest was nearly drowned. Soon after this, the travelers killed their first buffalo, tapping a source of food which served them well in the weeks ahead. Thus far, the Ramón-St. Denis party had followed a path beaten by the Espiñosa-Olivares-Aguirre expedition seven years before. Now they were striking out into a new country, for although De León and Terán had been in East Texas, they had gone by a different route, closer to the Gulf.

On Brushy Creek, between Taylor and Cameron, Ramón recruited two Indian guides. About the same time, two Mexican Indian servants, hunting the buffalo, were lost in the dense woods along Brushy Creek. (Why they were looking for buffalo in the woods is a mystery.) Says Espinosa, "Seven Masses were celebrated for the return of the lost ones. Not expecting, however, that they would appear miraculously, sixteen Indian friends went out with the soldiers to search for them." But still the strayed hunters could not be found.

More and more Indians were joining the party as it struggled on through dense woods, laced with grapevines, in the vicinity of the San Gabriel River. Finally, after nine days of such difficult traveling, the Spaniards came out at a large Indian village, where some 2,000 people of various tribes had congregated under several chiefs, one of whom had visited Ramón at his presidio across the Rio Grande.

Word of the missionaries' approach had preceded them, and the Indians had built them a bower of branches, where some 500 people of all ages came to kiss their hands. As for the secular members of the expedition, Ramón tactfully encamped them a rifle-shot away from the village, warning them to be fair in trading with the Indians and not too eager in pursuing the native women.

After a day's trading, the expedition moved on to the Brazos River, where it negotiated another difficult crossing. At the farther bank the two lost servants reappeared, and "though reprehended they were well received," says the chronicler.

While helping to build a rude barge for the crossing, one Indian was threatened by an alligator, which Ramón dispatched with a well-placed shot through the eye, said to be the only vulnerable spot. The Indians were greatly impressed with such marksmanship.

The first horse-races ever seen in Texas were held by the soldiers of the Ramón party to celebrate the Feast of St. John, June 24, 1716. Each soldier placed bets on his entry—a practice which has been alternately permitted and forbidden by the Texas Legislature in the present century.

The expedition was now approaching the land of the Asinai or Tejas Indians. Some of this tribe had already joined the party, and St. Denis had gone ahead with a son of Captain Ramón to inform the chiefs of the expedition's approach and ask them to assemble their tribesmen. On June 27, four days after crossing the Trinity River, the Spaniards were met by 34 Indians, with St. Denis at their head. At this ceremonial meeting, Espiñosa records in his diary:

"We arranged the soldiers in two files, placing our captain in the center with the religious, and in this order we went to greet and embrace them, our hearts overflowing with joy. In order to enter fittingly, the Indians left their horses behind; the bows and arrows and the firearms that some brought, they left in the hands of other Indians who ministered to them as servants. There was a general salute on our part, and in the meantime we went to the place prepared for the reception, which was a hut of boughs of trees, carpeted with blankets, the packsaddles serving as stools. There, all seated according to rank, a page of the Tejas drew out a pipe, filled with the tobacco which they cultivate in their fields. The pipe was very much ornamented with white feathers, a sign of peace among them. He lighted the pipe and made each one of us take a puff of smoke. We returned the compliment with the same courtesy and served chocolate to them. The function terminated with a very serious discourse by an Indian chief, in which he gave us to understand the pleasure with which all desired to receive us in their midst, as Don Luis de San Dionisio, who understands and speaks much of their language, made known to us. This day was most pleasing to us, holding out, as it did, such great prospects of attaining our end and achieving our purpose so much desired. That night the Indians gave a salute and feasted on an ox which the chief served them for their pleasure."

The next day the Spaniards had another call, this time from a party of 96 Indians. Again there was a formal greeting, and this time Captain Ramón bore a standard on which were painted the images of Christ crucified and the Virgin of Guadalupe. This delivered into the hands of Father Espinosa, after which Ramón knelt, kissed the holy images and embraced the *padre*. All the soldiers then did likewise, after which the military fired a salute while the priests marched in procession, singing a *Te Deum Laudamus*. After these ceremonies, the Indians brought gifts of corn, watermelons, tamales and cooked beans with corn and nuts, receiving in return gifts of blankets, sombreros, tobacco and flannel. All night the Indians expressed their joy in wild ceremonial pagan dances, but the next morning a "multitude" of them attended high mass in honor of St. Peter.

While the Indians remained in this hospitable frame of mind, Ramón addressed them through an interpreter, pointing out that the gifts he had brought them really came from the King of Spain, who desired them to choose from among their chiefs a captain general to rule among them as his representative. They duly elected a chief who, being young, was fairly sure to have a long reign if he was not killed in battle. Ramón recognized this new super-chief by presenting him with a baton as a symbol of office and one of the best coats from the Spanish captain's own wardrobe.

This done, an exploring party went out to find a suitable location for a *presidio*. A site was found in a clear space by the edge of a lake, on the west side of the Neches River, and within two days the Indians had built a small house for Ramón. This grass-roofed *jacalito* was completed on July 2, 1716—an important date, for it marks the beginning of continuous settlement in the Province of Texas. The new presidio was christened Nuestra Señora de los Dolores de los Tejas.

Meanwhile the priests occupied their time in saying mass, writing down words of the Asinai language, and discussing with the Indians (St. Denis serving as interpreter) the locations of the four projected missions. The first mission, a mere shanty, was built on July 3 near a spring of water in Cherokee County, probably on Bowles Creek not far from the Neches. It was named San Francisco de los Neches and was considered to be a reestablishment of the Mission San Francisco de los Tejas, in Houston County, which had been established by De León and Manzanet in 1690 and abandoned in 1693.

San Francisco de los Neches remained active until 1719, when it was temporarily abandoned because of war with the French. Reestablished in 1721 (See Chapter XI), it was transferred to San Antonio in 1731 under the name of San Francisco de la Espada. The latter establishment still stands, but the log huts in the East Texas woods that served as the original missions have long since rotted away.

Only four days after San Francisco de los Neches, another little mission, designated as Nuestra Señora de la Purísima Concepción, was founded near Linwood Crossing on the east side of the Angelina River, in Nacogdoches County. Concepción's future destiny duplicated that of San Francisco, for it also was moved to San Antonio, where it now stands. The third mission established by Ramón and Espinosa was Nuestra Señora de Guadalupe, founded at Nacogdoches on July 9, only two days after Concepción. Its first pastor was Father Fray Antonio Margil de Jesús, the saintly man who, prevented by illness from joining the expedition at its outset, had recovered sufficiently to hurry in pursuit and overtake the others before they arrived in East Texas. This mission, after a brief abandonment from 1719 to 1721, remained in operation on the original site until 1772.

The fourth mission, San José de los Nazones, near the present town of Dolores, was established the day after the Guadalupe Mission. San José de los Nazones followed the course of the first two missions, for it was temporarily abandoned in 1719-1721 and transferred in 1731 to San Antonio, where it became part of a new establishment, San Juan Capistrano, which still remains.

With the establishment of four missions and a presidio, the work of the Ramón-St. Denis expedition was completed, and success had come at last to Father Hidalgo, who had longed for this moment of return ever since the forced abandonment of the two original East Texas missions in 1693. And, although it had taken four years, Hidalgo's rash letter to the French Governor Cadillac had justified itself by making possible the return of the missionaries, though certainly in a most unexpected way.

Espinosa concluded his diary with a description of the Tejas Indians as he understood them:

"The particular traits which we have observed in this people are their loyalty to their lands and the skill with which they construct their houses. These have high beds for everyone, and compartments of wood where large baskets of nuts and beans are stored for the whole of the year. They are very charitable among themselves and assist one another in need. They recognize a superior head, who directs them when they have to work, and there is one who gives them orders and punishes them harshly when they do not go to work or if they are lazy. They have all the earthenware that is necessary for their service, and curious seats of wood for those who come to their houses.

From what we have observed it will require solicitude and labor to eradicate a number of abuses to which they are addicted, since they hardly ever take a step that is not directed by some particular abuse. Time will reveal minutely the good qualities as well as the evil propensities of these people. . . ."

The Tejas Indians, more properly called the Asinai or Hasinai, had been selected as the tribe to benefit by the first missions because they were recognized as the strongest, the best organized, most influential and probably most civilized tribe in Texas, besides which their country was strategically situated across the trade routes by which the French had been attempting to penetrate into territory claimed by Spain. But the Tejas had already been subjected to French influence, and they were clever enough to play off the French against the Spaniards, gaining favors from both sides in the struggle for empire.

The missions had hardly been established, but the Indians had received their gifts, when they told the *padres* they could not congregate and form settlements around the missions until their crops had been gathered in the fall. Later the majority of the Indians found other excuses for continuing their old, pagan habits, so that the East Texas missions were never highly successful.

In the fall of 1716, Ramón established his permanent presidio, about three quarters of a mile from the first mission, San Francisco de los Tejas. About the same time (though the exact dates are not given in this part of the record) two more missions were founded. One of these was Dolores de los Ais, near the modern town of San Augustine, and the other was San Miguel de Linares, across the Sabine River in what is now Louisiana, not far from the French outpost of Natchitoches.

Even before these last two missions were established, on July 26, 1716, Ramón wrote to the Viceroy, calling attention to the exposed position of the Spaniards in East Texas and asking for twenty-five more soldiers and $6,000 a year to buy gifts for the Indians. He also asked that the pay of the soldiers be increased from $400 to $500 a year because of the high cost of shipping provisions from Mexico. Ramón also suggested that more civilian settlers would be desirable. Should gold and silver be found in the province, as he hinted was not unlikely, the settlement of civilians would be made easier, but he asked the Viceroy to send only those of exemplary character, "for the good and bad habits and customs of our people are transmitted imperceptibly to those of the land."

In the first few months in East Texas four soldiers died and many deserted because of the hardships of life on this extreme frontier, many weeks' journey from civilization in Mexico. Evidently a halfway station was needed between the East Texas missions and the settlements on the Rio Grande. This was one of the considerations that led to the founding of San Antonio two years later.

As for St. Denis, when the missions were established he had hurried to Mobile with Ramón's son, Diego II, to obtain a new stock of trade goods. There it turned out that Crozat, the French concessionaire, was for some reason unwilling to entrust St. Denis with any more merchandise, even on the security of Governor Cadillac. The resourceful St. Denis thereupon organized a company, got his merchandise and, a year later, returned to the Rio Grande. Here he was again placed under arrest, his goods were seized, and he was sent to Mexico City for a hearing. There he was placed in prison for a time. It took nothing less than a royal decree to restore his goods. He escaped from Mexico City just in time to avoid being returned to prison. Once out of the capital, he followed a leisurely though secret course, returning to Natchitoches after six months. There he became commander of the post and played a prominent part in border affairs for the next twenty-eight years.

The Birth of San Antonio

Father Olivares, conspicuously missing from the Ramón-St. Denis expedition, was meanwhile busily engaged in selling the idea of a mission at San Antonio to the Viceroy. In November, 1716, Olivares made a detailed proposal for such an establishment, which he wished to call the *Mision del Río de San Antonio de Padua*. The mission was to be supplied with a "garrison" of two soldiers; specified numbers of cattle, sheep and goats; gifts for the Indians; tools, and various other equipment.

The idea that such a mission at San Antonio was already established in 1716, as suggested by one local historian, rests on a single ambiguous phrase in one of Olivares' letters. It was also alleged many years later that there had been a presidio and a civilian settlement in San Antonio in 1716, or even as early as 1691. This claim was maintained in statements made near the end of the 18th century by people interested in establishing their inherited rights to priority in the land. There seems to be not the slightest contemporary evidence in support of such theories, though the documents of the period have been well preserved and carefully studied.

Olivares predicted optimistically that his proposed mission would eventually make up a *pueblo* of three or four thousand souls. To begin with, he proposed to transfer from the Rio Grande his Mission San Francisco Solano, taking along a few Xarames Indians living there who could help him teach the San Antonio savages how to cultivate the soil. At a *junta de guerra y hacienda* in December, 1716, the padre's plans were approved with additions. Along with the mission at San Antonio there was to be well fortified *presidio* of at least fifty men; there was also to be an early occupation of Espíritu Santo Bay. These enterprises were to be financed with an appropriation of $6,000 annually. Apparently this figure did not include the pay of the soldiers, who received around $400 a year. Don Martin de Alarcón, an experienced soldier who had recently become governor of Coahuila—and who had been intriguing against St. Denis and the Ramóns—was additionally appointed governor of Texas and ordered to look after the colonization of the province. Nothing much was done about these plans for more than a year, while Olivares wrote endless letters complaining of Alarcón's dilatory tactics and the character of the men he was slowly recruiting for the new presidios. Of these men, the pious father wrote, " . . . Their customs are depraved and worse than those of the Gentiles themselves. It is they who sow discontent and unrest among them and come to control the Indians to such an extent that, by means of insignificant gifts, they make them do what they please. When it is to their interest, they help the Indians with their thefts and evil doings, and they attend their dances and *mitotes* just to get deer and buffalo skins from them."

Alarcón replied that unfortunately he did not have an Apostolic College from which to recruit his soldiers, and that good men were impossible to find in his Province of Coahuila. The governor finally left the Presidio of San Juan Bautista on April 9, 1718, a few days after the French had founded New Orleans. A week later, his final instructions caught up with him en route. He was then particularly ordered to bring in at least thirty families of settlers, whose presence would be most conducive to the propagation of the Holy Faith and the discouragement of the French. Both the settlers and the soldiers were to have their wives with them, "so as to prevent such excesses as resulted. . . during the earlier entries into the Province." Since these instructions arrived so late, it is little wonder they were not fully carried out.

After demanding an escort of soldiers, which Alarcón refused to grant him, Olivares left the Mission San Francisco Solano nine days after Alarcón had started from San Juan. On May 1, 1718, the priest reached San

Antonio, where the governor had arrived five days earlier. Within a few days, the combined expeditions had established a mission, a *presidio*, and a *villa*, or town. There is a statement by Alarcón which seems to say that the *villa* was already established when he arrived, but Fray Francisco Céliz, in his diary of the expedition, clearly states that the *Villa de Béjar* was founded at San Pedro Springs on May 5, 1718, and he does not speak of any previous settlement or mission.

The mission was named San Antonio Valero in honor of St. Anthony of Padua, a friend of St. Francis, and the Marqués de Valero, then Viceroy of Mexico. Among those present at the dedication was an Indian chief to whom Father Manzanet had given a horse in 1691. The combined settlement of mission, presidio and villa was called *San Antonio de los Llanos* (St. Anthony of the Plains) though later the town was known as San Antonio de Bexar and the mission chapel, abandoned to other uses, came to be nicknamed "the Alamo." The original site of the mission has never been precisely located. It was said to be west of the San Antonio River, three-quarters of a league down the San Pedro Creek from San Pedro Springs. In that case it must have been very near the site where a United States government arsenal was in operation from 1858 to 1948. The Spanish league was a rather elastic unit of measurement, but it was usually equivalent, in the 18th century, to 2.61 miles, so that three quarters of a league would be almost exactly two miles, which is the distance from the springs to the Arsenal site.

With the mission, presidio and villa duly established, Alarcón set out for the East Texas missions by way of Matagorda Bay, which he had been instructed to visit once a month during his time in Texas in order to warn away any Frenchmen who might be dallying in that vicinity. After traveling through or near the sites of modern New Braunfels, Seguin and Gonzales, Alarcón found a detail of topography that did not agree with his maps: the San Marcos River flowed into the Guadalupe and not into the Gulf.

Thrown into confusion by this unexpected development, as well as by the difficulties of struggling through tangled woods and swimming swollen streams, Alarcón was so stricken with melancholy that, when he saw two dozen buzzards circling over the camp, he called the chaplain, Father Céliz, and demanded of him, "Father, what are those birds looking for?"

To which the father replied portentously, "They may have come to make merry over the funeral rites of somebody present." This answer, whatever may have prompted it, did not help the governor's state of mind, and it was only with the most deliberate determination that he was able to attempt the next river crossing. Here he commandeered the strongest horse that could be found, placing himself in the saddle and his sergeant, Francisco Hernandez, on the haunches. Just as he reached the opposite shore, he reined the horse back and the current caught its hindquarters so that it was swept downstream half the distance of a musket-shot, with both riders submerged. They came up, still grasping the horse, but were submerged again, lost their grip and were swept downstream another half a musket shot, making a total distance of some three-quarters of a mile, according to contemporary estimates of the musket's range.

At this point, "The anxiety they experienced can well be imagined," says the chronicler with delicious understatement, especially as the governor did not know how to swim. This would seem to have made little difference, however, for the current was so strong that the sergeant, a good swimmer, was as helpless as the governor. Yet worse—the governor's knee-breeches lost their buttons, so that these nether garments fell down and hobbled his feet. But the two half-drowned men were finally rescued by what the priestly diarist regarded as a miraculous intercession when they came into contact with the branches of a submerged cypress tree, to which they were able to cling until ropes could be thrown to them from the bank.

The expedition returned to San Antonio and stayed a month, by which time the provisions had run low and the Indian members of the party had deserted, so that Alarcón found it necessary to return to the Rio Grande presidio for new guides and more supplies. By August 27 he was back in San Antonio de los Llanos, where he met Father Espinosa and Domingo Ramón, who had come from East Texas to ask about their long delayed supplies which Alarcón was to have brought. Joined by these men, Alarcón again led his expedition onward into East Texas, leaving San Antonio on September 5. On the 23rd they arrived at Matagorda Bay, now a few hours run from San Antonio by automobile. Here they found none of the expected Frenchmen, but only two Indians who fled at their approach and swam across a cove more than half a mile wide. Here also another miracle occurred when Alarcón lay all afternoon on a large snake, which failed to bite him or even move.

A few days later more Indians appeared. With some difficulty they were convinced of the Spaniards' pacific intentions, so that they finally came forward, embraced the governor ceremonially, and received presents of clothing and tobacco for which they returned a few dried fish—the only objects of value they possessed. Alarcón now took formal possession of the whole region and informed the Indians that the Spaniards would shortly settle the place, a promise which was fulfilled by another expedition three

109

years later. Although this incident was said to have taken place on the site of La Salle's colony, the place where Alarcón met the Indians was reported by him to be "two leagues from the bay toward the west," a description which is impossible to reconcile with any known theory regarding the location of La Salle's Fort St. Louis.

Throughout this part of the expedition, Alarcón's men had been finding stray specimens of European cattle, mostly black Castillian bulls, which they believed to be descended from stock abandoned by De León on on one of his expeditions some thirty years earlier. Whether the explorers were right or wrong in this guess, the fact that the cattle were not numerous at this time is a contradiction to the idea that the wild cattle of Texas were descended from Coronado's herds, for any animals left by Coronado in 1542 should have multiplied to respectable numbers by 1718. It is most likely that the wild cattle, which became plentiful by the time the first American settlers arrived in Texas, had strayed from more than one expedition, had wandered away from the Spanish settlements established in the 18th century, and had swum the Rio Grande from Mexico.

On October 14th, the Alarcón expedition arrived at the Mission San Francisco de los Tejas, the first of those established by Ramón and Espinosa two years before. Here the soldiers were greeted with a joyful ringing of bells by the missionaries and with gifts of food by the Indians. But the governor failed in an effort to persuade the Indians to congregate around the mission. This time the excuse was that their crops had failed and they had to go hunting buffalo for food.

At the Concepción Mission, the Indians were more numerous, and they greeted the governor with an elaborate ceremony. Lifting him from his horse, they took away his sword and pistols, and two men carried him by the feet and shoulders to a straw hut where he was to lodge. Here they gently washed his face and hands, dried him with a cloth and carried him into the hut. After smoking the pipe of peace, the chiefs told Alarcón in glowing terms how they had yearned for his coming because of the favorable reports of him which the priests had given to the Indians.

Alarcón replied in kind, telling the Indians of the great plans which his lord, the king, was preparing for the land of the Tejas, and he asked them to build a house in which he, Alarcón, might live throughout his stay in the province.

The house was built in two days, a pyramidal structure of timber, covered with grass. Now it was time for another celebration. All the Indians, men, women and children, assembled in their gayest dress around a

110

great bonfire at the front of the new house, the floor of which was covered with buffalo hides. The chiefs and principal men of the Indians, entering the house, took the governor by the arms and ceremoniously placed on his head a collection of the breast-feathers of white ducks and, across his forehead, a strip of black cloth which hung down to his cheeks on either side. They then placed him on the buffalo skins, his head against the knees of an Indian seated on a small bench. To the music of drums and timbrels, the Indians began to sing in what Father Céliz described as "a gentle though coarse harmony," the men sitting separately from the women and children, under the careful supervision of proctors bearing torches of burning reeds. From time to time one of the headmen would interrupt the singing to address Alarcón with a flowery speech, swearing eternal friendship and praying the help of the Spanish king against the enemies of the Tejas.

The gist of these speeches was reported by an interpreter to Alarcón, who replied by telling the Indians of the great love which the king bore them, and admonishing them to be grateful and submissive. With more singing and shouting, the festivities continued until three o'clock in the morning. The reciprocal pledges were renewed the next days and extended to still other Indians, but the Spaniards suffered some uneasiness when they counted the muskets fired by the Indians in salute to Alarcón and found them more numerous than the firearms on the Spanish side. The Indians' muskets, it was known, had been introduced by the nearby French in exchange for horses and skins.

The exchange of amenities continued in an atmosphere of great good will for more than two weeks. The spirit of harmony even extended to the French, for on November 3 Alarcón received letters from the French post at Natchitoches, in answer to courteous epistles of his own, in which the French commandant expressed a spirit of urbanity and cooperation which was not disturbed until war broke out the following year.

Don Martin de Alarcón was not the man to be lulled by French politeness, however, so he dispatched Sergeant Hernandez and another man to observe cautiously what might be going on at Natchitoches. These men reported that the French had only a simple stockade and a few cabins, and there were not more than twenty Frenchmen at the post. Seeing that the foreign outpost was not as formidable as it might have been, Alarcón conceived that he might have enough strength to persuade the Frenchmen to retire to lands well outside the patrimony of the King of Spain. But the missionary priests, wary of any conflict that might disrupt their work with the Indians, persuaded the governor that his orders from the Viceroy prohibited any militant action.

Meanwhile in San Antonio, Father Olivares plowed the fields on the east side of the river with the aid of the three Indians whom he had raised from childhood. He also erected a temporary *jacal* in which to hold mass. But the local tribesmen were slow in coming to the mission, and Olivares blamed Alarcón for their absence, although it was the season when the Coahuiltecans were accustomed to wander long distances in search of the *tuna* and other fruits. The padre charged, however, that the Indians had been discouraged by the long wait since May, 1717, when the mission had been promised them; that Alarcón had so mistreated an Indian guide that the fellow had run away and told his people, not that one Spaniard had dealt wrongly with him, but that "the Spaniards" had mistreated him; and that the gentleman Alarcón had antagonized the Indians by declaring, with an oath, that if they did not come to the mission he would go after them and put them all to the sword. "Imagine, your Excellency, such a method of congregating Indians and settling the land!"

Still, by January 12, 1719, when Governor Alarcón returned from East Texas, he found so many Indians living in the *pueblo* that he formally organized them into a "self-governing" community under the direction and care of the missionaries and the protection of the presidio. He then distributed presents among them, and remarked that they showed the effects of good Christian training in the alacrity which they responded to the call of the mission bell when gifts were to be distributed.

Alarcón also directed the construction of irrigation ditches for the villa and the mission. Traces of these *acequias* still remain in the modern city. At the same time, Alarcón ordered the planting of corn, beans and other grains when the season would permit, and he further commanded the importation of grapevines, fig trees, the seeds of various fruits, canteloupe, watermelons, pumpkins, chile peppers and other plants useful for food, as well as hogs, cattle, sheep, goats, and the necessary implements and munitions.

After his return to San Antonio, Alarcón was involved in yet more bitter quarrels with the missionaries, particularly Father Olivares, who bitterly resented what he considered Alarcón's wilful refusal to comply with the somewhat ideal requirements of his orders to garrison Texas with married soldiers of a superior type and to persuade the Indians to congregate around the missions. Early in 1719 Alarcón resigned his governorship and soon afterward returned to Mexico, where he lapsed into obscurity.

A year after the founding of the mission San Antonio Valero, Father Olivares was crossing a rude bridge when his horse stumbled and fell,

breaking the old priest's leg. Lacking medical attention, he became dangerously ill and had to send to the Rio Grande for one Father Muñoz, who
responded with such alacrity that he covered eighty leagues of the San Antonio Road, then under construction, in forty continuous hours at the terrific
speed of five miles an hour. When Olivares was able to make his confession to
Muñoz, he tells us, he obtained such an accession of divine grace that the leg
was eventually healed, though the padre had to remain in bed for a long time.
When he recovered, he removed the mission to the other side of the river,
"about two gunshots away," so that he would not have to use the rickety
bridge on his daily trips to the fields on the east side of the river. Besides, the
new site was on higher ground than the old one, and Olivares may have begun
to realize the danger of floods on the low ground between the river and the
creek.

Father Olivares was happy that he could bring salvation to the
gentiles on the San Antonio River, but he complained that none of the fifty
families who were to be established in the Villa de San Antonio de Bexar
were actually there. It is not clear what happened to the ten families which
Alarcón had reported present in the colony, except that, according to Olivares, Alarcón had removed one of them by force. What was more, the padre
again declared, the gentleman Alarcón had insisted on bringing in soldiers
who were not of good quality, had no families with them, and did not know
the Indians, nor did the Indians know them. Still worse, Alarcón had
threatened to cut the throats of the Rio Grande Indians in his expedition if
they would not return with him. The horses and cows of the expedition, said
Olivares, had been sold to the soldiers for $15 each.

Even while war was brewing between France and Spain, the
proposed Spanish settlement and fortification of Matagorda Bay were entirely
neglected, though they had been planned together with the presidio at San
Antonio as major bastions in a coordinated system of defense. So in 1719,
with war on the horizon, the entire guard of Texas, a country larger than
Spain itself, consisted of about 25 soldiers at San Antonio and the same
number of the eastern frontier.

When Fray Miguel Sevillano de Paredes arrived on a tour of
inspection in 1727, the Mission San Antonio Valero was inhabited by seventy
Indian families comprising 273 persons, although only 164 of these were
baptized Christians. Meanwhile 127 Christians had died—a figure which was
not due to high mortality alone, but to the fact that the missionary friars
were always on the alert to baptize Indians whom they found at the point of
death. Many others, once rounded up at the mission, had run away to the

woods because of their disinclination for work and Christian discipline. Besides its human complement, the mission had 307 head of branded cattle and 132 unbranded calves; 272 goats, 210 sheep, and seventy young goats and lambs; eleven horses, twelve mules, twenty-two burros and twenty-one yoke of oxen. The crops varied greatly from year to year because of drouth, insects, field mice, and the unreliability of the Indians who tilled the soil for the priests.

In 1724, after a hurricane had destroyed the mission, it had been rebuilt on its third site, on what is now Alamo Plaza in San Antonio. At the time of Father Sevillano's visit, the rough stone and adobe convent was under construction, but the buildings in actual use were mere *jacales* (shacks). Materials had been collected for a stone church but the work of erecting it had not begun, because no skilled mason could be induced to come from Mexico to this wild country to direct the work. Construction of an irrigation ditch to the fields south of the mission, though directed by Alarcón in 1719, was not started until 1724 and had just been finished in 1727, for the caliche rock was so near the surface that much of the digging had to be done with crowbars by the unwilling Indians, exposed to periodic attacks from the hovering Lipan Apaches.

The conditions found at San Antonio Valero were typical of those at all Texas missions in this period, except that most of the others were even more primitive. The handsome stone buildings that stand today were built much later, toward the end of the 18th century, and the mission chapel of Valero, itself, was never even finished before it fell into ruin.

10

A French Castaway in Texas

An interlude without consequences in the future history of Texas, but with an interest all its own, is the story of the lone French castaway who entered Texas at almost exactly the same point where Cabeza de Vaca was cast ashore two hundred years earlier, and whose adventures curiously paralleled the tribulations of the earlier traveler.

The Frenchman was Simars de Bellisle, a young man of 24 who left his native country in 1719 on an ordinary passenger ship, intending to become a colonist in Louisiana, but who had to spend a year or more as a slave of cannibal Indians and the "husband" of an Indian matron before he finally reached the French settlements.

Even his voyage before the shipwreck was an adventure, as most sea voyages were in those days. The first taste of adventure was a comparatively mild one—France and England being at war, the captain of Bellisle's passenger vessel felt justified in stopping an Irish ship and robbing it of two barrels of wine and two cases of raisins, over the lively protests of its

115

skipper.

Soon afterward, near Santo Domingo, the French ship was in turn attacked by a pirate. Seeing that the buccaneers could sail circles around him, the French captain stopped and invited them aboard. Bellisle thought at first that this maneuver was intended to outwit the pirate captain and take him prisoner, but the French skipper had other ideas. He accepted the apologies of the pirate chief, who said he had mistaken the ship for an English one, and the two captains then calmly sat down to a convivial dinner. As the evening wore on, they became friendlier and friendlier, and finally the pirate chief invited the French captain to join him in looting a nearby island.

"He would have accepted it if we had not prevented him," Bellisle wrote later. In any case the two captains had become fast friends and the pirate turned over to the Frenchman a prisoner who could pilot him through the difficult Old Bahama Channel, north of Cuba. After getting through the channel, the *Maréchal d'Estrée* sailed on for twenty more days, covering a thousand miles, before the lookouts saw land. The pilots warned the captain to take soundings, but seeing that the ship was still far from shore he decided this precaution to be unnecessary. He was wrong, for he had just finished answering the pilots when the ship struck some submerged object with terrific force. Since it was a brand-new vessel it did not split open, but it immediately began shipping water.

The pilots took more bearings and became convinced that this was not the Louisiana coast, as they had first thought. The ship sailed several days more, then grounded in seven feet of water when the captain again rejected the advice of his pilots and attempted to enter a large but unidentified bay. As the ship trembled with the gentle shock of settling into the sand, the captain, his lieutenant and his ensign all took to their cabins, presumably from embarrassment, while the mate, taking charge, commanded the rest of the crew and the passengers to rock the ship by running back and forth across the deck. In this manner the ship was freed from the sandbar, and the captain again took command.

Impatient and discouraged with the rate of progress toward their new home in the colonies, Bellisle and four other officers asked to be put ashore, imagining that in four or five days they could walk to the French post at Ship Island, near Biloxi, and send help to their stricken vessel. Actually they were at Galveston Bay, almost 400 miles west of Ship Island, across unknown forests and many wide rivers.

The five men landed one evening and remained to sleep at the point of landing, but by morning they could no longer see the ship. For five days they walked westward along the coast, until they came to a swamp where the mud went up to their necks. Finding no way around this obstacle, they decided to retrace their steps. Although they had arms and ammunition, they found little game, and for long periods they had nothing to eat. Using a rowboat which they found washed ashore, they ascended a river to its source in a small pond. Unable to go farther, they turned the boat around and, too weak from starvation to use their oars, they floated back to the sea, which they reached in eight days. In the bay at the river's mouth they found some oysters, which they cooked, and Bellisle killed a deer, but one of the men, Courbet, was so weak from hunger and exposure that he could not eat, and in a few hours he was dead.

The four survivors went on walking but during a rest stop one Legendre fell asleep and never awoke. This left two others, Alain and Duclos, with Bellisle. Eight or ten days later, Duclos was unable to walk, and the other two, after much hesitation, decided to go on without him, promising to send help if any could be found. They had not gone seven miles when Alain faltered and said he was unable to continue. "I told him," says Bellisle, "in order to encourage him, not to lose hope for so little reason, and that we would meet people if we continued, but if we stayed in the same place we would perish." Up to this time, at least a month after their landing, the castaways had seen no one, not even Indians.

Alain insisted on returning to the place where they had left Duclos. Bellisle pressed on until, on the fifth day, he came to a large river which seems to have been the Brazos. For the benefit of readers who know not Texas, it should probably have been explained before that all Texas rivers are fordable—or completely dry—when they are not in flood. Bellisle found the Brazos in flood stage so, for the third time in his Texas travels, he was forced to retrace his steps. Near the starting point of his latest sortie, he found the decomposed body of Alain, who had died without even reaching Duclos. Five miles farther along, under a tent which had fallen down, Bellisle found Duclos, dead but still warm.

"When I knew myself alone," says Bellisle, "I died a hundred deaths every quarter of an hour." For two days he could not even eat, but on the third day he gathered some oysters and also roasted some large yellow worms which he found in the driftwood. "I found that they tasted very good," he reported.

Two weeks later, on an island out in the bay, Bellisle saw some Indians who had come there to collect birds' eggs, for it was now the beginning of summer. Bellisle still had the rowboat which his party had found, so, using the last few ounces of his strength, he rowed the five miles out to the island. We may presume that he expected a friendly reception, for when he was in France he must have heard that the Indians of Louisiana were allied with the French. But if this was Bellisle's expectation, he was soon to be rudely disappointed. Finally reaching the island, he saw three men standing a hundred feet away, and he began staggering toward them. Approaching the nearest one, he prepared to embrace the strange but undoubtedly human fellow-creature, but the redskin drew back with a surprised and hostile look. Nothing daunted, Bellisle led the other two Indians to his landing place, but their answer to this friendly overture was merely to scoop up the entire contents of the boat—rifles, swords, silver knives and forks, a good coat, and other things that Bellisle had painstakingly saved in his wanderings.

Even this was not enough. The Indians next threw Bellisle on the ground and took off all his clothes, from his long stockings to his three-cornered hat, and left him naked as the day he was born. Yet, with what seemed to him to be strange inconsistency, they offered him some of the eggs which they had gathered and roasted, and some fish which they also had with them, so that he was able to eat until he was filled. Perhaps, he thought, they were trying to fatten him up so that he would be fit for a cannibal feast.

When night fell and the mosquitoes began biting, Bellisle had to squat in the water up to his neck to save himself from their stings, for the Indians only laughed when he begged them at least to return his shirt so that he would have some protection. Next morning the Indians took him to their village, where the party was greeted with such horrible yells that poor Bellisle thought he was about to be killed. They let him alone, however—so much so that for a day and a half he had nothing to eat. Finally they gave him some wild potatoes. From that time on, they kept him under close guard and drove him about the country with them as they wandered about in search of food. This state of affairs continued without change through the summer and fall. At the beginning of winter, for some unknown reason, the Indians began to treat Bellisle with more severity than before. When they needed water and wood they ordered him to go and get it, and when he talked back, as he sometimes did now that he was learning the language, they knocked him down with their fists or beat him with sticks.

About this time, under circumstances which are not explained in either of the two documents that Bellisle wrote for posterity, he was saved from death by an Indian widow—age not mentioned—who insisted on "marrying" him in the Indian fashion. From that time on, his life became easier, even though he was at the beck and call of the widow to such an extent that his uxorious state was hardly distinguishable from a benign form of slavery. At any rate, he still hankered for the comparatively civilized delights of Louisiana. Finally he wrote a letter intended for the nearest white man, whoever that might be. After writing the letter with an ink made from charcoal and water, he asked two Indians to take it to the white men, promising them they would be well rewarded. But instead of carrying the letter to the Frenchmen, Bellisle learned later, his Indians passed it about as an object of curiosity among the various tribes of the region.

Soon the Indians went hunting buffalo and took Bellisle with them. The Indians were on horseback, but the Frenchman had to travel on his bare feet, for "they told me it was not decent for a man of a different color to possess a horse." When sharp stones and thorns injured his feet so that he was unable to walk fast enough, the Indians would ride up and beat him over the shoulders with their whips.

Still more trouble was in store for the poor wandering Frenchman. When the Indians learned that he was able to write, they credited him with all sorts of supernatural powers, at least insofar as the acquisition of knowledge was concerned, though he was obviously incapable of mobilizing any familiar spirits to engineer his excape or defend him against mistreatment. At the end of the hunting expedition, the Indians saw a cloud of smoke several miles away on the prairie, and one of them asked Bellisle what was happening. "I told him there was a fire on the prairie," Bellisle recalled. "He asked me if there were people. I answered him that someone ought to be there and that no deer had lighted the fire."

Sure enough, when a small party of the Cocos went to the fire they found ten or twelve "Toyals", an enemy tribe, otherwise unknown. They were able to kill only one, whose body they brought back to dismember and eat at their camp. Bellisle indignantly refused to take part in the feast.

They blamed Bellisle for their small bag. If he had told them there were so many enemies at the fire, they would all have gone in pursuit and killed all the Toyals, they scolded him. When he protested that he could not possibly have known the number of enemies, they beat him for the obvious lie, since a man who had the marvellous ability to put words on paper would certainly know the answer to such a simple question. Later the Cocos gave Bellisle a meal of what they said was buffalo meat, and when he had swallowed it all they told him it was human flesh. Bellisle then threw up so violently that blood came from his stomach.

In spite of his sufferings, Bellisle observed that the part of Texas through which he and his captors passed was "the most beautiful country in the world." He noticed that the soil was almost black, and the grass grew to a prodigious height. These facts would indicate that the buffalo hunt took place in the blackland country of central Texas.

All this time Bellisle's letter had been passing from hand to hand among the Indians, who marveled at the strange markings on the paper and then passed it on to their friends, ignoring the fact that it was intended for the nearest French or Spanish commandant. Actually, as Bellisle knew from the Indians, the white men were not very far away. His adventures occurred in a region about halfway between the Spanish post at Bexar and the French fort at Natchitoches, which were some 400 miles apart. Finally, the letter reached some Asinai Indians in East Texas, more civilized than the Cocos and leagued in friendship with the French at Natchitoches, who supplied them with arms and other trade goods in exchange for skins. In this manner the letter at last reached St. Denis—by now the commander of the Natchitoches post—who immediately ordered his Asinai friends to find Bellisle and bring him back alive if possible, but to bring back his body if he was found dead.

So, one day when he was sitting by the fire with his Indian captors, Bellisle heard a rifle shot in the distance, and two strange Indians cantered into the camp, waving a letter which, though Bellisle did not know it at the time, came from St. Denis. The Cocos seized the letter before Bellisle could read it, but the Asinai finally took it away from them and handed it to Bellisle. At length the Cocos, who had great respect for the Asinai, reluctantly agreed to let Bellisle join the "great white chief" who had written to him. Not trusting the Cocos, however, Bellisle crept out of the camp at daybreak to join his new Asinai friends, who had agreed to meet him a short distance away. As he drew near the meeting place, he saw two Cocos running after him. Catching up, they took him by the throat and promised to kill him if he tried to leave, because they feared he would bring the white chief's warriors to avenge the ill treatment he had received. But the two Asinai rescued Bellisle, telling the Cocos that they, the Asinai, would destroy the whole Cocos tribe if any harm came to this Frenchman. What the widow said is not reported.

In four days, Bellisle and the two Asinai had reached the villages of the Bidais, another friendly tribe, and in 18 days, moving northeast, they arrived at the first Asinai village, where they were saluted with 20 rifle-shots. At the edge of the village a handsome Asinai woman came out, saluted Bellisle and spoke to him in Spanish, the first words of a civilized language that he had heard since the death of his companions, unless he had talked to himself in the long wilderness days and nights.

Bellisle gives this woman's name as Angelica, but actually she was the Angelina, often mentioned in Spanish chronicles, who occupied a distinguished position among the Texas Indians because she had been reared at the presidio of San Juan Bautista and had learned to speak Spanish, so that she was constantly being called into service as an interpreter and aide in winning the good will of the native Indians. She was later recognized by having the Angelina River named after her—possibly the only time that a native was ever honored by the Spaniards in naming features of the landscape. There is a hint in one of St. Denis' letters that this exceptional woman may have been the child of an Asinai mother by one of the soldiers of the Terán expedition of 1691.

Angelina, like the Cocos woman, was a widow when she met Bellisle. She was so much taken with the handsome young Frenchman that she invited him to stay in her lodge and rest for ten days, at the end of which time the Asinai would be returning from a war against a tribe called the "Sadamon" (Sijames?). Bellisle agreed to this dalliance, he says, "because my ankles were very much swollen from fatigue."

Angelina treated him as if he had been her child, says Bellisle. If she was a product of the Terán expedition she must have been well under thirty at this time, and in any case she could not have been much older, as until 1689 there were no Spaniards who could have taken her to Mexico as a child, and it is improbable that she would have been taken there by her own Indians. At any rate, Bellisle recuperated within eight days from the ill effects of his hardships.

But the ten days went by, then a month, then two months, and still the warriors did not return to escort Bellisle to the French fort. Between the lines, we can discern that he must have been fairly content with the long delay, for he was now able to get directions to Natchitoches and could have reached it alone in a few days. He says, however, that he was worried and impatient, so that he vehemently protested to Angelina, but she told him she could not understand why the men had not returned. At last, however, when the war party had been gone for two months and a half, Bellisle's nostalgia became so oppressive that Angelina took pity on him and promised to let two of her children guide him to the French post. The next morning she kept her promise, making ready three horses and food for the journey, but she still seemed reluctant to let him go, and asked him again if he was really sure that he wanted to leave. There were two great rivers barring the way, she told him, and how would he cross with the children, who did not know how to swim? He was sure that he could carry the youngsters on his shoulders, but Angelina was skeptical. So Bellisle demonstrated by carrying the children across the first river, which was near the village, while Angelina and the rest of the Asinai women watched from the bank. So Angelina had no more arguments, and Bellisle took off with the two youngsters. In six days he had arrived at Natchitoches, on the Red River, and reported to St. Denis.

"I leave it to the reader to imagine," says Bellisle, "whether I did not return to life after being dead. Of his "romance" with Angelina, which has been greatly inflated by some later writers, he has no more to say.

Bellisle finally reached New Orleans, and soon had become an officer in the service of Governor Bienville. By 1753 he was the town commandant of New Orleans. He died in Paris March 4, 1763, a year after he had been recalled to France because of a political quarrel.

Though it has been disputed, there seems to be no real doubt that Bellisle's adventure began in the vicinity of Galveston Bay. In 1720 and 1721 a Captain Béranger went out on two unsuccessful French expeditions to occupy the Baie St. Bernard, identified by the French with Galveston Bay, although the name "San Bernardo" was sometimes applied by the Spaniards to Matagorda Bay, farther down the coast. On his second voyage, Béranger was accompanied by Bénard de la Harpe, who had been appointed governor of the bay region, and by Bellisle as an interpreter. The Indians refused to cooperate, saying that if La Harpe remained there, they would be sure he had come "to revenge the bad treatment inflicted on Bellisle." So La Harpe sailed away again—for it was French policy to conciliate and not punish or antagonize the Indians—and never more did the Frenchmen attempt to occupy any part of Texas.

11

Aguayo and the Making of Texas

The war of 1719-1720, in which Spain had to fight against the Quadruple Alliance of England, France, Austria and the Netherlands, was the result of Philip V's dissatisfaction with the terms of the Peace of Utrecht, which had ended the War of the Spanish Succession in 1713. In the second war, Spain finally had to yield and sign a peace on somewhat humiliating terms in the early part of 1720.

During the war, in spite of a great deal of excited talk and correspondence, the Spaniards did nothing whatever to defend their settlements in North America. Fortunately the French were not yet numerous enough in America to pose a serious threat, although they captured Pensacola, made a minor sortie into Texas, and laid plans, which were never carried out, to take possession of Matagorda Bay, where La Salle had come to grief a generation before. They also consolidated their hold on the lower Mississippi by quickly importing 1,000 French settlers and 500 African slaves to their recently established colony of New Orleans.

The sortie into Texas, though trivial to the point of comedy, was important because it spurred the Spaniards, tardily as was their habit, to provide an adequate garrison and encourage civil settlement in this lightly held province. The raid took place in this fashion:

In June, 1719, a month after the capture of Pensacola, the huts of the Mission San Miguel de los Adaes, sixteen miles from the last French outpost at Natchitoches, drowsed in the noonday sun with only a lay brother and a ragged soldier in charge, the missionary father having taken the other soldier on an errand to the Mission Dolores, several miles away. At this quiet hour, the clergy and laity of the mission were suddenly roused by a furious cackling from their little flock of chickens. They turned in consternation to see seven French soldiers on horseback, led by Captain Blondel, then commander of the Natchitoches post.

The only resistance to this miniature invasion was provided by the chickens, who flapped their wings and cackled and crowed so lustily that the French horses reared up in fright and Captain Blondel was thrown to the ground, slightly bruised, but not too severely wounded to gather up the Spanish soldier and carry him a prisoner to Natchitoches, along with all the sacred vessels, ornaments and fixtures of the little mission. The lay brother was released after the French psychological warfare experts had been careful to inform him that they had a hundred more soldiers on the way from Mobile to drive the Spaniards back to the Rio Grande. The brother trotted all the way to Dolores and told his story to Father Margil, who realized that, even if the French threat were heavily discounted, it would be impossible for him to defend his isolated mission. Like Manzanet a generation before, Margil buried his bells and heavy equipment, packed the sacred chalices, and hurried to Mission Concepción, a few miles away, where there was a somewhat larger military force.

The news had traveled faster than the father, however. When he arrived at Concepción, the soldiers of Domingo Ramón were all but in retreat. Over the protests of both the priests and the Indians, the soldiers insisted on retiring to the Trinity River. This they did while the two mission presidents, Fathers Margil and Espiñosa, remained at Concepción to satisfy the Indians that they were not being wholly abandoned.

Within a month, however, the padres had to join the other fugitives, and before winter all the missionaries, settlers and soldiers had returned to San Antonio. So, for the second time in a generation, missions and settlements bravely established had been abandoned, and all of Texas, except the little cluster of mission, villa and presidio at San Antonio, had

124

been given back to the Indians or to the French if they cared to take it.

Even before the abandonment of the missions, however, the viceroy of Mexico received a royal order, written almost a year earlier, directing him to build a fort on Matagorda Bay and to reinforce the existing settlements in Texas with more soldiers and more missionaries. Six months after the war broke out, the viceroy first learned of it in an order directing him to put all forts and ports on a war footing to prevent surprise by the French. A month later he learned of the evacuation of East Texas.

Evidently action was necessary, even though belated. To put his orders into effect, the viceroy wisely chose Joseph Azlor Virto de Vera, the Marquis of San Miguel de Aguayo, a powerful nobleman of Coahuila, who had acquired his title by marriage with a descendant of the ennobled family of Don Francisco de Urdiñola, the founder of Saltillo. Aguayo was given his orders and appointed governor of Coahuila and Texas on December 19, 1719, only six months after the viceroy had received his instructions from the king. Preparations for an expedition were well under way by October, 1720, but by that time the war had ended and the original orders were changed to provide for purely defensive action on the Texas-Louisiana frontier. The changed orders were approved by the king himself in March, 1721. In this way it became possible for Aguayo to enter Texas less than two years after the frontier missionaries had been driven out.

Meanwhile, Father Márgil waited at the Mission San Antonio de Valero. With a certain impatience, he addressed a letter to Aguayo on December 26, 1719, asking for the establishment of a new mission at San Antonio for his organization, the College of Zacatecas, a more or less friendly rival of the College of Querétaro, which had established the Valero Mission. From this base, he pointed out, the Zacatecans could easily fan out to establish other missions in various parts of the province. After a well-reasoned exposition of the advantages of the site and the spiritual good that would be accomplished, he clinched the argument by suggesting that the new mission be named San José de San Miguel de Aguayo in recognition of the governor's great services to the Holy Faith.

The suggestion met with favor, and Aguayo commissioned Captain Juan Baldes to select a suitable site. Over the protests of the Quereteran missionaries, a place was chosen at the top of a little rise, a quarter of a mile south of the point where Highway No. 281 now crosses the San Antonio River, some five miles south of the Valero Mission. Captain Baldes nominally granted this property to the chiefs of the Pampopa, Pestia and Suliajame Indian tribes, who accepted it on February 23, 1720, with ceremonial acts of possession, such as pulling weeds, throwing stones and cutting branches, with eighty soldiers as witnesses. This was the beginning of the greatest and most successful mission in Texas, whose church, erected much later, is probably the finest example of Spanish architecture in the United States. Construction was begun immediately on the houses around a plaza 333 feet square, and it was not long before a granary had been erected out of rough stones, but not until 1768 was the cornerstone laid for the beautiful church.

The Marquis of San Miguel de Aguayo was a man of determination, as witnessed by more than one incident during the preparations for the Texas *entrada*. To prevent any exportation of Coahuila's scanty food supply, he decreed that anyone selling grain otherwise than to the government should be punished by a fine of $50, if a Spaniard, or by a hundred lashes if he were an Indian, a mestizo or a Negro. Soon afterward, using a small and hastily recruited force, Aguayo wiped out half of a tribe of Indians who had deserted a mission at Santa Rosa (now Muzquiz), Coahuila. Still later, he stopped desertions from his Texas force in process of recruitment by having two deserters shot in the main plaza of Monclova. (These desertions were less excusable than they might have been, for the men had accepted a year's pay in advance.)

Drawing upon his large personal fortune, Aguayo equipped his expedition of 500 men with 4,000 horses, 600 head of cattle, 900 sheep, and almost 800 mules, 600 of which carried loads of clothing, arms, munitions and other supplies, all brought from Mexico City. The little army carried six field pieces and three religious standards, bearing the images of Our Lady of Pilar, Our Lady of Guadalupe, and St. James the Moor-Killer, patron saint of Spain. Although disgusted with the changed orders directing him to wage only a defensive campaign, Aguayo told the viceroy that he was "willing to make the sacrifice as evidence of my blind obedience to His Catholic Majesty."

Before the expedition had crossed the Rio Grande, Aguayo received word that St. Denis, now indignant toward the Spaniards because of the shabby treatment he had received after his return from the expedition of 1716, was holding a convocation of many Indian tribes on the Brazos River, with the intention of leading them to attack San Antonio. Aguayo believed the story and promptly sent 116 men to reinforce the threatened outpost. He also sent Captain José Domingo Ramón with forty men to occupy Matagorda Bay and prevent its capture by the French.

The main expedition reached San Antonio on April 4, 1721, and Aguayo led the whole battalion to the Valero Mission to dedicate its

126

service in Texas to Almighty God, singing the Te Deum which contains the versicle, *"Benedictus qui venit in nomine Domini"* (Blessed is he that cometh in the name of the Lord). In order to rest the horses and provide time for administering to the spiritual needs of the soldiers during Holy Week, Aguayo decided to remain at San Antonio for a while. While there, he distributed clothing and other goods admired by the Indians to 240 *reducidos* at Valero, 227 at San José, and fifty wild Indians who had come in from the Rancheria Grande, near the Brazos River, to request a mission for their benefit.

Tightening his security rules to strengthen defense against the hostile Apaches who were now hovering nearby, the Marquis moved his army out of San Antonio toward East Texas on May 13. For many days' journey, the party did not meet a single Indian, hostile or friendly, but saw only abandoned huts, and the certainty grew that all the Indians had gone to be with St. Denis at his sinister convocation on the Brazos. Aguayo even sent a scouting party to investigate a fire which sent a column of smoke into the sky many miles off the course of the expedition, but it proved to be the work of some soldiers who had turned aside to hunt buffalo.

From time to time along the way, the expedition found more abandoned huts of branches and straw, and some cleared fields, but no Indians. At nightfall one day a messenger overtook the expedition to report that a ship had brought news to Mexico that Their Majesties were in good health, and Aguayo ordered a salute to be fired by way of rejoicing. These early expeditions, slowed down by their baggage trains and the cattle they drove along for food, were constantly being overtaken by faster-moving messengers along the way.

Not an Indian was seen until the morning of June 8, almost a month after the expedition had left San Antonio, when it had traveled something more than 180 miles through a region which normally held a fairly numerous native population. Here, at a point near the present town of Fairfield, a scouting party found several cultivated fields. There were no huts in sight, but Juan Rodriguez, the chief of the Rancheria Grande, who was with the expedition, called out in the native language, and an answer came back frm the nearby woods. After friendly greetings, the man with the fastest horse in the scouting party was dispatched to notify Aguayo, who came quickly although he took time to provide himself with a trumpeter and a man carrying a royal banner to precede him.

At the governor's approach, the Indians marched out carrying a French-made white silk flag, with blue stripes, and greeted the governor with submissive bows as they had doubtless been instructed by Juan Rodriguez and his Spanish friends. His lordship benignly directed the Indians to place their flag under the royal standard as a sign of submission and then to come forward one by one while he, without dismounting, placed his hand paternally on the head of each in turn. In this way some 200 Indians became the acknowledged wards of the King their Lord (May God Protect Him!). After explaining that his mission was one of peace, the governor added to the happiness of the Indians by distributing bundles of tobacco.

The next day several chiefs led their followers from the Ranchería Grande to wait upon the governor, who extolled their primitive virtues, admonished them to keep the peace, assured them they would be happy under Spanish protection, and promisd them that he would indeed erect a mission for them near San Antonio.

Further to impress the Indians, says Father Peña, the diarist of the expedition, "So that out of motives of love and fear, they might remain faithful to the Spaniards, the order to mount was given with a trumpet and the battalion was commanded to fall in line in the form of a square. The governor, having been requested to maneuver his horse in the Spanish fashion, in order that the Indians, who had never witnessed such horsemanship, might be favorably impressed by its advantages, did so with the greatest skill and in so many different ways that they marveled greatly."

The expedition was delayed sixteen days by a difficult crossing of the Trinity River, not far from the modern city of Palestine, but Aguayo made good use of the time, distributing two mule-loads of clothing, knives and other gifts to the Indians, and taking pains to spread to all four quarters of the compass the news that the Spaniards had come to Texas proclaiming friendship. The great chief of the Asinai, himself, visited Aguayo's camp with eight other chiefs and four women, one of whom was Angelina. Through Angelina the great chief, weeping for joy in the manner of his tribe, informed Aguayo that he had greatly missed the Spanish missionaries, and even Ramón's soldiers, after their abrupt departure from Texas. He had so much regretted the Spaniards' tardiness in returning to the province, he declared, that he would have gone to San Antonio to look for them if they had waited much longer.

Other meetings followed, at which the Indian women brought their customary gift of ears of corn, watermelons, beans and *pinole,* a drink made from parched corn, sugar and water. But at dusk on July 28, a French messenger cautiously arrived, bearing word that St. Denis was at the Adaes and desired a safe-conduct to come and lay before Aguayo the orders which, as commandant of the French forces on this border, he had received from the provincial capital in Mobile.

      This was the first word that the Spanish governor had received from the French captain, an almost legendary figure now, whose somewhat sinister shadow had lain on the expedition's horizon since it had left Mexico, and before. The words of the message were not reassuring. They sounded as if St. Denis had full confidence in his ability to enforce the orders of Mobile, regardless of what Aguayo might think, for St. Denis had not asked for a parley but merely an opportunity to inform Aguayo of his instructions. Aguayo knew that the war was over, for the time being at least, but the peace on this ill-defined frontier had always been an uneasy one, and there was no telling what St. Denis might do if he thought his military force was sufficient to overcome that of the Spaniards.

      Aguayo answered the messenger courteously and told him St. Denis might come whenever he chose, alone, without fear for the security of his person. The expedition moved on to the site of the first presidio of 1716, near the Neches River, where Aguayo was waited upon by a tribe of Indians under an old chief who had put out his own eyes so that he might become their high priest or medicine man. Eloquently the old man told the governor that what his people most esteemed was the sun, the moon, the stars and the Spaniards, and that the air, water, earth and fire could not compare with these. The interview was concluded with more gifts of Spanish clothing, glass beads, rings, mirrors, combs, awls, scissors, chain-links and blankets, as well as a silver-headed baton for the chief.

      On the 31st, three days after the French messenger, St. Denis himself arrived, swam his horse across the river and was received by the governor with the traditional Spanish expressions of courtesy. This done, St. Denis pleaded that he was very tired from the heat of the sun and the hard journey—as anyone who knows Texas in the summer will believe—and asked that he be permitted to rest overnight with the missionaries before discussing his business with Aguayo. As clerics, of course, the missionaries might be considered more trustworthy than the Spanish officers. Besides, they were old friends of St. Denis, from whom he might quietly learn how matters stood before he laid any of his cards on the table at an interview with the governor.

      In the morning Aguayo heard mass and then, careful to uphold his prerogative as the king's governor, sent word to St. Denis that he was ready to see him. The Frenchman, arriving at the governor's tent, faced a coolly polite semicircle made up of the governor, the lieutenant governor and captains of the expedition. When Aguayo aksed him formally to state the purpose of his visit, St. Denis replied that his intention was "to announce that, if his lordship was willing to do likewise, he, as commandant of the forces on that entire frontier, would observe most amicably the truce which had been published in Spain between the two powers, and which, according to letters that he had received from France, had probably already been established."

This was a fairly neat bit of diplomacy for a backwoodsman. In the first place, St. Denis implied that he had large forces at his command, and apparently made Aguayo believe it, although actually he had only a handful of men. In the second place, to "observe the truce" could only mean to retain the status quo, leaving the border where it was and the Spanish outposts deserted, whereas Aguayo had set out to reestablish the frontier presidios, start a new one at La Bahia, and, if the necessities of "defensive action" under his orders permitted it, he would also have dearly loved to invade Louisiana.

His lordship was as good a poker-player as St. Denis, even though he does not seem to have been aware that he had more in his hand. He rejected St. Denis' unconditional truce and replied that, as he had been ordered, he would observe the truce, as he understood it, on condition that the French commandant would immediately evacuate the entire province of Texas, withdraw his forces to Natchitoches, and interfere neither directly nor indirectly (through the Indians) with the reestablishment of the Spanish posts up to and including Los Adaes, sixteen miles from the French fort.

St. Denis readily agreed to "evacuate" Texas, where he had no soldiers anyhow, but he balked at the surrender of Los Adaes, so close to his home grounds, and directly across the trade routes to Texas and Mexico. He argued that the climate was unhealthy, and the soil unsuitable for farming, but Aguayo would not be swayed, so St. Denis gave in on this point, too.

The strangest thing about this little episode in woodland diplomacy is that Aguayo, firm as he was, apparently did not realize that his men greatly outnumbered the French in this part of the world, for he wrote to the viceroy, referring to St. Denis, "If he had seen our forces, he would not have abandoned his claims." Apparently the camp of the expedition must have been so distributed that Aguayo would assume that St. Denis, during his short stay, could not see how many men it contained. On the other hand, the missionaries must have informed him of the size of the expedition—the largest ever sent into Texas—or he would not have given in so easily. It was purely a poker game, in which Aguayo, though he failed to guess his opponent's hand,

and further handicapped by his royal orders limiting him to defensive action, won over St. Denis, not in spite of the latter's superior knowledge but because of it.

St. Denis went his way, promising to retire "with his people" to Natchitoches, and never again was there any real threat of a French invasion of Texas. The day after St. Denis' departure, Aguayo dispatched soldiers to rebuild the Missions San Francisco and Concepción. Three days later, he led his entire battalion to the site of the Mission San Francisco de los Neches for a ceremony of reestablishment which included a high mass, led by Father Márgil, and the firing of a salute by the whole battalion to impress the Indians. The main expedition then went on to the Mission Concepción for a similar ceremony. The Missions San José and Guadalupe also were reestablished. At all times, gifts and speeches were dispensed in equal numbers to make friends with the Indians. By August 21, the Mission Dolores de Los Adaes, of which not a vestige remained, had also been reestablished, a quarter of a league east of its former site near what is now San Augustine. On the 29th the expedition reached the last mission, San Miguel de Linares, near Robeline, Louisiana, which was reestablished as San Miguel de los Adaes.

Two days later a messenger arrived with a letter from M. Renaud, the acting commandant at Natchitoches, to the effect that St. Denis had gone to Mobile for further orders and that meanwhile M. Renaud must respectfully request the Marques de Aguayo to take no action toward reestablishing the settlement of Los Adaes. Evidently St. Denis had been "convinced against his will" when he had apparently agreed to the reoccupation of the Adaes.

On the pretext that the question could not be settled by correspondence, Aguayo dispatched two of his officers to talk with Renaud and, more important, to examine the French fort and the forces there garrisoned. The chief emissary, Lieutenant General Don Fernando Perez de Almazán, then clearly informed the commandant that the Spaniards would build a mission and presidio at any place they deemed proper. Renaud, handicapped by the slow communications of that period, replied that he had no express orders either to permit the establishment of a Spanish fort or to prevent it, and that he was willing to observe the truce if Aguayo would do likewise.

Work on the new presidio was begun immediately—a word that can only rarely be used in writing Spanish history. Both the fort and the mission, a quarter of a league away, were dedicated on October 12, 1721—a date then celebrated, not as Columbus Day, but as the Feast of the Apparition of Our Lady of Pilar in Zaragoza.

The expedition left on the return trip on November 12, and five days later Aguayo fortunately received a copy of the royal order authorizing him to make the expedition to Texas, the order having been signed by the king at Aranjuez, Spain, on May 6. After an arduous journey through snow and ice, in which he lost all but fifty of his original 5,000 horses, and all but 100 of the 800 mules, although all of the men came safely through, Aguayo reached San Antonio on January 23, 1722. Here he selected a new site for the presidio, which consisted only of a cluster of *jacales,* and personally drew plans for an adobe fort, 75 varas square with four bastions, between San Pedro Creek and the San Antonio River, facing the plaza which is the site of the present San Antonio city hall. During this visit to San Antonio, the governor also kept his promise to Chief Juan Rodriguez by establishing the Mission San Francisco Javier de Najera, although apparently no missionary activity was carried on at that location until the Mission Concepción was moved there nine years later.

After spending the rest of the winter in San Antonio, the expedition moved on to La Bahía, arriving at the temporary presidio on March 24. After a week's illness from the hardships of the journey, the governor began to draw plans for a permanent presidio, on the exact site of La Salle's Fort St. Louis. In digging the foundations, Aguayo's men found pieces of gun locks and other gear left by the French, although the cannon buried by the Frenchmen had some time previously been dug up by Spaniards and shipped to Vera Cruz by sea. Close to the presidio, Aguayo established the Mission Espíritu Santo de Zuñiga. He returned to San Antonio April 26, still in feeble health, and dismissed his men in Monclova on May 25.

The Aguayo expedition was undoubtedly the most significant single event in the history of Texas until the end of the Spanish regime. Aguayo found the great and fertile province, larger than Spain itself, wholly abandoned with the exception of the little settlement at San Antonio. In eight months, he reestablished six missions and founded three new ones; established two new presidios, reestablished one, and strengthened the fourth; placed 268 soldiers in an area where there had been sixty or seventy before, and left the Spanish power in Texas so firmly established that it could never again be threatened until the revolutions a century later. The history of Texas for the next hundred years was definitely determined by the Marquis of San Miguel de Aguayo.

Soon after Aguayo's return to Mexico, the presidios of Texas fell into varying degrees of neglect. That of San Antonio seemed impotent to prevent raids by the Apaches under its very walls. At Los Adaes—then and long afterward the capital of Texas—crops failed for two successive years, so that Captain-General Perez de Almazan had to go to San Antonio for help. At Espíritu Santo, commanded by Domingo Ramón, there occurred a chain of mischances which may bring an ironic smile to the lips of some who recall that Ramón's kinfolk, two centuries later, were San Antonio politicians.

After Domingo Ramón had died in what at first seemed a rather mysterious manner, his son, Diego, who was left in command of the presidio, wrote a letter direct to the viceroy in which he complained that the Indians were constantly harrying his presidio and the nearby mission; that they had killed a messenger en route from San Antonio and shot down two men at the presidio itself. Nevertheless, Ramón complained, the governor had failed to give him reinforcements.

Ramón's report was forwarded to Governor Almazan, who went to inspect the presidio on March 24, 1724, with interesting results. He found the soldiers in rags, spending all their time drinking and gambling, their guns rusty, the log walls pulled down for firewood, and the whole presidio in a state of decline which must have begun long before Domingo Ramón's death, although Aguayo had left the presidio well equipped two years before, and only the previous year a ship had brought ample additional supplies. What was more, the death of Domingo had come about through his own fault.

An Indian, waiting in a soldier's house for a handout of beef, had casually decided to shake the dust off his blanket. The dust fell in a cloud on the corn which the wife of the lieutenant of the presidio was grinding in a metate. Enraged, the woman called her husband and exhorted him to drive the Indian out of the fort. After a scuffle, the Indian took refuge in the mission village. Two soldiers, pursuing, wounded him with a knife, so that the rest of the tribe became alarmed and forty warriors took up their bows and attacked the soldiers, but wounded only a few horses.

After this, the Indians fled to the woods. José Domingo went after them, quieted their fears and persuaded them to return to the mission, but as darkness fell on the way back, half of the warriors again disappeared. Ramón then forced the remaining Indians—men, women and children—into a hut from which they were called out, a few at a time, to be placed within range of a cannon which was to mow them down while their fears were lulled with the sight of a steer being butchered, ostensibly to supply them with food. Such was the story elicited by Almazan in his investigation, at which he said all persons testifying were in full agreement.

The tribesmen became suspicious, and tried to escape en masse from the hut, but José Domingo and his soldiers forced them back into it. The captain then rashly entered the hut himself and tried to convince the Indians that nothing would happen to them. As they calmed down, the testimony went on, he called out to his soldiers, "At them, friends, and get them!"

At these words, one of the Indians picked up a large pair of scissors and stabbed José Domingo in the chest. The soldiers then attacked the hut, but only two of the Indians failed to make their escape. José Domingo, eight days later, died of his wound.

As a result of these happenings, the Governor learned, all the Indians deserted the mission on the bay, though later they were persuaded to return. The story that Ramón intended deliberately to have all the mission Indians shot down would seem incredible if it were not so well attested. It can be believed only on the supposition that he was roaring drunk, which is not improbable although it does not seem to be mentioned in the records. It is a curious and little noted fact that, in historic times, drunkenness was so often taken for granted that it is seldom mentioned as an explanation of irrational behavior. The worst atrocities, however, have been committed by abstemious men.

After such occurences, there was little to wonder at in the Indian depredations of which Diego Ramón had complained. Another formal investigation was held for the governor by his secretary, Manuel Malo de Mendoza, who carefully studied the happenings on the night of January 13, when the Indians had killed two soldiers and stolen a number of horses. The secretary found there had been advance warning of at least one Indian lurking suspiciously near the presidio, but the lieutenant in charge had decided that the man who made the report had mistaken a small palm tree for an Indian. The horses had consequently been allowed to go on grazing outside the presidio walls, and one of the four guards had gone to sleep. Among the four, they had only one rusty, useless gun and a short sword.

As a result of all these findings, both Diego Ramón and his lieutenant, Ignacio de la Garza, were removed from office.

12

War and Peace With the Apaches

Since long before the dawn of history, people have been on the move in all parts of the world, sometimes slowly, sometimes more rapidly. When two such movements clash, the result usually is armed conflict. The great movement of European emigration to the New World brought clashes with the native Indians which continued throughout the hundreds of years when the white settlements pushed westward from the Atlantic Coast and northward from Mexico. When these two waves of European expansion met, there were clashes between them as well as with the Indians.

At the same time the Indian tribes themselves continued on the move, as they had done since the progenitors of their race crossed from Asia. But, although North America was thinly populated, one tribe could not move out of its former limits without encountering another tribe which would put up stiff resistance. So it was with the Comanches and the Eastern Apaches. The latter, under constant pressure from the Comanche nation, were forced into Texas from the northern plains about the end of the 17th

135

century.

For a full generation, while defending themselves from the Comanches, the Apaches pressed against the Spanish settlements at San Antonio and raided supply trains or lonely travelers along the *Camino Real* that stretched across Texas from Eagle Pass to San Augustine. Sometimes they killed Spaniards and mission Indians for no apparent reason except bravado, but more usually they came to steal horses, cattle and any other object of value that they could lay hands on.

The prolongation of this long war with the Apaches was aided by Spanish inefficiency to some extent, and even more by the lack of unanimity as to what should be done to remove the ever-present menace. On the one hand, there were the military commanders, who usually believed in retaliating with as much violence as the limited forces at their command would permit, and who were not above going out deliberately to take slaves for their private use or profit. On the other hand, there were the missionaries and their friends, who believed that the Apaches, for all their known cruelty and treachery, would respond to a conciliatory policy.

For a generation after the founding of Spanish Texas, the Apaches and not the French were the real threat to the survival of the handful of little missions and presidios in the otherwise untouched wilderness. While the power of France, in the person of St. Denis, was only a more or less threatening shadow on the horizon, the Apaches were a present menace, swooping down time after time on the mission and presidio at San Antonio, which were so crucial a link in the line of supply that, without them, the missions in East Texas could not have lasted a year.

The Lipan Apaches, a Plains tribe who had gradually infiltrated Texas under pressure from the Comanches, were altogether different from the wretched Coahuiltecan Indians of South Central Texas and the equally miserable cannibal Karankawas of the Gulf Coast. There were at least 21 of the Coahuiltecan tribes, some having as few as 200 people and all speaking distinct dialects, so that they could communicate with each other only through the sign language. Since these tribes became extinct or were absorbed in the latter part of the 18th century, and since the early Spanish missionaries, intent on saving their souls, had not much interest in recording their customs, we know little about them. As one padre succinctly expressed it, "These creatures are of no interest except for the fact that they have souls to be saved." Of course, the friars did not even dream of the sciences of ethnology and anthropology. Even the classification of "Coahuiltecan" is based on language affinities only, and we do not know if these tribes were closely related in race.

Living much like the Digger Indians of Nevada, later described in Mark Twain's "Roughing It," these miserable creatures planted little or nothing and hardly even knew how to cook any meat that they might gain from the chase. Their food consisted principally of fish, prickly pears, mesquite beans, nuts and fruit. They went naked in summer, and in winter they covered themselves with buffalo robes. They lived in temporary huts made of woven branches and grass, plastered with mud. We are told that they, like the somewhat more civilized Tejas Indians to the northeast, were continually afflicted with smallpox, measles, other fevers, and pustules or buboes, which last an early visitor, Father Morfi, attributed to "some defect in the blood, mostly resulting from the excessive use of strong liquors and bear grease which they drink like water." They were dominated by medicine men, who seem to have had some good ideas, for Morfi tells us, "It is ridiculous how these barbarians thought they could get rid of the smallpox, which they considered a living being which followed them." Smallpox victims were isolated in the woods, given a supply of food and water, and left to themselves to die or recover. Though hard-hearted, the method had much to recommend it in a primitive world without isolation wards or nurses.

The Apaches were braver, prouder and more enterprising than the sedentary Indians of the Texas river valleys, and consequently they were more dangerous, for war and robbery were their profession. They were of course thoroughly misunderstood by the early Spaniards, who described the Apaches' raids on the mission livestock to sheer perversity resulting from the fact that their souls had not yet been saved. Actually, of course, war and larceny were the way of life of the Apaches, the only way they knew. They had raised themselves from savagery to barbarism when they learned to ride horses, being thus enabled to raid other tribes and improve their own standard of living. Bravery was their highest virtue, an ideal which it was said they realized in an abounding degree during battle, though they were not "constant" under torture, unlike Indians of some other tribes, who would curse and spit at their enemies even when their skin swelled and popped as they burned at the stake.

All the Indians—Apaches, Tejas, Coahuiltecans, and the rest— were passionately fond of the *mitote,* a kind of ritual dance, the impact of which on spectators may be deduced from the fact that its name has passed into the Mexican vernacular as a synonym for *riot* or *uproar*—compare the American word *shindy*. The Lipan Apaches in the middle 18th century were supposed to have 5,000 warriors, although it is possible that their rapid movements, raiding now here, now there, made them seem more numerous than they really were. They were described as being tall, well-formed, having regular features, intelligent, bold, perfidious, and "enemies of all living beings."

"It is said," Father Morfi reported skeptically, "the Coast tribes have an herb which keeps the blood from flowing from their wounds, and the Apaches have a branch to place behind their ears which keeps them from ever getting tired. But I believe that the true herb of the coast tribes is the poor aim of our soldiers, and the branch of the Apaches, their experience with fatigue." Despite their belief in medicine men and magic herbs, however, the Indians were suspicious of baptismal water: they had seen too many men die after receiving baptism *in extremis*.

As early as 1691, Father Manzanet remarked of the Apaches, "In the end they conquer all the tribes; yet it is said they are not brave because they fight with armored horses." The following year, a number of Spanish soldiers assisted the Tejas Indians in war against the Apaches and gained with the aid of their Spanish muskets a minor victory which was really a major disaster, for it taught the Apaches to regard the Spaniards as their enemies and settled them into a habitual attitude of hostility which nullified all attempts at conciliation for more than fifty years.

The Apaches were already regarded as a formidable enemy by 1718, when Governor Alarcón's instructions from the viceroy cautioned him to be on guard against them and to organize the neighboring tribes into a defensive alliance. Hardly had the presidio of San Antonio been founded when the Apaches began to attack the supply trains from Coahuila, and in 1720 they rejected Aguayo's peace overtures. Wisely, the Apaches avoided contact with the considerable army that Aguayo took with him on his expedition, but he had hardly crossed the Rio Grande, returning to Mexico, when a party of five Indians made off with fifty horses from San Antonio. Captain Nicolás Flores, the captain of the presidio, took after them and carried back not only the horses but also the heads of four of the raiders.

Because of his vigilance—so Flores boasted—no more horses were stolen for more than a year, but on August 17, 1723, a band of Apaches drove off eighty horses from the corral of the presidio itself, although there were ten soldiers on guard. Captain Flores followed the tracks of the raiders for thirty-six days and finally came to an Apache camp in the Hill Country northwest of San Antonio. After a pitched battle in which 34 Indians were killed, Flores and his men recovered the stolen horses with interest, taking 120 horses and mules, twenty Indian prisoners and a considerable stock of

138

saddles, bridles, knives, spears and other gear which were supposed to have been stolen by the Apaches.

Among the prisoners taken by Flores, presumably for use as hostages in negotiating peace, there was a woman who, when asked why the Apaches raided San Antonio, answered that they did this because of their friendship with "other Spaniards" in the north, to whom they traded horses and slaves for manufactured goods. These hostile "other Spaniards" could only have been the Frenchmen of Louisiana. Flores was encouraged to believe that it might be possible to make an alliance with the Apaches and turn them against the French, so he sent the woman back as a messenger with the promise that he would release the other prisoners if the chiefs would come and make peace. The woman returned in three weeks with five other Apaches, including a chief who presented Flores with a gold-headed Spanish cane and murmured "Dios! Dios!" The chief said he had come to verify the woman's report that the Spaniards decided to make peace, after which he would notify "the other five chiefs" so that all of them could come and conclude a treaty.

When the chief had departed, a disturbing report came to the presidio from San Juan Bautista—that the Apaches' talk of peace was only a ruse designed to gain the return of the captives, after which they would attack in great force. Two months later, thirty Apaches arrived at San Antonio and peaceably asked for their hostages. The priest at Valero Mission, Father Joseph Gonzalez, was willing to give up the prisoners, who were in his care, but Flores refused to consent to their liberation until all the chiefs agreed to make peace, and he was firm in this decision even though Gonzalez accused him of wanting the Indian women and children as servants, not hostages. Upset by the loud argument, the visiting Indians retired, leaving a young girl as an additional hostage.

Gonzalez's complaints resulted in a letter from the viceroy to Captain Flores, suggesting that the presidio was in a run-down state and that, if conditions had been as they should be, the Indians could never have stolen eighty horses from under the captain's nose. Flores appealed to Gonzalez to bear witness for him, but the missionary only renewed his complaints, and was joined by Father Hidalgo, then also living at Valero, who declared that the Apaches could have been converted years ago if the presidio had been properly managed. "Now again," he added, "the captain of this presidio has disturbed the so greatly desired peace by not releasing the children of the Apaches."

Gonzalez won, and on April 6, 1724, Flores was replaced in

command by one Mateo Perez, whom Gonzalez had recommended, although the fellow, a private in the same presidio, could barely write his name. The Apaches, apparently having lost hope of recovering their hostages by peaceful means, renewed their raids after seven months of quiet. Even Father Hidalgo remarked, "Little by little the Apaches are showing their claws." The return of Flores to the captaincy a year after his dismissal made little difference. On Aguayo's advice, the viceroy now announced a definite policy of attempting to conciliate the Apaches, but at the same time preparing for decisive military action, with the aid of the Tejas Indians, if the Apaches refused to be conciliated. This policy was accepted, without any deep conviction of its probable efficacy, by the officials of the province, while Father Hidalgo, though he was now an old man, prayed for permission to go to the hiding places of the Apaches, with only a single lay brother for companion, to convert this people to the Holy Faith and thereby secure the peace of the province.

For several years, from 1726 to 1730, there was a period of relative quiet, marred only by a few sporadic raids. This condition led Don Pedro de Rivera, who made a general inspection of the frontier presidios in 1727, to underestimate the strength of the enemy, so that he recommended drastic retrenchment in the garrisons at San Antonio, Dolores, Adaes and La Bahia—tiny forts, each with a handful of men, which were the sole defense of the Spanish Empire against the French on the east and the Apaches on the north and west.

Events moved slowly in those days. Rivera made his ill-advised recommendations in 1728 and they were put into effect in 1729, but it was not until January, 1731, that the evil effects of the retrenchment were felt in renewed raids by the Apaches.

At the same time, there was slowly moving toward San Antonio a little band of immigrants from the Canary Islands who, under the direction of the paternal Spanish government, were to establish the first civil municipality in Texas. Aguayo, immediately after his expedition, had recommended serious colonization of Texas, declaring that one permanently established Spanish family would do more to hold the country than a hundred soldiers. It was indispensable, he said, to populate the country with 200 industrious Spanish families from Galicia, the Canaries or Havana, together with an additional 200 Tlaxcaltecan Indians, the peaceable and intelligent tribe who already had been transported in large numbers to do the work of the mining settlements in northern Mexico.

Although Aguayo's recommendations were accepted in principle, their execution fell short of completeness. The king, or his ministers, decided that the whole 400 families should come from the Canary Islands, where the poverty of the land made it difficult for the inhabitants to gain a living. Orders to this effect were issued in 1723 but were not carried out until a further order had been issued six years later.

The qualities attributed to the Canary Islanders were expected to make them far superior to the indolent and licentious soldiery in developing the colony and setting an example for the native Indians. They were believed to be industrious in their habits and pure in their morals, with a high respect for women. They were people of Spanish race, whose ancestors had been settled in the Islands after the extirpation of the native Guanches. As early as 1686, proposals had been made for settling Canary Islanders at Matagorda Bay, but the plan at that time had fallen through.

After a crossfire of orders and reports which lasted seven years, the final and total result of the king's order of 1723 was the embarkation of ten Canary Island families, consisting of fifty-two persons, who landed at Vera Cruz in the late summer of 1730 and reached San Antonio on March 9, 1731, after the original number of families had been increased by intermarriage and by the accession of two other families, also originally from the Canaries, after the party arrived in Mexico. The final list included three families named Leal; two named Rodriguez, and one each named Curbelo, Santos, Padron, Nis, Alvares Travieso, Rodriguez, Arocha, Delgado and Cabrera; the widows Granado and Delgado, and two pairs of unmarried brothers, named Armas and Peres, the four of whom were counted as one "family" for the purpose of allotting land. These immigrants were the ancestors of many people now living in San Antonio, and are sometimes mistakenly referred to as the "first settlers," although there were at least forty-five soldiers and their families, amounting to some 200 in all, resident in San Antonio before the Islanders arrived.

The *Islenos,* as they were called, were hardly the stuff of Pilgrim Fathers, and their descendants are more of a credit to them than they are to their descendants. This is as it should be.

At home in the Islands, the colonists had been *labradores,* or small farmers, and only one or two could write their names. Threatened with starvation in the Canaries, these people were given free passage to the New World, along with a fairly generous cash allowance; they were given free land and granted the right, as "first colonists," to call themselves *hidalgos,* which is roughly equivalent to the term *gentlemen* as it was formerly used in England. Thus to personal and family feuds that the colonists brought from their isolated islands were added the causes of anger that would arise when anyone slighted their newly acquired gentility. Naturally, they held themselves above the soldiers who had preceded them into San Antonio. They quarreled constantly with the military, with their neighbors, with the friars at the missions, and even with the royal governors. They also quarreled with each other. Not even in fighting off Indian attacks were these colonists ever fully united. The quarrelsome tradition then established is not without its bearing on San Antonio's public affairs today.

The new arrivals were temporarily bedded down in the houses of the soldiers and a temporary division of lands was ordered, so that planting could begin at once. By June the Islanders had finished planting their corns, beans, barley, cotton, chiles, melons and squash, and in July they proceeded to lay out their permanent settlement, which the viceroy had ordered to be established with the rank of a *ciudad*. Each head of a family was alloted for cultivation a space 105 *varas* (nearly 100 yards) wide, its length being the distance from San Pedro Creek to the San Antonio River, which varies somewhat but is of the order of half a mile. Besides the land, each settler was given seed, oxen, implements, and a money allowance of fifty cents a day for the first year, with the doubtful privilege of buying provisions from the commander of the presidio at the same excessive price that was charged the soldiers.

The *villa* proper was established on the east side of San Pedro Creek, with the church to be built on the west side of the plaza at a point which remained the precise geographical center of San Antonio for more than 200 years. The *villa* was given the name *San Fernando* in honor of His Serene Highness, Don Fernando, Prince of the Asturias, who later became king of Spain. According to the viceroy's order, based on the general law of the Spanish colonies, the streets of the new town were to be laid out "straight, according to the map." That map must have been mislaid, however, as anyone can testify who has seen the badly bent streets in the older portion of San Antonio, some of which actually were laid out to follow the routes of irrigation ditches, or which turned aside from the straight course to avoid some natural obstacle such as, perhaps, a mesquite tree.

The residential portion of the city, as distinguished from the cultivated fields and the pastures, was to be a square of 1,093 varas on a side, divided into 144 blocks, each 240 feet square. Each family was given a block on which to build its house and was directed to line the borders of the lot with shade trees.

The viceroy's order, which might be considered the charter of the new city, went into meticulous detail regarding the duties of the settlers, though little if anything was said about their rights. The *hidalgos* were even

142

prohibited from leaving the immediate vicinity of the settlement, although other settlers could move about unhindered. One of the Islanders was unable to obtain a pass to go to Saltillo for urgently needed medical attention, and another had to obtain special permission from the governor to go and round up some cattle thirty miles from San Fernando.

It would appear, strangely enough, that the establishment of San Fernando was completely illegal, because the Laws of the Indies provided that any new settlement must be at least five leagues distant from any *ciudad, villa,* or *lugar de Espanoles.* There had been a mission, a presidio, and *villa* since 1718.

In any case, the viceroy's decree directed Governor Perez de Almazan to select six *regidores,* or councilmen; one *alguacil mayor,* or town marshal; one *escribano de consejo y publico,* or city clerk-secretary, and one *mayordomo de los bienes y propios,* a combination of treasurer, tax collector and city attorney. The council was to select from among its own number a first *alcalde* and a second *alcalde*—municipal judges with a few administrative duties—the second to act in the absence of the first. The term alcalde, often thought to be equivalent to the English and American *mayor,* thus can be seen to refer to a quite different office. It is true that the *alcalde* presided over the sessions of the *cabildo,* or council, and in that capacity was equivalent to mayor under the modern council-manager form of government, but he had no executive powers corresponding to those of the mayor under the commission or aldermanic forms.

Appointment of the *cabildo* by the governor, for life, was another violation of the Laws of the Indies, which made an exception to the generally absolutist political arrangements of the time by providing that the council should be elected by the people. Under the San Fernando arrangement the *cabildo,* as the older members died or retired, became a self-perpetuating body, though it does not appear that offices were ever sold or handed down from father to son, as often happened in other parts of the Spanish empire in the 18th century.

Installed as members of the *cabildo,* on August 1, 1731, were nine of the older, married members of the Canary Island colony: Juan Leal Goraz, Juan Curbelo, Antonio Santos, Salvador Rodriguez, Manuel de Niz and Juan Leal Alvares, *regidores;* Francisco de Arocha, *escribano;* Antonio Rodriguez, *mayordomo,* and Vicente Alvarez Travieso, *alguacil.* Leal Goraz was immediately elected as first *alcalde* and Rodriguez as second *alcalde.* The choice of Arocha as secretary was apparently due to his being the only colonist who could write a legible hand. Of the nine officers, only four could even sign their names. When Arocha retired in 1757, his place remained vacant until near the end of the century, presumably because no other qualified secretary could be found among the citizens of San Fernando.

There was no city hall at first, and as late as 1783 the council met in the jail. As for the character of the town elders, Governor Teodoro de Croix wrote in 1778: "The officers of San Fernando form a most ridiculous *cabildo,* because of the ignorance of all, and do many absurd and shameful things, because of the difficulty of appealing to distant superiors."

By the time the members of the new *cabildo* had settled in their seats, new reports of threatening action by the Apaches began to trickle in from the Hill Country. Early in August, an Apache prisoner declared that a great number of his people were assembling in the *Lomería Grande,* preparatory to a combined attack. Six weeks later, the captain of the presidio, Juan Antonio Perez de Almazan (possibly a son of the governor) and his 25 soldiers were ambushed by 500 Apaches in what is now a placid northwestern residential district of San Antonio, a league from the presidio. Almazan reported that he had sent five scouts to chase a party of Indians who had stolen sixty horses. When he joined the scouts with his "main force" of twenty men, he found the scouts engaged in battle with some forty Apaches. Just as he arrived, however, an army of 500 Apaches came out of their hiding places in the mesquite thickets, all on horseback and well armed with bows and arrows, forming their line in the shape of a crescent and gradually surrounding the little band of Spanish soldiers. The fight continued for two hours, during which two Spaniards were killed and thirteen wounded. The entire troop of Indians then suddenly turned tail and fled, an event which Almazan attributed to the intervention of Divine providence. Actually it was a characteristic reaction in the economical type of limited warfare practiced by the Indians. Despite their numbers, the Indians were at a disadvantage in that the Spaniards were armed with guns while they had only bows and arrows, and the chiefs knew that many more of their own warriors would be lost if they fought to a decision.

Reporting this skirmish to the viceroy two months later, Almazan asked for reinforcements and complained that the civilian settlers could hardly be persuaded to assist in a campaign, since the enslavement of captives had been prohibited.

A year later a new governor, Juan Antonio de Bustillo y Zevallos, led a force of 157 Spaniards and 60 mission Indians by a circuituous route to a great encampment of the Apaches near the San Saba River. Fighting began the moment the Spanish force crossed the stream, when they were

144

attacked by 700 warriors, all well-disciplined and extraordinarily brave, Bustillo said, mounted on horses and armored with leather breastplates which were proof against lances and arrows but not against the Spanish rifles. However, the Indians waited until the Spaniards had discharged their single-shot weapons, which were awkward to reload, and then closed with them in hand-to-hand combat. After five hours of battle the Indians retired, driven not only from the field but from their camps, which stretched for a mile and a half along the river. The Spaniards took only thirty prisoners, for most of the women and children had fled, but they recovered 700 horses and captured 100 mule-loads of furs and other plunder. Not a single Spaniard was killed.

In the next few years, the frequency of Apache attacks generated such fear that in 1736 the governor was compelled to issue an order that no one should discharge firearms in the Villa de Bexar unless he should see Indians entering the place, and that a shot would be the agreed signal of an Indian attack. The continual raids did not by any means end with the capture, in 1737, of Cabellos Colorados (Red Hair), a chief who had been largely blamed for the persistent hostility of his people. After being held as a hostage for many months, during which the Apache raids continued from time to time, Cabellos Colorados was sent into Mexico and thence, like many other hostile Indians, was probably transported to slavery in the West Indies. Although the law forbade enslavement of the Indians as a general policy, it made an exception of those captured in "rebellion" against the king.

By now, the Bexar presidio was commanded by Captain Joseph de Urrutia, probably the most experienced Indian fighter in Texas, who had lived on the frontier, part of the time among the Indians themselves, since he went with the Terán expedition as a boy in 1691. Petitioning the viceroy for a free hand in dealing with the Apaches, Urrutia wrote that the people of San Antonio lived in constant terror, and no wonder, for "Those who can enter a presidio at night as far as the center of the plaza, and who without being heard can safely remove the horses from the corral in which they are tied to the doors of the houses, are to be feared." Urrutia went on to say that many white settlers had left the region and that most of the mission Indians had fled to the woods or to the coast, where the Apaches did not go. After an unsuccessful campaign in 1739, Urrutia died and was succeeded as captain at Bexar by his son, Toribio, who led new campaigns against the old enemy in 1743 and 1745.

In retaliation for the latter campaign, a band of 350 Lipan and Natagés Apaches tried to burn down the presidio on the night of June 30, 1745, while the soldiers were asleep. Luckily a boy saw the Indians and aroused some of the citizens of San Fernando, who held off the enemy for a time, until 100 mission Indians came to the rescue and drove off the Apaches. What the soldiers were doing all this time is not recorded in the archives.

This little battle had an unexpected result. One of the Indians who came out from the mission was an Apache captive, who immediately joined his tribe and told the Lipan chief that his daughter, who was being held as a hostage in the care of Father Santa Ana, was being treated very kindly, and that the Spaniards were anxious to make friends with the Apache tribes. Hearing this, the chief at once ordered his followers to refrain from renewing the attack, and he persuaded the Natagés chief to do likewise. For two months the Apaches troubled San Antonio no more. A squaw, bearing a cross and a bundle of gifts, came to Urrutia to assure him that her people would keep the peace.

While these two branches of the Apaches made peace with the Spaniards, however, others remained troublesome. Three years later in 1748, Apaches attacked the San Xavier Mission (near Rockdale on what is now called the San Gabriel River), killing several soldiers and Indians and creating such terror that more troops had to be summoned, both to guard against the Apaches and to keep the mission Indians from running away.

Long before this, Father Santa Ana and Father Vergara, ten years apart, had pleaded for the establishment of missions among the Apaches. Santa Ana sagely mingled piety with practical arguments, pointing out that the Apaches lived in mortal and growing fear of the Comanches, and no doubt could be induced to enter the walled missions for their own protection, after which they would make valuable soldiers to protect the Spanish settlements from both the Comanches and the French. By 1746, some of the Apaches themselves were asking for missions, though it seems doubtful if those who were heard from carried any authority. Circumstances, however, were gradually developing in the missionaries' favor. For one thing, the authorities in Mexico now recognized the truth of Santa Ana's contention that the retaliation to be expected from the Apaches was in direct proportion to the severity of the Spanish attacks against them. It was finally ordered that, in all future campaigns, the Spanish soldiers should kill no Indian except in self-defense, and that all captives should be kindly treated. These policies were tried out by Toribio de Urrutia in two expeditions in the spring of 1749, in which a number of prisoners were taken but apparently nobody was killed. Immediately after this, Urrutia and Santa Ana chose two women and a brave from among the prisoners to go and tell their chiefs that, if they would make peace with the Spaniards, all the Indians held captive at Bexar would be released.

Three months later, the emissaries returned with word that four chiefs and 400 of their tribesmen were waiting at the Guadalupe River, thirty miles north of San Antonio, for permission to enter the settlement and begin peace talks. Urrutia sent word back to the Apaches that they were welcome, and that they should send up a column of smoke as a signal when they were ready to leave their camp, so that they might be properly received. In the meantime he had a large temporary building erected in the plaza to receive the visitors. On the evening of August 15, 1749, great columns of smoke were seen in the northern sky, and the following day Captain Urrutia went out five miles from the settlement, followed by the entire military, civilian and clerical population of San Antonio, to meet the Apache chiefs and people.

After elaborate ceremonies of greeting, the entire assemblage went to the pavilion in the plaza, where they enjoyed a feast of beef, corn, squash, and various fruits. The following day, after a mass in the parish church, formal discussion of peace terms began. The prisoners were released the following day, and the terms of perpetual peace were finally ratified by both sides on the fourth day of the visit.

After thirty years of intermittent war, a new age seemed to be dawning as the plaza filled with a crowd of excited and jubilant people who came to witness the ceremonies that would usher in the peace. The soldiers, priests and citizens lined up on one side of the plaza, the Apaches on the other. In a great hole which had been dug in the center of the square, there was placed a live horse, a hatchet, a lance and six arrows, symbolizing all the equipage of war. Captain Urrutia and the four chiefs danced ceremonially around the excavation, after which the citizens and the Apaches, joining hands, also danced in a great circle around the place of peace, and then again retired to their places. Finally, at a signal, all rushed up to the open grave and scooped handfuls of earth over the poor horse and the weapons, so that all were buried in a few minutes, while the Spanish "Viva el Rey" echoed the whoops of the Indians. The next day the Apaches went back to their hills, promising to treat all Spaniards as their brothers from that time forward.

13

Trouble and Progress on the Frontier

The boundary between Texas and Louisiana, that is to say between the dominions of Spain and France in North America, was the subject of lively disputes for more than a hundred years. An innocent victim of this almost interminable controversy was Captain Don Manuel de Sandoval, governor of Texas from 1734 to 1736, who was sent to prison and emerged broken in health and with a lasting blot on his reputation despite the fact that he was officially cleared of any failure to use proper diligence in defending the frontier.

Sandoval, a veteran of twenty years' service in the royal armies, came to Texas after serving a term as governor of Coahuila. His orders from the viceroy specified that "the French are always to be checked and prevented from advancing and settling beyond the country which they now possess," but that he should do this "without committing a definite hostile act" and "so as not to cause a break or disturbance." It will be observed also that the orders gave no precise boundary beyond which the French would not be allowed to advance. There was excellent reason for this omission, since the boundary had never been officially determined, much less surveyed. At the only point where Spanish and French settlements stood close together, the boundary was locally and unofficially understood to be the Rio Hondo, a small stream halfway between the French post of Natchitoches and the Spanish mission and presidio at Los Adaes. Not many years before this, the French had claimed all the territory to the Rio Grande, while the Spaniards had originally laid claim to the whole of North and South America, west of the line by which the Pope in 1493 had divided the New World between Spain and Portugal.

Although Los Adaes was then the capital of Texas, Sandoval spent most of his time at San Antonio to direct the presidial soldiers in fighting off the troublesome Apaches. In a letter dictated at Los Adaes on November 12, 1735, Sandoval was informed by his "lieutenant general," an illiterate sergeant named José Gonzalez, that St. Denis, the French commander at Natchitoches, had moved his fort "the distance of a musket shot, or a pistol shot, or something less than one-third of a league" (three quarters of a mile) toward the west into what might be claimed as Spanish territory.

In the disputes which followed, it was often said that St. Denis had moved the fort from the east side of the Red River to the west side. Actually, he had moved it across a back channel which held water only in flood-time, for the fort had always been west of the main channel, on a piece of ground which became an island during high water only. Furthermore, the ground to which he moved it had been occupied for a long time, without any protest from the Spaniards, by the huts and fields of several poor French settlers. Meanwhile the relations between the neighboring colonies were so friendly that St. Denis' Spanish wife was godmother to most of the children born at Los Adaes. In 1731 the Spanish governor, Bustillo, had sent eleven soldiers to help St. Denis defend his fort in a twenty-two-day siege by the Natchez Indians.

St. Denis never explained why he had moved the fort, except to say that he had done so in compliance with orders from his superiors, but the object may have been to make the headquarters more accessible, to protect it from floods, or to make the former site available for growing corn, since the low island was more suitable for farming than the hilltop where the new fort was built.

The next day after receiving the letter which Gonzalez had dictated to the local priest, Sandoval wrote to his lieutenant, directing him to send a series of three formal protests to the French commander. Gonzalez accordingly sent the first notice, warning St. Denis against "the harmful consequences that may be expected from such an unlooked-for innovation."

"I reply to you," St. Denis wrote, "for the first, second and third time that I obey and shall obey always the commands of my superiors." In his reply to the second demand, St. Denis again minced no words, but declared, "We shall not move the said presidio back so much as a foot." To the third demand he replied at somewhat more length, presenting his arguments for French rights to the land in question, and demanding that the Spaniards "show their title" before asking the French to move back.

Meanwhile Sandoval had also written direct to St. Denis objecting in polite but positive terms to the removal of the fort. In his reply to this, St. Denis not only repeated his general arguments for French priority but recalled that he himself had "founded" the Spanish missions in the vicinity. He also defended himself and his king against the calumny that they were introducing "innovations." St. Denis' tone in this letter was not serious enough to please Sandoval, who wrote back in an injured tone, "You make a joke of this, as if the arguments which support me and which I advance were of no weight whatsoever for holding the land under dispute as belonging very properly to His Catholic Majesty."

Nevertheless, in his next letter, St. Denis wrote, "The difficulty amounts to nothing whatsoever, and in case there should be one, its decision belongs to the crowns. In what I am writing here, I shall give an account of this pointless disturbance." He generously granted, however, that "Notwithstanding that as far as the Rio del Norte I did not find [in 1714] any vestiges of Spanish settlement (if there were such), it does not follow that we Frenchmen claim all the territory to the said Rio del Norte as our own. I admit unreservedly that the Spaniards have legitimate possession of it."

In the meantime, relations between the French and Spaniards on the Texas-Louisiana frontier were not helped by a minor incident which occurred while Sandoval and Gonzalez were busily engaged in writing letters and St. Denis was just as busily building his new fort. "Lieutenant General" Gonzalez, despite his illiteracy, was a Spaniard of great pride, and consequently he did not react favorably when one Baptiste d'Herbanne, a Frenchman from Natchitoches, paid court to his daughter, Victoria. In conformity with the etiquette of that day, when Herbanne thought of marriage, he first spoke to the Jesuit priest at Natchitoches, Father Pierre Vitry, although this good father was already in bad odor with the Spaniards because he was supposed to have instigated the removal of the presidio. When Herbanne asked him to "speak" to Gonzalez, Father Vitry replied that he would not dare to suggest such an alliance to the haughty lieutenant general. Undiscouraged, Herbanne himself went to Gonzalez's house to speak to the old man, who politely brushed him off by saying that he could not consent to the marriage without the approval of the governor, who was away at San Antonio. In telling of the incident, Gonzalez declared, "I told him this so as not to hurt his feelings, for even though I would not say he is not a gentleman, if he were of the highest French nobility I would refuse to have my blood mixed with his."

On Sunday, April 8, 1736, while Gonzalez was talking with the Spanish priest after mass, a sergeant came running to tell him that, while he was at church, several Frenchmen had come to the house and "abducted" his daughter. They had taken off in a canoe, through the lakes, swamps and little rivers that laced the region, to evade the pursuit that would not have failed to catch them if they had gone by land. While the Spaniards searched the sloughs, the eloping party paddled to Natchitoches and arrived there at midnight, when Father Vitry was still up and waiting to marry Jean to his Victoria. It later turned out that they had been helped by one Cerda, a foster-brother of the girl's mother, who thereupon deserted the presidio in fear of being punished by his brother-in-law, who was a judge as well as a lieutenant general. Another Spanish accomplice, Juan de Mora, was jailed by Gonzalez to await sentencing when the governor came to Los Adaes.

"The least of the matter," said Gonzalez in a long, dictated letter to Sandoval, "is my aggrieved and suffering paternal affection. I give up everything, for I do not recognize such a daughter, and only resent the manner and contempt with which they snatched her away from in front of my very eyes, it not being sufficient to scorn our arms."

Gonzalez also charged that, the last time a group of Spanish officers had gone to Natchitoches with another demand for the removal of the fort, St. Denis had pointed to their ragged clothes, reminded them of the fact, reported by the Indians, that no supply trains were on the way from Mexico, and asked them, "with great boldness, what they were doing, what they were waiting for, and why, fleeing from such tyranny, they did not all come to his presidio, where they would find shelter, rest, and relief for all the needs which their governor did not supply."

In his correspondence with Sandoval, St. Denis was gradually moving from tolerant amusement to mild exasperation. In August, 1736, he wrote, "I am surprised and shall always be surprised that the right of the French to remove their presidio a stone's throw is disputed. Who set boundaries between us and you? We are not taking your lands from you; leave us

151

ours." He had also reacted to the Spanish threats by building an extra stockade around the new fort for its defense.

Sandoval, on his part, ordered a rupture of all normal relations between his post and Natchitoches, so that, theoretically at least, not a bushel of corn could pass between the two colonies. By August, however, the French had not only completed their fort but had erected a church and fourteen houses at the new location. Sandoval still took no overt action and all remained quiet on the border until April 28 the following year, when Don Carlos de Franquis y Lugo arrived at Los Adaes in full panoply with an escort of soldiers from Bexar. Don Carlos flourished a viceregal order appointing him governor in place of Sandoval, and immediately had his unhappy predecessor placed in stocks in the middle of the plaza, along with Franquis' own lieutenant general, Don Firmin de Ibíricu.

Franquis and Ibíricu had taken office in September, 1736. In February, 1737, Ibíricu, commanding at Los Adaes, had given a passport to one Jean Legros, a Frenchman. While on his way to trade with the Cadodachos Indians, however, Legros had been arrested on Ibíricu's orders. Taken to Los Adaes, he was put in the stocks and escaped a ramrodding only by some unknown intercession. Ibíricu confiscated his trade goods, however, and burned part of them in the presence of witnesses.

St. Denis furiously wrote a Latin letter in his own hand to Ibíricu: "Perhaps we are at war, or perhaps you mean to prevent us from going to the Cadodachos. What is meant that five soldiers should be sent by a sergeant to arrest one of my Frenchmen who was going to the Cadodachos by the direct road? Did you know that he was sent by me? For, if you were ignorant, you should know that he was. You confiscated all his goods. On what grounds? You put him in the stocks; perhaps he is a Spaniard? You wished to ramrod him; where is your justice? You were wise that you did not do so, that's all I have to say."

When Franquis came to Los Adaes, he learned that jealousy over an Indian woman Legros had taken on his journey might have played a part in Ibíricu's change of face. It was also charged, and believed by the governor, that his lieutenant general had been unduly intimate with the French and had kept French women at the *Casas Reales* in Los Adaes. Franquis had Legros compensated for his goods, and St. Denis assured fourteen Indian chiefs, who had complained to him at this interference with their trade, that they had nothing more to fear.

The next month, Franquis turned his attention to Sandoval and, after a hearing which lasted several days, indicted the former governor on seven charges, of which the most important was that he had failed to use proper diligence in preventing the removal of the French fort. It was not until six years later that a decree of the viceroy finally cleared Sandoval of this piffling charge. The same order also cleared Franquis, who had been arrested only three months after Sandoval and charged with several counts of misfeasance in office.

Sandoval, in his defense, pleaded the orders which had required him to avoid actual war on the frontier. Further, he said, in spite of the vehement arguments contained in his letters to St. Denis, he had never really believed that the Spaniards had any cause for offense, "because the site which is said to be ours by ill-informed common report, the French as well as the Indians have occupied with cattle and houses for a long time past."

It was through fear of malicious gossip, such as went on constantly on the frontier, that Sandoval had put up a great show of maintaining that the west bank of the Red River was Spanish territory. "In order not to give the malice of those who have never looked upon me with favor an opportunity to accuse me of being negligent, an abetter of crime, or of anything else detrimental to my unblemished honor in such a delicate matter, I took all possible measures to keep the French from continuing with their fortifications, as is seen in the documents," he wrote.

Sandoval had certainly convinced St. Denis that he was in earnest, even if the Frenchman could not be scared into retreating, and Sandoval's summary as given just above is undoubtedly a true statement of the case as it appears in the detailed record which filled thirty volumes before the case was finished. There are some indications that the "malice" Sandoval had most to fear was that of the Franciscan missionary priest at Los Adaes, Father Francisco Vallejo, who feared that the removal of the fort was a Jesuit plot engineered by his French rival, Father Vitry. There is a strong suspicion that the whole dispute, with its six-year prosecution, its thirty volumes of records, and its historical repercussions over the next hundred years, may have grown out of a hostility which arose between these two men when the French priest had opposed letting the Spaniard baptize St. Denis' newborn son, Louis Charles, in 1732. "From trivial causes dire offenses spring." If the truth were known, wars have been fought over less.

Even the boundary dispute, itself, was trivial enough, but in spite of Sandoval's acquittal it left a permanent shadow on his reputation as a colonial governor and soldier, and it remained a lively subject for discussion throughout New Spain and New France for 27 years, or until Louisiana was ceded to Spain. The affair was revived in the discussions of the boundary

153

after Louisiana was sold to the United States in 1803, and the uneasy ghost of Sandoval was not permitted finally to rest until the boundary became completely meaningless after the annexation of Texas had been confirmed in 1848 by the treaty of Guadalupe Hidalgo.

During the whole period from the first settlements on the Texas-Louisiana border until the cession of Louisiana, the French from Louisiana regularly traded with the Indians in Texas, and often had the connivance of local Spanish officials. Even when the governors and presidial captains were honest, they believed, with good grounds, that the Indians could not be kept under control unless they were allowed to trade with their French friends, who had more goods than the Spaniards and who pleased the Indians by living among them on equal terms, often assuming the habits of the Indians even to running naked and painting their faces.

Although the younger St. Denis was only twelve years old when his father died in 1744, it was said that the Indians of the region "danced before him in preference to the commander of the post." As an illustration of the power he inherited, witnesses in a Spanish investigation said that in 1750 the Indians of East Texas had gone into open rebellion and threatened to drive out the Spaniards merely because the Spanish Governor Barrios, had interfered with the younger St. Denis' trade. Soon afterward, 500 Nadote warriors gathered and threatened to massacre all the Spaniards on the frontier because the governor had sent a scouting party to report on the operations of the Frenchmen.

Nevertheless—and even while Franco-Spanish relations in Europe became more and more friendly—a few Frenchmen were arrested for trading west of the vague Louisiana-Texas boundary. In 1754, after three Frenchmen and two of the Negroes were captured near the Trinity River, their leader, Blancpain, died in prison in Mexico and his companions were sent to Spain. The king then ordered that if any more Frenchmen entered Spanish territory without permission they should be imprisoned on the Isle of San Fernandez (Juan Fernandez?) or at the presidio of Valdivia.

Meanwhile, in one of those violent passages that are not the warp and woof of history but are often the colored thread that makes it easier to discern the pattern in the cloth, the murder of one Father Ganzabal was the climax of a long passage of unsuccessful development in the Texas mission field during the middle part of the 18th century.

After long argument over the feasibility of the project, three missions were established on the San Xavier (now San Gabriel) River near Rockdale in 1748-1749 and a presidio at the end of 1751. The presidio,

154

though garrisoned for the protection of the missions, proved to be their ruin. Don Felipe de Rábago y Terán, the captain of the presidio, immediately showed what was interpreted by the priests as an attitude of hostility toward the missions, and recommended that they be consolidated into one. What was more, Rábago brought with him a woman, the wife of one of his soldiers, Juan Joseph Zevallos of San Antonio. On the way to San Xavier, Zevallos had apparently learned for the first time of his wife's infidelity and made a protest which resulted in his being placed in chains for the remainder of the march, while Rábago jeered at him. Arriving at San Xavier, Rábago had the poor fellow placed in a dirt-floored cell and tied prostrate on the ground with four stakes at his hands and feet and three at his neck, while the captain had a bed brought into the room and there "abused" Señora Zevallos before her husband's eyes. The whole scandal quickly became known to Spaniards and Indians alike.

On Christmas night, 1751, Zevallos managed to escape to the Mission Candelaria, where he demanded sanctuary. The next day Rábago, leading a squad of eight men, rode into the church on his horse, dragged Zevallos back to prison, and put him under torture. Father Miguel Pinilla spent the next ten days arguing with Rábago, explained to him the enormity of his crime in violating the right of sanctuary, and finally put him under formal ecclesiastical censure before the captain could be induced to restore Zevallos to the church, where he became a voluntary prisoner as the only means of escaping Rábago's persecution. Meanwhile the captain continued to quarrel with the clergy, who wrote to their parent College of Querétaro that "the indecent rage of Don Carlos de Franquis, the impostures of Barrios, the craft of Don Jacinto, the plots of the Islanders, the machinations of Don Juachín, and the entanglements of the Provinces, all combined, are outdone by the malice of this man [Rábago]."

While steps toward conciliation and compromises on various practical issues were being taken, a new climax occurred. After a quarrel over the missionaries' accusations of concubinage among many of the soldiers, the priests posted on the door of the presidio a bill of excommunication against the captain and all his men. The soldiers tore down the document and burned it, but nevertheless replied to it with a petition "demanding" absolution. When the priests refused the demand, Rábago assembled the soldiers for a conference at which some of them threatened to desert so that they might seek absolution at the cathedral in Guadalajara. The conference ended with the taking up of a collection to send two of the chief offenders as couriers to Mexico as proxies for the rest. Finally, however, the soldiers agreed to beg for

155

absolution in the proper penitential spirit and it was granted by Father Ganzabal with the approval of Father Pinilla. Peace now reigned for a time,
although Captain Rábago declared what he really regretted was that he had
not ejected Father Pinilla from the missions.

Meanwhile the two emissaries of the garrison were proceeding
to Mexico. Eventually the case reached the viceroy, who took substantially
the side of Rábago, for he decreed that all the missionaires then on the San
Xavier should withdraw, to be replaced by others. But before the order
reached the San Xavier, Zevallos and Father Ganzabal, standing at the door of
the Mission Candelaria, were both shot to death, the soldier with a ball from a
blunderbuss and the priest with an arrow through his heart. The identity of
the murderer or murderers was a complete mystery. Within a month after the
murders, all but one of the missionaries had fled, and so had all the Indian
neophytes at Candelaria, who perhaps were not pleased with what they had
seen of the blessings of civilization.

Some time later, there appeared at the Mission San Juan Capistrano, near San Antonio, an Indian named Andrés who had been reared since
boyhood by Father Ganzabal, had acted as his personal servant and interpreter, and had disappeared from Candelaria two days before the murders.
Confronted by Captain Urrutia, Andrés confessed—without tortue, say the
archives—that he and four soldiers had committed the double murder at the
instigation of Captain Rábago. The investigation of the case continued for
eight years, during which time Rábago remained not only as large but in good
standing, though of unsavory reputation, as the commander of the presidio of
Santa Rosa (now Muzquiz) in Coahuila. Finally, in June, 1760, the viceroy's
court acquitted Rábago of complicity in the murders. At the same time the
missionaires were declared to be innocent of any misconduct in the whole
melancholy affair.

Meanwhile signs from heaven, interpreted in the spirit of the
times, had led to the removal of the missions. As Father Mariano Francisco de
Dolores y Viana wrote in an official report: "The sacrilegious homicides
having been perpetrated, the elements at once conspired, declaring divine
justice provoked; for in the sky appeared a ball of fire so horrible that all
were terrified, [which] circled from the presidio, when it exploded with a
noise as loud as would be made by a heavily loaded cannon. The river ceased
to run, and its waters became so corrupt that they were extremely noxious
and intolerable to the smell. The air became so infected that all who went to
the place, even though merely passing, became infected with the pest, which
became so malicious that many of the inhabitants died, and we all found

ourselves in the last extremes of life. Finally, the land became so accursed that what had been a beautiful plain became converted into a thicket, in which opened horrible crevices that caused terror. And the inhabitants became so put to it, in order to escape the complete extermination which threatened them, that they moved more than thirty leagues away, with no other permission than that granted by the natural right to save their own lives."

The Mission Candelaria was eventually moved to the upper Nueces River and along with it there was established another called the Mission San Lorenzo de las Amarillas, both intended for service to the Apaches. Strangely enough, they came under the protection of Captain Rábago, now in command of the San Saba region, where he built the presidio which can now be seen in a restored form at Mendarville. Because of the breach between Rábago and the Texas missionaires, the mission work in the San Saba and Nueces regions was directed by Father Diego Ximénez, president of the Rio Grande missions.

The Mission San Lorenzo was founded January 23, 1762, on a little knoll near the Nueces River at a place which is now in the northern outskirts of the little town of Camp Wood. The site is now suggested by a modern historical marker, and a few yards away another stone marks the site of Camp Wood, a United States Army post of pioneer days. A ridge of earth, outlining what is presumably a ruined wall enclosing a space 100 yards square, together with the buried foundations of a few small buildings, is all that remains of either the mission or the fort, and there is no way of telling one from the other.

Of the Mission Candelaria nothing remains but a slight mound, identified by two modern markers, in a pasture on the C. T. Stockley ranch, beside the highway a hundred yards north of the one store in Montell, a "town" which is easy to miss on the road between Uvalde and Camp Wood. Bolton says that the San Lorenzo Mission continued in operation seven years and that of Candelaria about four years. The Indians not only disliked the laborious life of converts; they also found that the brown-robed Franciscans could not frighten away the enemy tribes, who attacked them even in the immediate vicinity of the missions. Hence there were many desertions. The neophytes would wander away as they pleased, returning to the missions only when they expected presents.

The boundaries of Spanish Texas extended only from the Medina River on the southwest to the Rio Hondo on the east. Hence they excluded not only the Nueces and San Saba regions, which have just been

157

mentioned, but two other areas which are much more important in the modern State of Texas, although they remained outside the sphere of Texas history during the Spanish period. The region of El Paso, on the upper Rio Grande, was then a part of New Mexico, and the only important settlement in the vicinity was in what is now Ciudad Juarez, on the Mexican side. At the lower end of the same river, the region that later came to be called "the Valley" was part of the province of Nuevo Santander, which also included the site of Laredo and territory as far into Texas as the Nueces River. The boundary between Texas and Mexico was not fixed at the Rio Grande until after the Mexican War.

The history of the lower Rio Grande Valley, though important for future development, was uneventful. The region on both sides of the river was settled on an ambitious scale by José de Escandón under a royal commission granted him in 1746. After thorough preparations, Escandón set out from Querétaro on November 16, 1748, with 755 soldiers and 2,515 colonists. In the first two months of 1749 he founded several colonies inland in what is still a part of Mexico. In March he had arrived at the Rio Grande and founded Camargo and Reynosa, both on the Mexican side. In the next few years he founded many more towns, but the first one in what is now Texas was Laredo, established May 17, 1755. Meanwhile the ranches of Escandón's colonists were spreading out on the left bank of the Rio Grande as far as the Nueces, and eventually to the lower San Antonio River. All told, Escandón founded twenty towns with more than 3,600 Spanish settlers, as well as fifteen missions with an estimated 3,000 converts. All of the towns except Laredo were on the Mexican side, but the rural settlers provided the beginnings of population on what was to be the American bank of the river.

Cabeza de Vaca passed near El Paso on his way to Mexico about 1535, but the first permanent settlement in the vicinity dates from 1659, when Father Garcia de Zuñiga established the Mission Nuestra Señora de Guadalupe in what is now Juarez. This was a way-station on the long road from Chihuahua City to Santa Fé. In 1680, Spaniards of northern New Mexico and their friendly Indians were driven out by a revolt of the Pueblo tribes. Stopping near El Paso, the exiled Indians established themselves in three villages a few miles down the river on the American side. Twelve miles south of the present city of El Paso stands the first village, Isleta del Sur (now called Ysleta), where the Mission Corpus Christi de la Isleta del Sur was soon built for their spiritual welfare—the first permanent mission in what is now the State of Texas. The town, though settled only by Christianized Indians, is in a sense the oldest Spanish settlement in Texas. El Paso itself was not founded until long after the end of the Spanish regime.

Three miles south of Ysleta is the second village, Socorro, where the Mission of La Puri´sima Concepción was established in 1683. The third village, San Elizario, three miles farther south, no longer stands on its original site but has been moved several times because of floods. The churches of all three of these villages are modern structures, the originals having disappeared.

14

Spanish Texas at the Zenith

Less than fifty years after the first permanent settlements in 1716, the Spanish Province of Texas had reached the most stable and flourishing—if these terms can be used—conditions that it was ever to know. In later years there was some growth in population and an increase in the sort of events that fill the pages of conventional history, but never again was the province to enjoy the sort of equilibrium that it reached in the early 1760's for a moment of time on the eve of the day when the cession of Louisiana to Spain would change the course of development in Texas by converting it overnight from a frontier to an interior province of the Spanish Empire, temporarily freed from the need for defense against a potential enemy on its eastern border.

The cession took place in 1762, as part of the peace settlement ending the Seven Years' War, when France and Spain ceded to England nearly all of their possessions east of the Mississippi River and Spain received from her ally, France, the vast territory of Louisiana, consisting of substantially the whole area drained by the Missouri and Mississippi Rivers and their tributaries to the west of the latter. Owing to Spanish lassitude and the opposition of the French colonists of New Orleans, the cession of Louisiana did not become fully effective until 1769, when Governor Alejandro O'Reilly had a group of these dissidents tried for rebellion, with the result that five were condemned to be hanged but were finally shot by a firing squad when no one willing to act as a hangman could be found.

For several years after 1762, the nominal cession of Louisiana remained unknown in Texas and there are some indications that it was deliberately concealed from the public to maintain the Mexican officials' monopoly on trade, a task which would not be difficult in that isolated province, where there were no newspapers and few literate citizens. So, for a considerable time, life in Texas went on as it had before the Louisiana cession, with little to excite the populace except occasional minor raids by the Indians and rumors of trading incursions by the French or the English. Even after the cession had become effective, trade with Louisiana was strictly prohibited for reasons connected with the official monopoly on trade between Spain and Mexico, but the prohibition was largely ignored on both sides, just as it had been when Louisiana was a French possession. As for the Indians, the chief enemy was now the Comanches. The Apaches had kept the peace concluded in 1749, although they cunningly used it for their own purposes, carrying out cattle raids and other thefts with impunity, since they knew that the Spaniards were unlikely to retaliate so vigorously as to bring back the former state of war.

Early in 1766, the Marqués de Rubí was commissioned by the viceroy to make an inspection of all the frontier settlements from Lower California to the Louisiana border. Accompanied by an engineer, Nicolás de La Fora, Rubí visited all the then existing missions, presidios and civil settlements in the Province of Texas, as well as those farther west. Rubí's reports, together with the journals and maps of La Fora, present one of the most complete records ever made of conditions in Texas in the period after its first settlement and before it was shaken by revolts and filibustering expeditions. The account which follows is based on these reports, filled out with observations from other visitors of about the same period.

After visiting the settlements in Chihuahua, Sonora and New Mexico, Rubí crossed the Rio Grande near the present site of Del Rio on July 14, 1767, and advanced to the Vallé de San José (Nueces Canyon). He began his Texas inspection at the Mission Candelaria, where he found a handsome adobe chapel and friary near a spring that flowed into the Nueces River. A large *jacal* served as a granary and warehouse. Surrounding these buildings were the temporary brush huts of the neophytes, destined never to be replaced with more substantial dwellings. A few fields had been cleared in the vicinity, but although there were some 400 Indians—mostly Apaches—about the mission, the crops were not well cultivated.

Ten miles farther north along the Nueces, Rubi found the Mission San Lorenzo guarded by a detachment of thirty men from the presidio at San Saba. This mission had a rude quadrangular fortification and two small cannon, but Rubi criticized the site as being badly chosen for defense, since it was on a slight knoll with higher hills close by.

"These buildings," La Fora wrote, "were constructed by the Lipanes to please and flatter the missionaries, making them believe they would subject themselves to the discipline of permanent settlement, which they never did do, taking advantage of the simplicity and credulity of the missionaries." Even the official Franciscan chronicler, Arricivita, admits that the conversion of these Apaches was "imperfect." He tells how the Indians made continual raids across the Rio Grande and brought back their stolen horses and goods under the very eyes of the fathers. Neither of the Nueces missions was ever approved by the viceroy and both were abandoned within a year or two after Rubi's visit.

The marquis and the engineer went on northward to the headwaters of the Nueces, through the rocky, semi-arid canyon, then cut across the hills and reached the Llano River somewhere below the modern town of Junction. After following the Llano for two days, they crossed over to the San Saba and reached the presidio of San Luis de las Amarillas, commanded by our old friend Captain Rábago, now fully cleared of the San Xavier murders, but broken in health although he was only forty-five years old. The ninety-four men of Rábago's garrison, Rubi found, were virtually peons, kept at their post because they were heavily indebted to the commander, although many were unfit for service and thirteen were entitled to retirement on a pension. It was undoubtedly the worst company of soldiers in the entire kingdom, in Rubi's experienced and usually temperate judgment. There was barely one horse per man, although each soldier should have had five or six remounts. Their guns and other equipment were poorly maintained. Their uniforms, consisting of blue breeches and red cloaks with silver buttons, were dirty and ragged, for they would have been charged $80 for new ones. All other kinds of supplies were charged to the soldiers at prices which were exorbitant for those times. The fort was poorly situated and its walls were too low. All in all, Rubi feared that if the true condition of the fort became known to the Comanches, they would be emboldened to wipe it off the map.

But the inspector must have been an expert in the aristocratic art of dissimulation, for on the very day that Rubi made his secret report, Captain Rábago was emboldened to write to the viceroy, asking that he be promoted to colonel in recognition of his distinguished services. The following year, however, after barely fighting off several Indian attacks, Rábago abandoned the presidio.

From San Saba, Rubi went on to San Antonio, which, although it did not become the capital until 1772, had the largest and most flourishing group of settlements in Texas. The garrison, however, consisted of only twenty-two men, of whom fifteen were generally stationed in the five missions stretched out for a distance of nearly eight miles along the river. The prosperity and success of these missions now redounded to their disadvantage, for it was Rubi's opinion that they should be secularized and their property distributed among the Indians and settlers. Secularization was not ordered by the viceroy until 1793, however, and it was not made fully effective for many years after that.

Perhaps the Indians appeared civilized by contrast with the Spanish soldiers of the presidio. At any rate, Rubi was horrified at the conditions he found there. Each man had chosen his own costume with no attention to uniformity, but rather the reverse. Shades of red were most popular, and although the clothing was ragged and dirty, the men wore costly silk handkerchiefs, lace and silver buttons. Like the men at San Saba, they were deeply in debt, chiefly because of their fondness for costly ornament. Moreover, one out of three pistols and rifles was found to be useless, and so were most of the horses. The presidio itself was half in ruins, while the missions had strong walls and were capable of defending themselves unaided.

Five years earlier, the Bishop of Guadalajara also had found that the presidio of San Antonio de Bejar offered no protection whatever to the settlers and the missions. It had no stone buildings, although it had been established for 44 years, and it was not protected by even so much as a stockade of logs. Cannon lay rusting on the ground in front of the captain's house. Even if the guns had been in working order, they could not have been used without wrecking the settlement, for the houses were built at random, contrary to the Laws of the Indies, which provided for straight streets where cannon could be used against invaders.

In 1762, when Luis Antonio Menchaca assumed command of the presidio, he found twenty-two men on the military payroll, of whom only five were effectives, and 100 adult male civilian settlers, including the aged, the sick and those who lived on ranches as much as sixty miles away. So the presidio and the villa together could muster only thirty able men to repel an attack.

Between Indian scares, the hidalgos of San Fernando occupied themselves with acrimonious disputes over questions such as that of whose ox had trodden down whose corn. The parish church, provided in the orders for the first settlement of San Fernando in 1731, had finally been completed in 1757, but the sixty families of the settlement managed to eke out a living "only by the Grace of God," and the bishop feared that 200 Indians, armed with guns, could easily wipe out the whole establishment.

The five missions in 1762 sheltered 1,242 Indians from twenty-three different tribes, but by the time of Rubi's visit in 1767 the number had been reduced to 809. Up to the time of the bishop's inspection in 1762, the five missions had baptized five thousand Indians, buried three thousand, and married seven hundred. All of the missions had now acquired permanent stone buildings. They raised corn, beans, chile, potatoes, cotton, lentils, melons, sugar cane, peaches and other vegetable crops. On their outlying ranches they had a total of five thousand cattle, 17,000 sheep and goats, 1,600 horses, and a number of donkeys and mules. They operated sixteen looms for weaving wool and cotton cloth.

All of the Indians at each mission were assembled to listen to sermons three or four times a week, and daily they recited portions of the catechism. The unconverted Indians were taught separately through interpreters, receiving baptism when they became fairly well grounded in doctrine and showed some inclination to remain permanently at the mission. All of the Indians received rations of meat and vegetables from the produce of the communal effort. The surplus was sold to buy cloth, hats, knives, cooking ware, tobacco, glass beads, tools, harness and other necessaries which could not be produced at the missions. Although the Indians were required to work, it was impossible to drive them for fear they would run away, and it was said that one Spaniard could do the work of four Indians. Comparing this with what we know of the habits of Spaniards at the same time and place, it is apparent that the Indians must have been slow indeed. They also required close supervision to avoid costly blunders.

Father Santa Ana wrote in 1740, "The conversions are not difficult but they are vexatious, for it is necessary to deal with them like a mother instructing a child. Until after five, six or seven years they are unable to enter into a perfect understanding; and thus it is rare that one does not flee into the forest twice or three times, and so far that they sometimes go inland as many as a hundred leagues. But we have the patience to seek them, and as soon as they see the Father they come like lambs."

Dr. Bolton adds, however, that the fugitives sometimes fought and even committed suicide by throwing themselves from cliffs rather than return to the flogging which they feared as punishment for their flight. It was considered essential to have soldiers at the missions, not so much for protection against raiders as to inspire the resident Indians with "respect" until they acquired the habits of civilization and became willing members of the community.

The largest and most flourishing of the San Antonio group of missions was San José, of which Father Morfi said, "This mission can justly be called the metropolis of all those in New Spain; not because of the antiquity of its origin, but for the beauty of its plan, the strength of its construction, the grace and beauty of its edifices, the abundance of its defenses: there being absolutely no other in all the line of the frontier which deserves even a comparison with San José."

San José can serve as a type of all the missions although, being larger and more firmly established, it contained elements not found in all the others. A good stone and mortar church had been built by 1762 but was already being torn down to make room for a better one, the present structure, whose cornerstone was laid in 1768 although the building was not completed until the eve of secularization in 1793. The church of 1762 had "a good chime of bells." It was ornamented with statues and furnished with gold and silver ornaments, altar furniture and vestments of excellent quality.

Around the thick stone walls of the mission enclosure, 200 yards square, were arranged eighty-four two-room huts for the Indian families. The mission was even provided with two swimming pools which used water from the irrigation ditch before it was allowed to spread out over the fields.

Subject to the veto power of the padres, the Indians managed their own affairs, electing their own "governor," a *cabildo,* and other officials. Those who neglected either their work or their prayers were tried and punished by their own officials. What the punishment consisted of can only be guessed, for the mission did not have a jail and was not equipped with shackles or stocks.

By 1768, Father José de Solís could exclaim, "This mission is in such a flourishing condition, both spiritually and materially, and so beautiful that I cannot find words or figures of speech with which to express its beauty." The Indians of San José had now progressed to the point where they were able to work without Spanish overseers. In addition to their farming and ranching, they operated a carpenter shop, a blacksmith shop, a tailor shop, a mill and a lime and brick kiln. The mission sold supplies not only to the presidio of San Antonio but to those of La Bahía, Orcoquisac and Los Adaes. "The able-bodied men attend to the manual labor," Solís explained, "the old men make arrows for the warriors, the grown-up girls weave cloth, card wool and sew, the old women catch fish for the padres, and the younger boys and girls go to school and recite their prayers."

All of the Indians now spoke Spanish and most of them played the guitar, the violin or the harp. On certain regular occasions a choir of four voices, with instrumental accompaniment, sang while marching in procession between a double file of warriors. The Indians also danced well—perhaps more gracefully than the Spaniards—Solís reported.

Next in importance to San José among the missions was San Antonio de Valero, the largest of the four establishments of the College of Querétaro. Here in 1762 were 275 Indians carrying on substantially the same activities as the 350 at San José. There was a substantial friary and other buildings, but the church had caved in because it was "built without knowledge" and a new one was started some time before 1762, but never finished. The granary that was being used as a church in 1762 was handsomely furnished, however. The walled compound of the mission extended over what is now Alamo Plaza in San Antonio. The present park at the rear of the church is a modern development which never was part of the mission enclosure.

At Concepción, one league south of Valero, the present church building had been completed before 1762. Over the main altar it had a fresco, long since obliterated, of the *Cinco Señores*, and there were two statues of the Virgin in different manifestations as Our Lady of Sorrows and Our Lady of Pilar. The whole sanctuary was richly furnished. At this mission lived 207 Indians carrying on the usual work of agriculture and handicraft.

Next in the line of missions along the river road was San José, and after San José came San Juan Capistrano, on the east side of the River at what is now Berg's Mill, just inside the present city limits of San Antonio. This was a smaller establishment than the others, but the church was well furnished and it even had several oil paintings. Partly because of its isolated location, exposed to frequent attacks, it had made less progress than the other missions, but in 1762 it had 203 resident Indians, or almost as many as Concepción.

Still farther removed from the doubtful protection of the presidio was the Mission San Francisco de la Espada, a mile and a quarter

166

south of San Juan on the west side of the river. Here there were 207 Indians in 1762, although San Francisco, like San Juan, was smaller and apparently less ambitious than the three other missions. The foundations had been laid for a church but the work had been delayed because of a lack of suitable materials. A quarry had just been discovered nearby, however, and work on the church was again going ahead.

Rubí and La Fora, having completed their inspection of San Antonio, moved on toward Los Adaes. At Santa Cruz de Cíbolo, near the present town of Stockdale on Cíbolo Creek, 26 miles east-southeast Antonio, they passed beyond the farthest ranch and went on through country inhabited by bands of thieving but otherwise harmless Indians until they reached the Mission Nuestra Señora de Guadalupe de los Nacogdoches, deep in the Piney Woods of East Texas. At this mission they found a priest, two soldiers, their families and a few servants, but no Indian neophytes whatsoever. Forty-five miles farther east, the travelers arrived at the Los Ais Mission, where again there were no "reduced" Indians. They did find a few Indians living at the Mission of Los Adaes, 73 miles northeast of Los Ais, but the presidio was in a deplorable condition. Even the suave marquis could not restrain his astonishment when the 61 soldiers were lined up before him and presented only two serviceable rifles and only two swords that could pass inspection. Although each man should have had a shield—mainly for protection against arrows—there were only six in the whole garrison. Only a few soldiers had powder-horns, and hardly any of them had a hat, a shirt or a pair of shoes. Only twenty-five horses were fit for service.

When the accounts of the absent governor, Don Angel Martos y Navarrete, were examined, it was found that he had profited in eight years to the extent of $8,400—a substantial amount for those days—by selling to his men, at 1,000 percent profit, supplies which he had purchased from the nearby French post of Natchitoches in defiance of laws and regulations. He had also bought droves of horses in San Antonio at $10 each, sold the poorest ones to his soldiers at $16, and disposed of the best mounts to French traders for as much as $60. And this did not complete the chronicle of his abuses.

Such practices were common on the frontier. Martos may have shown less moderation than some governors and presidial captains, but according to Bolton "The administration of Texas, as of other provinces, was corrupt with 'graft.' The positions of governor and presidial commander were made attractive largely by the opportunity which they afforded for making money in addition to the fixed salaries. The pay of soldiers was made chiefly in food, clothing and equipment, purchased by the governor and commanders, and charged to the presidial soldiers at enormous profits. Thus the post of governor or captain was scarcely less that of merchant than of soldier."

Through woods and marshes, Rubí next made his way to the new presidio of Orcoquisac, near the mouth of the Trinity River, about 200 miles south-southwest of Los Adaes. Here, although the presidio had recently been burned down as the result of violent differences between Governor Martos and Captain Rafael Martínez Pacheco, it had been restored to a fair condition, and the uniforms and arms of the men were the best in Texas. Still, both the presidio and the nearby Mission Nuestra Señora de la Luz were having a hard struggle to survive, and it passed all understanding why such a site, almost inaccessible in the windswept marshes, had ever been chosen for settlement, Rubí declared in his report.

From the Trinity, Rubí traveled on to the presidio of Nuestra Señora de Loreto, better known as "La Bahía," which after two moves was situated on a hill just outside the present town of Goliad, on the lower San Antonio River. Here, when the fifty soldiers lined up for inspection in their dress uniform of red jackets and red flannel trousers, Rubí noted that the clothes were threadbare and soiled. The armaments were in good condition but, as in all the other presidios, the guns were of various calibers, making it difficult to keep them supplied with ammunition, and the men lacked shields, cartridge belts and lances.

The two missions in the vicinity, Espíritu Santo de Zuñiga and Nuestra Señora del Rosario, were in a prosperous condition, although Espíritu Santo had only ninety-three Indians and Rosario had only ninety-one. Supposedly as a result of "bad air" caused by proximity to the sea, twenty miles away, the citizens were frequently incapacitated with malaria and a dreaded "plague" called *mal de loanda,* which was scurvy resulting from improper diet.

Father Solís, a year after Rubí, found that neither of the Bahía missions had yet erected stone churches, but they did have buildings of neatly plastered wood, well furnished. The difficulties encountered by the padres in weaning their charges away from the pagan life were augmented by the Apaches, who had recently come into the region, and who often insolently butchered stolen cattle within full view of the missions, taking only the choicest parts. As at San José, the priests had introduced Spanish dances to distract the Indians from their beloved heathen *mitotes.*

Rubí returned to Mexico in 1768 to write no less than twenty-four separate reports on the presidios visited; seven volumes of extracts and depositions he had gathered along the way, and an advisory opinion on the reorganization of the frontier defenses. Before examining these recommendations and their results, let us consider another and far different visitor to Texas at the same period.

This was Pierre-Marie-Francois de Pagés, described as a captain in the French Navy, Chevalier of the Royal and Military Order of St. Louis and corresponding member of the Academy of Sciences at Paris, who passed through this region in 1767 in the course of a tour around the world, and who reported on his journey in a book which was translated into English and published at Dublin in 1791. This was the first detailed report on conditions in Texas that the English-speaking world had received since the publication of a translation of Joutel's *Journal of La Salle's Last Voyage* in 1714. Consequently the "Travels" of Pagés probably had a distinct influence in turning the thoughts of Americans toward the Southwest, although we have no information as to how widely it was circulated either in the British Isles or the United STates.

Coming from Santo Domingo by way of New Orleans and Natchitoches, Pagés entered the Province of Texas at Los Adaes, where he found "half-savage Spaniards" occupying a collection of forty *jacales*, surrounded by a stockade for defense. These people lived poorly, their diet consisting mainly of tortillas, for although all of the men were in military service their pay was hardly enough for subsistence. Their clothing in many cases was nothing but rags, yet men who did not own a hat or a shirt would still decorate themselves with gold or silver buttons, lace, and spurs five or six inches long. In battle they were armored with deerskin and equipped with a carbine and a long broadsword. To hold themselves steady in the saddle when fighting, they used stirrups weighing at least fifty pounds, which were likely to dislocate the knee-joints of riders unaccustomed to them. As for personal character, the people of Los Adaes were more notable for friendliness and hospitality, Pagés discovered, than for honesty and truthfulness.

Allowance must be made here for the fact that Pagés was a disciple of Rousseau. He was consequently prepared to admire the Indians of Texas more than the "civilized" people, and he was not disappointed in his expectations. At the first Indian village he came to, he was much impressed with the kindness of the noble savages, who gave him fruit cakes in exchange for some of his corn, and took great pains to show him the trail to Nacogdoches. Soon afterward he heard of a poor Spanish traveler who, when a group of white men refused to help him on his way to San Antonio, was given a horse and provisions by the Indians.

San Antonio, Pagés found, was a settlement of perhaps two

hundred houses, two-thirds of them build of stone but many in ruins, standing on a small peninsula which sloped gently to the river and was surrounded by thick mesquite woods. The houses on the perimeter of the town served as walls for defense, the gaps being filled with stockades. The people raised horses, mules, cows and sheep, which were usually allowed to run at large in the woods. Pagés took a lively interest in the process of lassoing cattle, which he had not seen before although he said the custom was described in Anson's "Voyages" as being peculiar to the coast of Patagonia. Horses in San Antonio were so cheap that one would be exchanged for a pair of shoes, yet the inhabitants would track a strayed or stolen animal as much as fifteen or twenty leagues.

As for the missions of San Antonio, Pagés found the Franciscan fathers to be far less "liberal and conciliating to the minds of the savage proselytes" than were the missioners of the Jesuit theocracy in Paraguay, but he left this criticism unamplified and unexplained. He probably meant that the Franciscans were less willing to adapt heathen traditions to Christian uses.

While Pagés was at San Antonio the Indians (presumably Comanches) raided the town and drove away 400 horses. The troops of the garrison were unable to catch the raiders though they followed their tracks for a hundred leagues. On the return, crossing the Guadalupe, the soldiers were attacked by another party of the same tribe, losing 150 horses and some other property. By this time, says Pagés, "the governor began to see the necessity of putting the fort in a better state of defense." The Comanches by this time were using fire-arms, though the Apaches and the coast tribes still employed the bow and arrow.

Pagés lived with a friendly Indian family in San Antonio, and was so impressed with the virtues of his hosts and the beauty of his surroundings that he contemplated staying there for life—"But however much impressed with the excellence of those pure and gentle manners which are the result of freedom, a decent mediocrity of fortune, and the advantages of a pious education; and however sensible I might be to the charms of their women, the amiable qualities of their minds, and the beauty and fertility of the surrounding country, the strong partialities I still retained for my native soil were not to be subdued." So Pagés went on down the *Camino Real* to Mexico, and after four years returned to his native France by way of the Philippines, Java, India, Arabia and Syria.

The celebrated French naturalist, the Count de Buffon, who was working on a series of supplements to his encyclopedic "Natural History," was deeply interested in the stories his friend Pagés told after his return. Pagés had seen many strange things, including unheard-of animals. For example, in describing his journey from San Antonio to Mexico, he recounted, "Another inconvenience which awaits him [the traveler] in this this country is the abominable smell of an animal without the agility but nearly of the same size with a rabbit. This creature, when hard pressed, and finding himself in jeopardy of being taken, emits a most intolerable stench, which threatens suffocation to his pursuers, and is only eluded by precipitous flight."

When Pagés had such marvels as this to tell about, it is little wonder that Buffon and other friends gave him no rest until he had reluctantly agreed to write a book. Unfortunately, his reporting is annoyingly vague in many details. For this reason it has been suspected that he never toured the world at all, but pieced his narrative together from second-hand accounts. This does not follow, however. The book was written nine years after the end of the tour from probably inadequate notes which, as Pagés implies in his introduction, were not intended for publication. This fact, alone, would probably account for the paucity of names, distances and other concrete data. The entire story of Pagés' five years of travel and adventure makes a book of only 437 pages in rather large type, so there was hardly room for exhaustive detail. Then too, there is merit in Pagés' protestations that he is no writer, and that we must "excuse the style of a military man, who has long been a wanderer in wild and savage countries . . . who, little concerned for the ornaments of composition, is, of all literary talents, ambitious of perspicuity alone." Certainly his account of Texas, as far as it goes, is consistent with what we know from other sources.

To return to the Marqués de Rubí, the most important recommendation in his long and carefully drawn report was that the outer defense line, stretching from the Gulf of California to the Gulf of Mexico, be shortened by reducing the number of presidios from 24 to 15. In Texas, this meant the abandonment of the Presidio of Los Adaes, some 400 miles beyond the Presidios of San Antonio and La Bahía, which were to be retained. The more recently established presidio of Orcoquisac, on the lower Trinity, was also to be given up. Both of these forts, the marquis correctly pointed out, lay far beyond the really effective limits of the king's domain.

Los Adaes was practically, but not completely, evacuated in February, 1770, and Orcoquisac was abandoned the same month. Meanwhile a new post, satellite to the Presidio of Bexar, had been established under the name of Santa Cruz del Cibolo at the point where the road from San Antonio to La Bahía crossed Cibolo Creek, in a region where the citizens of San Antonio had established a number of cattle ranches which were in need of protection.

The recommendations of Rubí were officially adopted in a long royal *cedula,* generally referred to as "The New Regulations of the Presidios," on September 10, 1772. Since the missions and civilian settlers in East Texas were to be left unprotected with the removal of the presidios, the order provided that the four missions in that region should be suppressed and the civil inhabitants, though many of them had been born and had spent their entire lives on the eastern frontier, should be moved to the vicinity of San Antonio, which now replaced Los Adaes as the capital of Texas.

When, in the glacier-like course of Spanish colonial administration, the king's orders reached Los Adaes in June of 1773, there was despair among the 500 settlers, who were to be required to abandon their lands and houses, their herds and their ripening crops, and start life anew in a strange community, because of considerations of imperial policy which they could hardly understand. They may also have felt that the withdrawal of the protection of the presidios was not so much of a loss in reality as it might appear in theory. Governor Baron de Ripperdá, though he was sympathetic, could not help but enforce the king's order.

The retreat to San Antonio was a tragic march in which many died from illnesses contracted along the road, while even those who did not become ill suffered torture from the summer heat, the insufficient water and the gradual exhaustion of the food supply. The survivors, barely able to walk a step farther, finally arrived in San Antonio on September 26, three months and one day after they had left Los Adaes.

Once safely in San Antonio, however, the Adaesaños were either unable or unwilling to find lands in that vicinity on which they could settle. It was said by some that their reluctance to leave the Louisiana border had really been due to the opportunities which that frontier, unlike San Antonio, offered for contraband trade. It was true, in any case, that many of the Adaesaños had to beg for bread in the streets of San Antonio and more than thirty of them died within a few months after their arrival in the new capital.

Antonio Gil Ybarbo, the richest of the Adaesaños, and Gil Flores were deputized to go to Mexico and seek the viceroy's permission for a return to the border. This petition was refused, but the Adaes colonists were finally granted permission to return as far as the Trinity River, halfway between San Antonio and Los Adaes. Here, in September, 1774, they established the new settlement of Nuestra Señora del Pilar de Bucareli (named for the Virgin and the viceroy) at the point where the *Camino Real* crossed the Trinity. When Don Hugo de Oconor, the commandant inspector of presidios, heard of this, he expostulated that the site of the new colony "better than any other, enables them to engage in illicit trade and to encourage the northern Indians in stealing droves of horses from the presidios."

Whatever facilities it may have offered, however, Bucareli lasted only five years, for the Comanches harassed the settlers so closely that they hardly dared go out to plant and harvest their crops. Early in 1779, without asking official permission, the Adaesaños fled from Bucareli and established a new settlement farther east, near the site of the abandoned Nacogdoches Mission. The town they established, called Nacogdoches, played an important part in later Texas history.

15

Philip Nolan: The Forerunner

Apologizing for his mistake in using the name "Philip Nolan" for the protagonist of his patriotic fable, *The Man Without a Country,* Edward Everett Hale paid tribute to the actual owner of the name in these words: "The part which the real Philip Nolan played in our history is far more important than that of many a man who has statues raised in his honor."

This is very true, for when Nolan led the first American expedition into Texas, he set in motion a train of events which more than doubled the area of the United States. It is also true that Nolan was the greatest wholesale horse-thief in history and a confidential agent of Major General James Wilkinson, the man who tried to sell the American frontier territories to Spain.

Nolan was not the first American to enter Texas, but he was by far the most important up to his time. Most of the handful of others who dared to cross the border in the late 18th Century were either driven back or carried away to the mines of interior Mexico. To cross the Spanish iron curtain of that day, without a special license from the King of Spain, was in fact a capital offense, though there is no record that the extreme penalty was ever enforced. Especially after the American Revoluation were the King's officials nervous at any hint of infiltration from the democratical and deistical young Republic to the East. The captain general of one of the eastern Mexican provinces even declared, only half jesting, that if he had the power he would prevent the birds from flying west across the boundary.

In 1768, during the period when Louisiana was a Spanish province, the Spaniards were reliably informed that certain English traders had penetrated as far west as the Texas border. This news took on an added significance from the fact that some 68 years before—or only yesterday in the Spanish calendar—an English vessel sent by Dr. Daniel Coxe had made an abortive attempt to possess the mouth of the Mississippi, and English horse-traders had been sent to the mines before 1715.

By 1769, four "Englishmen" were found openly living in Nacogdoches. In August, 1771, four others—Joseph Dickson, James Sherman, Neill McMillan and Arch McKenzie—and two Negroes, all from the bark *Two Friends,* were found shipwrecked at the mouth of the Nueces and taken to San Antonio. In some manner they obtained permission to proceed overland to Natchitoches, driving 133 head of cattle and more than forty horses which they had purchased in San Antonio with three pipes of rum and three barrels of sugar.

In the next three years, parties of "English" merchants were reported to be on the Trinity and Neches Rivers, buying horses and mules which the Indians had stolen from the Spaniards. One of these parties remained long enough to harvest a crop. By 1777, English (possibly Anglo-American) traders had alarmed the Spanish Governor of Texas, Ripperdá, to such a degree that he summoned the Bidais tribe to San Antonio and ordered them to allow no English landings on the coast. About this same time, an English ship, which had carried some building materials as if to establish a colony, was stranded on the coast. The crew and passengers fled in other vessels, but one man, named Miller, who said he had been shipwrecked on still another craft, was carried in chains to Bexar.

Despite the severity of the exclusion law, there were ways in which Americans could obtain exemption. If they were not too scrupulous or too proud of their nationality, they could claim to be Irishmen, a favored race in the Spanish Empire of this period, especially in Texas, where a recent governor had been Don Hugo de Oconór, and a well-known missionary priest had been Fray Juan Agustin Morfi, to say nothing of Governor O'Reilly of Louisiana. The Americans might also claim to be former French subjects in Louisiana, or at least they could become converts to the Catholic Church and marry Spanish-Mexican girls of the Province.

Unlike the laws of the Medes and Persians, the laws of New Spain altered themselves as freely as the wind, in practice if not in theory. The only fixed rule was that circumstances alter cases. There was one law for Spaniards; another for Creoles; another for Indians; and still others for foreigners. Exemptions could often be obtained by appeal to higher authority — to the viceroy or to the King himself. Though local officials were supposedly allowed little discretion, their superiors were far away across the North Mexican desert, and the compelling force of legal and moral arguments could be assisted with cash or a share in the foreign trader's business, as we have seen long since was suspected in the case of St. Denis.

The confusion always characteristic of the absolutist Spanish government reached its height around the end of the 18th Century. Decisions of the provincial governors in Texas were subject to review, if on military matters, by the commandant general in Chihuahua; if on fiscal affairs, by the intendant at San Luis Potosí; if on ecclesiastical matters, by the Bishop in Nuevo León, and if on civil questions, by the Audiencia of Nueva Galicia. As George P. Garrison has keenly remarked, "Any attempt to enforce rights by law was like a shot at the moon: it might be started in the proper direction, but there was little prospect of reaching the mark."

The compensatory advantage in this chaos of arbitrary decisions and overlapping jurisdictions was that the government was less oppressive in practice than its theory required. Hence a good many Americans were able to slip through the holes in the iron curtain long before the King's rule in Texas began to dissolve into anarchy and revolt.

In addition to the Americans already mentioned, and those concerned in the story of Nolan which is to follow, there was a "Francisco Connichi" (Francis McConnaghey?), born in Philadelphia in 1754, who with his wife and four children was counted in the census at Nacogdoches in 1794. The same census also shows as Americans Antonio Buquer, Francisco Borman, and one Fil, first name not given. It goes without saying that names of foreigners in the Spanish archives are almost always grotesquely misspelled. An exception was another "Englishman," one Jones, who was reported living in Nacogdoches in 1793.

The Comanche chief *El Cojo* (the Cripple) came to Bexar in 1794, bringing one "Juan Culbert," a Presbyterian silversmith from Philadelphia, who said that he had been roaming the Southwest for three years, but now wished to settle in San Antonio, become converted to the Catholic faith, and practice his trade. Governor Muñoz waited a year for instructions from Chihuahua, then chained Culbert incommunicado in the *calabozo*. What happened during the following months is unknown, but in October, 1795, Muñoz informed the commandant general that the American, who now spelled his name Calbert, or Galbes, and claimed to be a first cousin of the Count of Galvez, had a passport to continue his journey to San Juan Bautista del Rio Grande. Culbert, Calbert or Galbes arrived at Valle de Santa Rosa on October 9, 1795, and further history sayeth not.

Stephen and Mordecai Richards, of Pennsylvania, who took part in Nolan's last expedition in 1801, appear in the San Antonio records as early as 1799, and Stephen claimed to have been in Chihuahua for nine years before that date.

Except for the Hispanicized names in the archives, however, these others left hardly a trace on history, and the rumor of Philip Nolan's achievement, reaching Thomas Jefferson, that must have helped to turn the President's mind toward the Louisiana Purchase. This, in turn, placed the United States hard against the borders of the Spanish Empire, a collocation which led by successive steps to the Americanization of Texas, the Mexican War, and the extension of American settlement to the Pacific. The ripples which Nolan started in the pond of history even now have not ceased moving, for if the United States had not grown to face both oceans, our war with Japan and subsequent complications in the Pacific would have been most unlikely.

To understand Nolan, it is necessary first to know something about James Wilkinson, a man whose treachery was matched only by his colossal effrontery, and whose machinations make the plottings of Aaron Burr, in the same period, look like a half-hearted attempt to rob a henhouse.

Wilkinson had become a colonel in the Revolutionary army at twenty-one, and soon afterward was breveted a brigadier general by special act of the Continental Congress, over the heads of the 47 other colonels in the army. Meanwhile he was associated with Benedict Arnold, though if he had any part in Arnold's treason, no evidence of it has ever been allowed to come to light.

After being mysteriously forced to resign his brevet, Wilkinson made a fortune as clothier-general of the army. After the war, having gambled away his fortune, he went to Kentucky as a penniless adventurer. Here, about 1787, he met and made a protege of Philip Nolan, then only sixteen years old. Mystery surrounds Nolan's parentage and early life. He claimed to have been born in Belfast, Ireland, but this is a statement which he made to a Spanish census taker in Texas, and may have been his way of avoiding the stigma of being a *Norteamericano* in Spanish territory. He also claimed to be a relative of the former governor, Oconór. People who knew him said he was born in Kentucky.

When Wilkinson, with young Nolan as his confidential clerk, went into business as a Kentucky trader, the Spaniards, then in possession of Louisiana, were levying a forty percent tax on all merchandise shipped down the Mississippi. This was easy for them to do, since they controlled the whole west bank of the river, the lower part of the east bank, and the port city of New Orleans. The purpose of the tax was not to gain revenue, but to prevent the Americans on the east side of the river from building up their trade along the boundary.

Wilkinson did not care to pay tribute, however, so one day he loaded a string of flatboats with tobacco, bacon, whiskey and flour, bought on credit, and set out for New Orleans, taking Nolan with him. By dint of wheedling and browbeating his way past the Spanish patrols, he finally landed his cargo at the Spanish capital, where Governor Miró immediately ordered it seized. Wilkinson, however, invited the Governor to dinner and convinced him that a man of Wilkinson's potent influence among the wild Kentuckians should be permitted to sell his cargo duty-free.

That was not all. After a few more winings and dinings, Wilkinson advanced a proposition which sounds fantastic today, but which made a certain kind of sense in that period when the turbulent frontier states were straining at the leash of the feeble young Republic. Turning on all the winsome charm that had made him a boy general, Wilkinson confidentially informed Miró that the people of Kentucky, not to mention Tennessee and Mississippi, deeply resenting the Federal government's failure to negotiate a treaty for free navigation of the great river, were almost ready to split off from the Union and conclude a separate treaty which would make them virtually a Spanish protectorate. Wilkinson, of course, was the man who could deliver these three American territories to the Spanish crown. In return for acting as Spain's secret agent in the enterprise, he asked nothing but free trading privileges, for himself alone, a pension of $2,000 a year, and a $12,000 advance payment for "expenses."

Miró agreed, and Wilkinson set his right-hand man Nolan to work drawing up the "papers." What he concealed from Miró, and probably also from Nolan at first, was that his dream went farther than merely acting as a traitor to the United States. A man of vision, he saw that Spain's hold on its American provinces was weakening. After he had split off the western territories of the United States, it would be no trick at all to raise an army of 20,000 frontiersmen to conquer Texas and the country beyond, making himself, James Wilkinson, the dictator of an empire reaching from the Alleghenies to the Pacific. Yet, besides being a man of vision, Wilkinson was also a man of sense. Even if none of these grandiose schemes worked out, he would still have his pension and his chance to make a fortune through exclusive free-trading rights on the Mississippi.

Returning home, Wilkinson drew several prominent Kentuckians into his plot and made some public utterances which were disloyal enough to satisfy Miró when he heard of them, yet not so treasonable as to get Wilkinson arrested. The plotting went on for many years, becoming hotter and colder by turns and changing its form in accordance with political developments and alterations in the mood of the principals. In 1791, when Carondelet replaced Miró as governor of Louisiana, Wilkinson gave up his trading enterprises to rejoin the United States Army as a lieutenant colonel. Nolan was left on his own, but remained in touch with his former protector, who still drew his $2,000 yearly traitor's pay.

Nolan then went to Texas on his first trading expedition. He was still only twenty, and it was probably due to his náiveté and his ignorance of such old Spanish customs as *la mordida* (the bite) that he had his goods confiscated in San Antonio and was forced to flee to the woods. He lived among the Indians for two years, finally acquiring enough beaver pelts to pacify the Spanish authorities and buy 250 horses which he drove back to Louisiana. At twenty-two, he was already sure of a place in history as the first American to penetrate so successfully the vast Spanish territories where now live nearly half of the people of the United States.

Yet the enterprises that made Nolan a hero of American history were strictly forbidden by the laws then prevailing in the Spanish Empire. All unbranded animals were the property of the king, and although under certain conditions the governor of Texas could authorize the sending of horses and cattle to Louisiana, their shipment across the Mississippi into the United States was never contemplated. But the horses were so plentiful and so easy to catch, law or no law, that there was a fortune waiting for anyone who could transport them to the growing young Republic.

A few years after Nolan, Zebulon M. Pike said of the wild horses of Texas, "They go in such large numbers that it is requisite to keep an advance guard of horsemen, in order to frighten them away; for, should they be suffered to come near your horses and mules which you drive with you, by their snorting and neighing, they alarm them, and are frequently joined by them and taken off, notwithstanding all the exertions of the dragoons to prevent them."

Pike also described the Spanish method of capturing the wild horses: "They take a few fleet horses and proceed into the country where the animals are numerous; they build a large enclosure, with a door which enters into a smaller enclosure. From the entrance of the large pen they project wings out into the prairie to a great distance, and then set up bushes, etc., to induce the horses when pursued to enter into these wings. After these preparations are made, they keep a lookout for such a drove; for if they unfortunately should start too large a one, they either burst open the pen or fill it up with dead bodies, and the remainder run over them and escape, in which case the party is obliged to leave the place, as the stench arising from the putrid carcases would be insupportable, and in addition to this, the pen would not receive others. But should they succeed in driving a few, say two or three hundred, they select the handsomest and youngest, noose them, and take them into a small enclosure, then turn out the others. . . . They subdue them by degrees, and finally break them to submit to the saddle and bridle. For this business I presume there is no nation in the world superior to the Spaniards of Texas.'"

In 1794 we again find Nolan in Texas, where he boldly allowed himself to be counted by the census taker at Nacogdoches and presented a passport to the Governor, Don Manuel Muñoz, in San Antonio. It can safely be presumed that Wilkinson's friendship with the Spanish authorities in New Orleans was a great help to his protegé in obtaining this passport.

In 1796 we find Nolan in Kentucky, where he accepted 9,000 Spanish silver dollars for Wilkinson from a man named Power who had brought them in barrels of provisions from New Orleans. Nolan allowed the messenger to keep $640 for his labor, after the barrels were opened in the store of Montgomery Brown in Lexington. The rest of the money Nolan delivered to Wilkinson for his past commercial transactions, but actually it was bribe money. At other times, the money came in sacks, and it was said that Nolan could lift a sack of 2,000 silver dollars with one hand. His strength, it was said, also helped him in taming drunken Indians. He had grown into a tall, handsome man with dark hair and a ruddy complexion.

The following year, Nolan returned from a trip to Missouri with some maps he had drawn, which were so greatly admired by Governor Carondelet that he granted Nolan a passport to go to Texas on an expedition with the combined objects of "buying" horses for the Spanish garrison in Louisiana and drawing maps of the province.

At the same time, Wilkinson gave Nolan a letter of recommendation to Don Manuel Gayoso de Lemos, the Spanish Governor of Natchez. This short but pointed letter will bear quoting as a typical example of Wilkinson's style:

"This will be delivered to you by Nolan, who, you know, is a child of my own raising, true to his profession, and firm in his attachment to Spain. I consider him a powerful instrument in our hands, should occasion offer. I will answer for his conduct. I am deeply interested in whatever concerns him, and I confidently recommend him to your warmest protection. I am evidently your affectionate

WILKINSON"

Unimpressed by this letter, and suspicious of both Wilkinson and his "child," Gayoso wrote to General Pedro de Nava, the Commandant General of the Interior Provinces, urging him to arrest any foreigners who might enter those provinces, because he, Gayoso, was aware that some Americans intended to visit that country for the purpose of making friends with the Indians and starting a revolution. This letter took six months to reach Nava through governmental channels.

In the meantime, Nolan received his passport, dated July 17, 1797, and hurried to San Antonio, where he again met his old friend Governor Muñoz, who now helped him to obtain from General de Nava a permit to buy horses both in Texas and Nuevo Santander, a province of Mexico which overlapped present-day Texas on the south. This sounds very regular. The joke is that Nolan, older and wiser than at the time of his first trip, had no intention of *buying* horses. Not when there were millions of wild mustangs running the plains of the Southwest. Of course, these creatures were the property of the King of Spain, who might have frowned from the throne if he had been told that an American adventurer was lassoing his horses and selling them to the citizens of the upstart Republic. But the King was far away, and Nolan, through the help of his great and good friend Wilkinson, had most of the Spanish officials eating from his hand.

When Gayoso's letter finally reached General de Nava, the latter ordered Muñoz to arrest Nolan. But Muñoz meanwhile had died, and the Governor pro tem, Irogoyen, had a delicacy about opening his mail, hence did not read the order. At least that was the story.

So, in a little more than a year, Nolan had rounded up 1,297 head of horses which he drove back to Louisiana. Some of these he sold to a new regiment then being organized in New Orleans; others he loaded into flatboats to be sold in American territory, though this last was contrary to the terms of his permit. There is no record of how much he made on the transaction, but it may have run into twenty or thirty thousand dollars for his year's work.

Meanwhile Thomas Jefferson (then vice president) had written Nolan a letter, asking him to prepare a paper on the habits of wild horses for the Philosophical Society of Philadelphia. Jefferson, an interested dilettante in all the sciences of the time, wanted to know in what respects the habits of wild horses were different from those of animals which had been trained by men. Someone had told the great Virginian that Nolan, because of his unique experience, was the man to answer this question.

Mail was slow in those days, and Nolan had departed on another horse-catching expedition before Jefferson's letter reached New Orleans. It was answered by Nolan's friend, Daniel Clark, who wrote on February 12, 1799: "That extraordinary and interesting man [Nolan] is now and has been for some years past employed in the countries bordering on the Kingdom of New Mexico, either in catching or purchasing horses and looked for [sic] on the banks of the Mississippi at the fall of the Waters with a thousand head, which he will in all probability drive into the United States."

Clark, a Spanish subject of Irish origin, deeply involved in Nolan's and Wilkinson's intrigues, evidently did not believe in letting his Spanish right hand know what his American left hand was doing, for he told Jefferson, with considerable presumption, "In the meantime I must suggest to you the necessity of keeping to yourself for the present all the information that may be forwarded to you, as the slightest hint would point out the Channel from which it flowed and might probably be attended with the most fatal consequences for a man, who will at all times have it in his power to render important Services to the United States, and whom Nature seems to have formed for Enterprizes of which the rest of mankind are incapable." He explained that Nolan had asked him to open his mail so that no "suspicious" matter would be forwarded to him in Spanish territory.

All this was not mere brass, but was evidently intended to maneuver the great Jefferson, soon to be President, into the position of a fellow conspirator. The method, so reminiscent of Wilkinson, suggests that Clark, too, had studied at the feet of the man who, still drawing his Spanish pension, had become the head of the entire United States Army in the field, with the rank of brigadier general. Washington and Hamilton, his only superior officers, both recommended him for promotion to major general, but

Congress turned down the recommendation, ostensibly for reasons of economy. Washington and Hamilton both know that Wilkinson's loyalty was at least doubtful, but they felt that promotion might be one way to hold him in line.

Whether or not the suspicious-minded Spaniards learned of Jefferson's inquiry, Gayoso sent another letter to Nava, on June 1, 1799, warning him that Nolan should not be permitted to work in Texas; that he had obtained his passport through fraud; that he was a sacrilegious hypocrite who posed as a Catholic among Spaniards but laughed at this religion when he was with Americans; that he had been commissioned by Wilkinson to spy out the land and bribe the friendly Indians to rebel against the Spaniards.

In November, 1799, Clark wrote a second letter to Jefferson. In this he reported that Nolan had just returned from Texas, once more, with 1,000 head of horses. He did not explain why Nolan could not answer his own letters now, and it is possible that he deliberately withheld this important contact from his dear friend. In this letter, Clark referred to Nolan in a definitely patronizing manner, telling Jefferson that he, Clark, would "send" Nolan to Monticello and would reimburse him for the time he spent on the mission. Clark also said he was sending Jefferson a barrel of oranges and a sack of "paccan nuts."

During the minor portion of his time that he spent in the American settlements, Nolan met Frances (Fanny) Lintot, the redheaded nineteen-year-old daughter of an old French Creole family in Natchez, which had been ceded to the United States in 1798. Fanny was greatly taken with the dark, handsome adventurer, and although her family viewed Nolan with considerable reserve, they were married on December 19, 1799.

Nolan went east the following summer, and enjoyed a visit of several hours with Jefferson. He was armed with a rather non-committal letter of introduction from General Wilkinson. It was said that Nolan sought aid both from Jefferson and the British minister for his and Wilkinson's ambitions to conquer the Spanish Southwest.

While Nolan was in the East, the Commandant General ordered the new Spanish Governor of Texas, Don Juan Bautista de Elguézabal, to arrest Nolan if he ever returned to the Province. The death of his friend, Governor Muñoz, was to have a decisive bearing on Nolan's ultimate fate.

The Spanish authorities of those days, knowing the insecurity of their hold on the vast territories of North America, were, as we have seen, almost morbidly sensitive to the slightest hint of aggression by the wild men from the East. It is quite likely, therefore, that Nolan's incursions into Texas played a part in deciding the King of Spain, Carlos IV, to enter into negotiations with Napoleon for the retrocession of Louisiana, which had been ceded from France to Spain 28 years before. With the trackless wastes of Louisiana exchanged for a cozy principality in Italy, His Majesty could breathe easier, for the land would serve as a buffer forever between New Spain and the upstart American Republic, with its nonsensical but dangerous ideas about human freedom.

These negotiations were started secretly at San Ildefonso, Spain, on October 1, 1800. Six days later, the captain of the presidio at Concordia, Louisiana, across the river from Natchez, wrote to the commander at Nacogdoches, Texas, that Don Felipe Nolan was, under pretext of a horse-buying expedition, organizing a force of thirty or forty armed men to enter the province of Texas, and that the American authorities at Natchez refused to do anything about it. This message was forwarded to the Spanish commandant general in Chihuahua, and from him to the Viceroy.

In Natchez the Spanish consul, Don José Vidal, protested Nolan's scheme to the American governor, Winthrop Sargent. Called before the Governor and Federal Judge Bruin, Nolan flourished the passport he had obtained to enter Texas three years before. Vidal objected that the permit did not have indefinite duration, that it was granted for a business trip in 1797 and not for a filibustering expedition in 1800. But the Americans were not convinced by the consul's argument, and they allowed Nolan and his men to depart without hindrance.

Vidal then wrote to the commander of the post at Nacogdoches, urging him to arrest Nolan, and adding, "Nolan has many friends there and in San Antonio, and none of them, not even excepting the government officials, should be advised, because the last time that Nolan was in those parts he was able to learn the steps that had been taken and the reports that had been made of his conduct. Nolan is active, enterprising and bold, and knows these localities better than the natives themselves."

From this point to the end, the story of Nolan begins to fill out. Previously it has had to be pieced and patched together from a few scattered letters and reports, with long gaps that represent burned documents and well-guarded secrets. But from now on, for what little remains of the story, we have detailed testimony.

Rebuffed by the Americans, Consul Vidal sent a man on a fast horse to carry warning of the "invasion" to De Neva, the captain of the presidio at Ouachita, Louisiana, with the added information that Nolan was a dangerous character who had long been plotting with Wilkinson against the

Spaniards.

Nolan, with forty men, left Natchez in October and headed northwest through the Mississippi River swamps, toward a point near the Ouachita post. They had gone about forty miles when they were stopped by a party of fifty well-armed Spanish militiamen. Nolan parleyed with the officer in charge and convinced him that he had a valid permit to go to Texas. Expecting, perhaps, that the militia captain would change his mind when he had talked with the captain of the presidio, "Don Felipe" avoided going nearer to the Ouachita post, six miles away. Instead, he led his men in a wide circle through "a fine country, but without roads or inhabitants," as his follower, Ellis P. Bean, said in the memoir he wrote fifteen years later. They crossed the Ouachita River the next morning, and stopped to kill some deer for provisions along the way before pushing on to the Red River. While hunting, three of the men "got lost," according to Bean, and could not be found, though the main party stayed several days to search for them.

This was no wonder, for the three men had "lost" themselves intentionally, and turned up at Natchez while Nolan was still beating the bushes for them. Their leader, Mordecai Richards, then crossed the Mississippi to the Spanish post at Concordia and made a voluntary statement that set the seal of disaster on Nolan's enterprise.

Richards said that after the militiamen had gone, Nolan had taken him aside and told him, "You are a man on whom I rely to carry out my plans, and for that reason I appoint you third in command. If we succeed, you will make your fortune." Don Felipe then told how he would explore Texas, return to Kentucky with a herd of horses, and there "receive authority to conquer the Province of Texas." He added, "I will be the General, Mr. [David] Fero [of New York] the second, and yourself third in command." Nolan did not know his man, however, for it was Richards' panic over this bold proposal that drove him to desert, though he had a son and nephew in Nolan's company.

The party pushed on into the country of the friendly Tehuacana Indians, from whom Nolan purchased some tame horses to replace the expedition's own mounts, which were already worn out from the hard journey and the many rivers they had had to swim. After six more days the party crossed the Trinity River and emerged from the Piney Woods into the open prairies of Central Texas. Meanwhile more of Nolan's followers were drifting away.

The party's provisions had given out and there were neither deer nor buffalo in this new country, so they were compelled to kill wild horses for food. They had lived on horse-flesh for nine days when they arrived at the Brazos River, where they found plenty of deer and elk, a few buffalo, and thousands of wild horses. Finally, on the banks of the Blanco River (not the river now called by that name, but apparently the Navasota) they built a pen and drove into it some three hundred mustangs.

They were not left alone for long. After a few days, two hundred Comanche Indians dropped in on them for a social visit, and invited the Nolan party to go with them to the south fork of the Red River to see their chief, Nocoroco. The invitation was of course accepted, though Nolan must have been reluctant to leave his captured horses without care. The Indians treated the men of the expedition kindly, but it was a month before the Americans felt free to return to their corral. By that time, many of the captured horses had died. A group of Indians came back with Nolan, stayed a few days, and then left in the night, taking with them the eleven tame horses that the party depended upon to see them through the expedition.

Nolan and five other men, including a Negro slave named Caesar, set out on foot to catch the thieves. After nine days they found four of the Indian men, with some women and children, encamped by a small creek. Friendly greetings were exchanged, and an old Indian told Nolan the horses had been taken by a fellow descriptively named One-Eye, who was just then out hunting buffalo. When One-Eye came back that evening, Nolan's men grabbed him and tied him up, without interference from the other Indians, who this time did not outnumber the palefaces.

Nolan kept One-Eye tied up all night, but in the morning his wife ransomed him by turning over all the horses. After threatening the Indians with a "whipping" if they tried to steal the horses again, Nolan and his party returned to their camp, riding hard to cover in four days the distance which had taken them nine days on foot.

Meanwhile their doom was approaching from another quarter. An abstract of Richards' revelations had been forwarded to the Spanish presidio of Nacogdoches, and Lieutenant M. Múzquiz, with sixty-eight regular army men, thirty-two volunteers and a few Indian guides, set out from there in pursuit. This was on March 4, 1801, about the time than Nolan returned to his camp from Nicoroco's village. It was also the day of Thomas Jefferson's inaguration as President of the United States.

On the 12th, near the Brazos River, Múzquiz found a chief of the Tejas Indians who knew where Nolan was, but who refused to give the Spaniards any information. Five days later, at eight o'clock on the morning of the 17th, the sergeant commanding the vanguard galloped back to inform

Múzquiz that two men on horseback had been seen, and immediately had plunged into a thicket. The men were soon caught, but they proved to be Indians. Múzquiz questioned them closely, however, and they finally told him that Nolan was nearby with twenty-five men. They also agreed to guide the Spaniards to Nolan's camp.

The Spanish force traveled all day on the 18th, and again on the 19th, while Nolan's party, all unknowing, were resting their mounts in preparation for going out to round up more mustangs. On the night of March 19, Lieutenant Múzquiz sent eighteen men to spy out the Nolan camp. They returned promptly to tell Múzquiz they had found a wooden "entrenchment" and pasture, with some horses, on the banks of the Blanco.

The whole Spanish company sallied forth and reached the corral at daybreak, but Nolan and his men were not there. Two Indians told Múzquiz that Don Felipe and his men were in a house without a roof, at a place between a creek and some hills. Waiting until night, Múzquiz led his men to this place, and surrounded it before daybreak on the morning of the 21st. It was precisely on this date, on the other side of the Atlantic, that Lucien Bonaparte signed he second of the three treaties of San Ildefonso, which ultimately cleared the way for Napoleon's cession of Louisiana to the United States in 1803, two years later. So history marched on while the Spanish lieutenant stalked the sleeping freebooter.

The final scene can best be told in the military prose of Lieutenant Múzquiz's diary. Ellis Bean gives a somewhat different story, but the differences are not fundamental, and Bean's recollections may have been modified by the lapse of fifteen years' time, to say nothing of his natural tendency to embroider. Múzquiz reports:

"At sunrise, having divided my force into three bodies, one commanded by me and carrying a four-pounder, I marched on Nolan's entrenchment. When I was at a distance of about thirty paces from it, ten men sallied from the entrenchment, unarmed. Among them was Nolan, who said, in a loud voice, '*No lleguen, porque seremos muertos unos o otros.*' [Do not approach, because one or the other of us will be killed.] Noticing that the men who accompanied Nolan were foreigners, I ordered Mr. William Barr, an Irishman, who had joined my company as interpreter, to speak to them in English and say to them that I had come for the purpose of arresting them, and that I demanded their surrender in the name of the King. Nolan had a brief conversation with Barr, and the latter informed me that Nolan and his men were determined to fight. Nolan immediately entered his entrenchment, followed by his men, and I observed that two Mexicans (Juan Jose Martínez and Vicente Lara) escaped from the rear of the said entrenchment. Soon afterward they joined us, stating that they had brought with them Nolan's carbine, which was handed to me. At daybreak Nolan and his men commenced firing. The fight lasted until nine o'clock a.m., when, Nolan being killed by a cannon ball, his men surrendered. They were out of ammunition. His force at the time of the engagement was composed of fourteen Americans, one Creole of Louisiana, seven Spaniards or Mexicans, and two Negro slaves. Nolan had three men wounded and several horses killed ... Nolan's Negroes asked permission to bury their master, which I granted after causing his ears to be cut off, in order to send them to the Governor of Texas."

Such was the end of Philip Nolan's dream of empire. As William Dunbar, the Natchez planter and scientist, wrote to Jefferson: "Altho' his eccentricities were many and great, yet he was not destitute of romantic principles of honor united to the highest personal courage, with energy of mind not sufficiently cultivated by education, but which under the guidance of a little more prudence might have conducted him to enterprises of the first magnitude."

Nolan's followers were taken in irons to San Antonio and thence to the mines of Mexico. Fanny Nolan did not long survive her husband. Three months after Philip was shot down, she gave birth to a son, and died. The son died at twenty-one, without issue. General Wilkinson lived to a ripe old age, scheming to the last. The spot where Nolan lies buried has never been found.

A Spanish statesman of the period remarked, "Wherever these Americans go, they spread out like oil upon a cloth." So it was in the lands west of the Mississippi. Within two years after Nolan's death, the United States had annexed through the Louisiana Purchase the areas of thirteen of our Middle-Western and Western States. Within forty-five years, Texas and the eight Far Western States had been added, completing the Union as we know it today. But it was Philip Nolan, forgotten though he was, who had dropped the first oil on the cloth.

Edward Everett Hale was, in a sense, right the first time. Nolan, the disciple of Wilkinson, was in fact a man who knew no country, but in following his own distorted ends he unconsciously served the future of the United States.

16

Nightmares of Empire

Fear of French invasion or infiltration was, as we have seen, the ruling motive of Spanish colonial policy in Texas from the first rumors of La Salle's expedition in 1684 until Louisiana was ceded to Spain in 1762. Thereupon ensued a period of stagnation and retrenchment, when there appeared to be no urgent reason for developing the resources of this remote province. But with the retrocession of Louisiana to France and its immediate sale to the United States in 1803, all was changed, and at this date began the slow but substantial fulfillment of a remarkable prophecy made twenty years before in 1783, the very year when the United States won recognition of its independence from England.

This prophecy, the first known record of Spanish apprehension from the expansionist proclivities of the young American Republic, occurs in a letter written with remarkable foresight by an Indian in the Spanish service, Jean Gasiot, a Frenchman, to the commandant general, Felipe de Neve:

"It is necessary to keep in mind that a new independent power now exists on this continent. It has been founded by an active, industrious and aggressive people who, free from the war sustained for many years against their mother country, from which they have at last succeeded in gaining independence, are already considering the means that will cause it to be respected in the future. These men, freed from the hardships of war that have engaged them so long, will turn their industrious genius to agriculture, the arts and commerce. Their development will constantly menace the dominion of Spain in America and it would be an unpardonable error not to take all necessary steps to check their territorial advance by strengthening the outposts of Spain, particularly in Texas, Coahuila and New Mexico. If we fail to do so, your lordship will see that the citizens of the United States of America, led by the advantages for trade offered by the uncontrolled Indians in the territories lying between their frontiers and our provinces of New Mexico and Texas, will make frequent incursions and establish trade relations with the natives, who will thus become attached to them. They will next establish forts among them and will continue to advance until they reach the limits of our possessions, where they will have to be checked. By this time, they will have become formidable by their new acquisitions and the winning of numerous allies."

To resist this threat, Gasiot wrote, it was necessary for the Spaniards to form stronger alliances with the Indians and increase their trade with the tribes in the north and east of Texas as a means of holding their good will. He continued, in a vein that was almost subversive, coming from the agent of an absolute monarch, "The character of their [the Americans'] republican government has great influence over the individual. The voice of public interest binds them and moves them as one, and in this union of action their strength is found. Such a people may be exposed to suffer more internal disturbances than any other, but they are likewise capable of undertaking and accomplishing greater things than any other. A Senate that is ready to meet at any time, that is always ready to deliberate upon anything that may benefit the states, and that has the necessary means at its command for the accomplishment of the desired purposes, must keep the people of a monarchical government always on the alert, with the spring of its resources far removed and the need of waiting for decision and resources that must come from more than 2,000 leagues away."

Surely no statesman in history has made a wiser long-range prophecy than did this obscure frontiersman. If the Mexican revolution had not intervened, his prophecy of future conflict between Spain and the United

States could have been fulfilled in every detail. As it was, the forecast still came true, but with Mexico and Santa Anna standing in place of Spain and the king.

In 1795, the viceroy must have heard garbled reports of Citizen Genet's unsuccessful efforts to raise troops in the United States and attack Louisiana and Florida on behalf of the revolutionary government of France. Attributing the movement to the United States government, the viceroy issued an order in which he declared he had been informed that the United States was planning to send emissaries to Mexico to instigate a revolution. The order gave instructions for the exclusion of all Americans as well as all other foreigners and all suspicious characters whatsoever. The Genet affair had another echo two months later, in September, 1795, when Bernardo Dortolan, captain of the post of Natchitoches, learned from the Iowa Indians that Genet had sought American aid in an attempt to invade Louisiana.

From this time forward until the end of the Spanish regime, the archives show continual references to fear of American attack. Documents are cited to this effect from 1796, 1800, 1801, 1804, 1805, 1806, 1811, and 1812, after which time the theme becomes ever present.

To strengthen Texas against the supposed threat of American military invasion—a fear which was based partly on the subterranean machinations of General Wilkinson, partly on the open American claim that the boundaries of the Louisiana purchase extended to the Rio Grande, and partly on the usual Spanish nervousness in the face of any foreign power on the frontiers of the empire—the immigration policy was liberalized in the first years of the 19th century and efforts were made to found additional colonies in Texas.

The new immigation policy was náive in its inception, for it assumed that Americans who represented themselves as Catholics and swore allegiance to the king of Spain would, by these facts, be desirable colonists in the territory over against the borders of the new Republic. Perhaps because of its náiveté, the policy was never fully accepted by the responsible Spanish authorities, nor was it consistently carried out for any considerable time. A substantial number of American, Louisiana French, and Irish immigrants were admitted under the liberalized policy, however. One was Daniel Boone, a nephew of the celebrated Kentucky pioneer of the same name, who swore that the government of the United States did not "suit" him. He became a gunsmith for the soldiers at Bexar and was killed by the Indians about 1817. Another immigrant was one Miguel Quinn, who, soon after he was admitted to Texas, wrote to a friend in the United States to inquire how far the

Americans would go when they invaded Texas, so that he might buy cheap land in what was to be United States territory. Still another figure of the time was a Dutch adventurer, the Baron de Bastrop, one of the greatest land speculators of the early Southwest, who in 1805 spoke contemptuously of "the daring land-hunger of this infamous class of Americans." At the same time that he wrote in this way to the Spanish governor, however, Bastrop was selling a million acres of land in Louisiana to Aaron Burr, and later he supported Moses and Stephen Austin in their colonization projects.

The few settlements made under the new policy never got fairly started and were extinct in a few years, with the exception of the tiny village of Palafox on the Rio Grand, which was founded by local officials against the orders of the Commandant General of the Interior Provinces. The Villa of Santísima Trinidad de Salcedo, founded in 1805 on the Trinity River near the *Camino Real* (not far from the abandoned settlement of Bucareli), and the Villa of San Marcos de Neve, founded on the San Marcos River in 1808, both seem to have become extinct by 1812. The projected colony of Nueva Jaen, on the *Camino Real* at the crossing of the Frio River, seems never to have been actually established. A port was legally opened under the name of San Bernardo on Matagorda Bay, but because of the restrictions on commerce it never flourished and was soon abandoned.

In 1805 and 1806, war between Spain and the United States was as close as it has ever been between two nations which did not actually come to blows. On the Spanish side, the motive for hostility was fear. Although Spain was still a great empire, its dominions were so widely scattered, and its forces in Europe were so preoccupied with Napoleon, that it could hardly have repelled an American invasion of Mexico. The Spaniards' fear of armed might, of course, was mingled with their hatred for democratic and Protestant—or worse—ideologies. On the American side, the diplomatic claim that Texas had been included in the territory bought from France was only a thin cover for the real motive, which was a blend of revolutionary ardor and expansionism. To free the suffering millions of Mexico and at the same time to open up fabulous moneymaking opportunities for red-blooded Americans—that was an enterprise worthy of heroes.

President Jefferson hardly troubled to conceal his hope that a war would be "forced upon us," in which case, he said, the United States would be practically compelled to occupy all the territory from the Sabine to the Rio Grande, and Florida as well. Burr and Wilkinson went even farther in their dreams. The Commander in chief, as we have seen, had for many years

192

hugged to his breast the notion of leading an invading army to the City of Mexico, like a new Cortez. The former Vice-President, forced out of politics because of his fatal duel with Alexander Hamilton, now took over Wilkinson's dream and, unlike Wilkinson, took serious steps toward realizing it. In short, he began to organize a private army, in the hope that, on the outbreak of war with Spain, he would be authorized by the United States government to lead the invasion. Later it was charged that Burr also thought of adopting the other part of Wilkinson's dream—that of splitting off the western territories of the United States—but there is no evidence that he ever acted toward that treasonable end. Burr's second in command of the proposed invasion was to be none other than General Wilkinson, who presumably would give up his routine job as head of the Army for the sake of the greener opportunities to be found in the land of Montezuma.

Meanwhile a small Spanish force, led by Governor Antonio Cordero of Texas and Governor Simon de Herrera of Nuevo Santander, crossed the Sabine River and reoccupied the old presidio of Los Adaes, in territory to which the claim of the United States had not previously been disputed. The Spaniards had evidently been aroused to this action by the widespread and exaggerated rumors of Burr's activities.

In May, 1806, Wilkinson was ordered by the war department to proceed frm St. Louis to Natchitoches to repel this invasion of American territory. On one slight pretext or another, despite the clear and urgent order from the Secretary of War, Wilkinson delayed his departure. Burr was preparing his expedition at Blennerhassett's Island in the upper Ohio River, and it seems fairly evident, although beyond proof, that Wilkinson was waiting to see how much support, in men and money, Burr could command before he, Wilkinson, decided whether to obey the orders of his government or to throw in his lot with the adventurer. But the general grew increasingly skeptical of Burr's chances, and in September, four months after the order, he finally decided to do his duty as a soldier and repel the Spanish invasion.

Wilkinson was a perfect weathervane, and at no time in his life is it possible to discover any consistent principle except his stupendous effrontery and his opportunistic devotion to a not very enlightened self-interest. At this period his lifelong unscrupulousness seems to have been modified in form but not in substance by emulation of Napoleon, whose personality made a bad model for far too many ambitious men in his time and long afterward.

Dressed in a showy uniform, Wilkinson approached the Louisiana border with a great deal of sabre-rattling, denounced the Spaniards as invaders, and demanded that they retreat beyond the Sabine. On this man now depended the issue of peace or war between Spain and the United States.

Governor Cordero, in Nacogdoches, temporized by writing to Wilkinson that he could not act without the approval of Captain General Nemesio Salcedo in Chihuahua, but Governor Herrera, the field commander at Los Adaes, took matters in his own hands and retired west of the river. In spite of this compliance, Wilkinson quickly wrote to Jefferson that "I have not the least doubt, we shall soon be engaged in hostilities." He also, for the first time, gave Jefferson a report on the Burr conspiracy—a matter concerning which he had been fully informed for two years and which had been common talk for almost as long.

By now, Wilkinson was anxious to go to New Orleans, halt the Burr expedition, arrest Burr and thereby appear as the savior of the nation. But the Spaniards were still inconveniently sitting on the right bank of the Sabine, and in spite of their withdrawal the issue which might lead to war had not been settled. So Wilkinson arranged a meeting with Cordero and patched up what was probably the most hasty, ill-advised and unauthorized peace treaty in modern history. Under the terms agreed upon between the border commanders, the Spaniards were to remain where they were, on the west bank of the Sabine, while the Americans agreed not to enter the unoccupied territory between the Sabine and the Hondo. This strip of land was to remain "neutral ground," ungoverned by either of the two countries. Wilkinson's pact remained in effect for 13 years, during which time the Neutral Ground became a nesting place for smugglers, highwaymen, filibusters and other undesirable characters, obnoxious to both nations.

Wilkinson wrote to Jefferson that the Spaniards had agreed to retreat into Texas, but he carefully neglected to mention that he had committed the United States to remain east of the Hondo. At the same moment that he wrote to Jefferson, Wilkinson dispatched a personal emissary, Walter Burling, to Mexico City on an errand that was as neat a piece of multiple dealing as has ever been recorded in the annals of rascality. To make the nature of this transaction perfectly clear, it will be desirable to summarize it under numbered headings, for otherwise the reader might be overcome with dizziness at the gyrations of Wilkinson's agile mind:

(1) Ostensibly, Burling was to go into Texas to purchase a number of mules for Wilkinson's army.

(2) Actually, Burling was to continue all the way to Mexico City (with two passports, one from Wilkinson and the other from Wilkinson's friend Stephen Minor, a Spanish officer) to hand to the viceroy a detailed

report of Burr's projected expedition.

(3) But the "report" really placed its major stress, according to the viceroy's own summary, "on the measures which he [Wilkinson] has taken at the risk of his life, fame and fortune in order to save, or at least protect, this Kingdom from the attacks of the insurgents." In Wilkinson's own words, he had risked his life "by the change I have made in the military arrangements without the knowledge of my government." Wilkinson here implied that he had been acting in the Spanish interest when he made peace on the Sabine. By his own estimate, this was treason.

(4) For his alleged monetary outlay in defeating the schemes of Burr, Wilkinson asked the viceroy to "reimburse" him to the extent of $121,000.

(5) Wilkinson was careful to call attention to the fact—approximately the only true statement in the whole letter—that "I am risking my life, my good name and my property by the means I have adopted." The juxtaposition of this statement with the request for money made it quite plain that he was really asking for a bribe.

(6) At the same time that Burling was carrying this message, he was directed by Wilkinson to spy out the country from Louisiana to Mexico City and prepare maps which the general might use in a future invasion of Mexico.

(7) While Burling was still in Mexico, Wilkinson sent Jefferson a supposed report of conditions in that country, falsely alleged to have come from Burling. With the report went a request for $1,500 to cover the cost of the expedition. Jefferson approved the expenditure of his faithful servant, but the viceroy was less easily taken in. He wrote to Wilkinson, very politely and with admirable restraint, that the "revolutionists" had not caused him any alarm; that he could not pay such an amount of money without definite orders from the king, and "In conclusion I thanked him for his martial zeal, and insinuated that I wished him happiness in the pursuit of his righteous intentions."

With matters settled on the Sabine, Wilkinson proceeded to New Orleans, where he declared martial law, arrested many of the most prominent citizens on suspicion of complicity with Burr, and generally conducted himself as a military dictator. When Burr drew near New Orleans, Wilkinson covertly offered a henchman $5,000 for his assassination, but the scheme came to nothing.

The story of Burr's arrest and his trial, with Wilkinson as the chief witness for the prosecution and defender of virtue, is a fascinating chapter in American history but has too little relation with Texas to be told here. Suffice it to say that Burr was acquitted of treason, but was forced to leave the country, while Wilkinson, cleared by a court of inquiry, continued to enjoy the uneasy confidence of Jefferson and other high-placed patriots.

It is often thought, by people who have not made a special study of the subject, that Burr was acquitted on a technicality and that he was "really" guilty of treason. Unbiased modern scholars, led by Walter F. McCaleb, have thoroughly exploded this notion, which originated in the partisan political comment of Burr's time. Actually, whatever Burr's thoughts may have been, it is clear from the evidence that he never committed a treasonable act. His culminating expedition, with less than sixty men in flatboats, could not sanely have been intended as a revolt against the United States, and was too feeble even for a filibustering expedition against Texas and Mexico, which seems to have been Burr's real intention.

Thirty years later, when Burr was a lonely old man in New York, he read in the newspapers that the American settlers in Texas had begun their struggle to set up an independent state. "There!" he exclaimed. "You see? I was right. I was only thirty years too soon. What was treason in me thirty years ago is patriotism now." Even on his deathbed he denied that he had ever intended to make war against the United States or give aid and comfort to its enemies.

The independence of Texas and its annexation to the United States can better be understood when viewed in the light cast upon them by the conspiracies which began with Wilkinson about 1784, and continued with incursions by Nolan and other Americans around the turn of the century; the border conflict, the Burr expedition and (to be discussed in a later chapter) the filibustering activities of Magee, Long and others, all of which occurred before the end of the Spanish royal dominion and long before the conditions had ripened for the successful and, under the dictatorship in 1836, thoroughly justified revolt. It was Wilkinson, that stupendous scoundrel, who plotted the first tentative, subterranean stirrings of the southwestward movement which eventually, becoming irresistible, resulted in the extension of American domain to the Rio Grande and to the Pacific.

American interest in the mysterious lands west of the Sabine received an added impetus when Captain Zebulon Montgomery Pike published, in 1810, his report of the expeditions which he had made by order of General Wilkinson in 1805-1807. Although Pike's explorations were undertaken under such dubious auspices, the assignment seems to have been bona fide. It was approved by the president and recognized later by Congress, which, after investigation, granted Pike's petition for reimbursement of expenses.

Attempting a topographical survey of the territory recently acquired from France, Pike first discovered what he thought to be the source of the Mississippi at Cass Lake, Minnesota, only a few miles from the real source in Lake Itasca. When Pike returned, Wilkinson immediately sent him off again on an expedition through the Southwest, where he discovered the peak now called by his name. Going too far into Spanish territory, he was quietly taken into custody by the Spaniards near Santa Fé, transported to Chihuahua and then escorted with all courtesies through northern Mexico and Texas, back to the Louisiana border. In his detailed and well organized report, Captain Pike gave a factual but sufficiently alluring account of Texas as well as of the other northern Mexican provinces through which he passed. Texas, he declared, had "one of the most delightful temperatures in the world." Much sickness was caused by the large amount of putrescent vegetation, but this condition vanished gradually as the land was cleared, with the loss of only two or three members of each family.

San Antonio, said Pike, was "laid out on a very grand plan," but most of its 2,000 souls resided in "miserable mud-wall houses, covered with thatched grass roofs." At this time the garrison was housed in the abandoned Mission San Antonio Valero, called the Alamo. Of the other missions, two were entirely depopulated; a third had barely enough Indians to perform necessary household labor for the resident priest. Yet the remains of the missions, "for solidity, accommodation, and even majesty, were surpassed by few that I saw in New Spain."

Pike estimated the population of the entire province at 7,000, including a few Americans and French besides the Spaniards, Indians and mestizos. Nacogdoches, he said, had only 500 people and was merely a "station for troops."

The abundance of buffalo and wild horses, in Pike's view, had produced a more "wandering" disposition around San Antonio than anywhere else in Mexico. By declaring a closed season on buffalo for part of the year, and requiring every head of a family to cultivate the land, Governor Cordero had succeeded in enforcing some of the habits of "urbanity and suavity of manners" which apparently was much needed in those parts. Although the civil *cabildo* of San Fernando still met, Pike described the government as "perfectly military, except as to the ecclesiastical jurisdiction." Of troops, however, there were only 888 in the vast expanse of the province.

The women of New Spain, Texas included, were inclined to "enbonpoint," and "none or few [were] elegant figures." The observant young explorer added, "Their dress generally is short jackets and petticoats and high-heeled shoes, without any head-dress. Over the whole dress they have a silk wrapper [*reboso*], which they always wear and, when in the presence of men, affect to bring over their faces, but from under which you frequently see peeping a large sparkling black eye." Near the border, some Spanish women wore American dresses, which they conceived to be the height of fashion. The men, in the cities, dressed nearly in the European or American style. The countrymen of the lower classes favored wide-brimmed hats, short coats, large waistcoats and breeches left unbuttoned at the knees for comfort in horseback riding, which was their occupation for at least half of each day. They wore high boots of soft, pliable leather.

When not on horseback, the men diverted themselves with gambling at cards, billiards and cockfighting, all of which are popular sports around San Antonio to this day. Both men and women were fond of music, singing and performing the fandango and other Spanish dances to the music of the violin and guitar, accompanied by voices singing the songs of the country. As today in Mexico, every town had a public walk, where the unmarried men and women would meet in the evenings. The siesta in the afternoon was in favor then as now in Mexico.

Pike was hospitably received in San Antonio by Governors Cordero and Herrera. In the evening, Pike was entertained at a levee in the governor's house, where he met Father McGuire, an Irish priest, and Doctor Zerbin, a former resident of Natchez who had migrated to Texas "in consequence of pecuniary embarrassments." After supper the gentlemen went out to the plaza, "where might be seen the two governors joined in a dance with people who in the daytime would approach them with reverence and awe." At dinner the next day, a large party toasted the President of the United States, His Catholic Majesty, and General Wilkinson. Pike was impressed with the "superexcellent" qualities of Cordero. Herrera, too, was "in all his actions one of the most gallant and accomplished men I ever saw." Herrera had once been introduced to George Washington. Both were unquestionably loyal to their king, "But should Bonaparte seize European Spain, I risk nothing in asserting that those two gentlemen would be the first to throw off the yoke, draw their swords, and assert the independence of their country," Pike declared.

At Nacogdoches, Pike noted down a favorable estimate of the commandant, Don Francisco de Viana, but observed that "He unfortunately does not possess flexibility sufficient to to be useful [to the United States] in the present state of the Spanish Kingdoms." Near Nacogdoches, Pike found a French-speaking family who first professed great attachment to the Spanish regime but, when they were convinced that their interrogator was an American, changed their tune to hatred of everything Spanish.

In his summary, Pike placed emphasis on the great extremes of wealth and poverty in Mexico, a feature which, notwithstanding a century and a half of revolutions, can still be observed today. He called attention to the severe restrictions on commerce, then enforced to protect the Spanish monopoly. Freed from these hobbles, he saw no limit to what the Mexicans might accomplish, both in the arts and in the manufacture of woolen, silk and cotton goods, since "their dispositions and habits are peculiarly calculated for sedentary employments."

Pike concluded his book with the following calculations: "Twenty thousand auxiliaries from the United States under good officers, joined to the independents of the country, are at any time sufficient to create and effect a revolution. These troops can be raised and officered in the United States, but paid and supplied at the expense of Mexico. It would be requisite that not only the general commanding, but that every officer, down to the youngest ensign, should be impressed with the necessity of supporting a strict discipline, to prevent marauding, which should in some instances be punished with death, in order to convince the citizens that we come as their friends and protectors, not as their plunderers and tyrants. Also, the most sacred regard should be paid not to injure the institutions of their religion . . . Should an army of Americans ever march into the country, and be guided and governed by these maxims, they will only have to march from province to province in triumph, and be hailed by the united voices of grateful millions as their deliverers and saviors, whilst our national character resounds to the most distant nations of the earth."

Pike's "Expeditions," with this ringing peroration, was widely read when it was published in 1810, just on the eve of the outbreak of revolution in Mexico. The book, giving a clear direction to the vague pressure that had pushed Americans up to and beyond the Sabine for many years past, probably had a farther reaching effect on the future of Texas than any other book ever written. The men who made Texas history were practical men and not bookish. But the second volume of Pike's "Expeditions" was a useful guide that was read like a Baedeker by a whole generation of adventurers.

17

A Generation of Struggle

The revolution and counter-revolution of Texas in 1811, picayune events on the surface, were important for their far-reaching side-effects in two directions. On the one hand, if the revolutionists of San Antonio had been able to maintain themselves in power a little longer, holding open the ways of communication between the Mexican revolutionary leaders and their willing friends in the United States, the course of events throughout Mexico might have been altogether different, in that the revolution might have been finally consummated by the liberal forces of Hidalgo and Morelos rather than the reactionary armies of Iturbide. In the other direction, the San Antonio outbreak was important because it ushered in years of disorder during which filibusterers from the United States were able to start the process that culminated in the independence of Texas and the Mexican War.

To understand the situation in 1811, it is necessary to backtrack a little. Seeds of insurgency had been present in Mexico since the days of Montezuma, but only in the worldwide ferment following the American and French revolutions were these seeds able to germinate. Instead of the usually recognized two social classes, the rich and the poor, Mexico had four classes whose positions were based ultimately on national origin. At the bottom, in some ways, were the Indians, but worse off were the *mestizos,* who were not rooted in the land and had no recognized position in society. Above these two more or less submerged groups was a ruling class of Spanish descent that was split within itself by the division between the creoles, or native-born Mexicans, and the *gachupines,* immigrants from Spain. The latter enjoyed special privileges under law and custom, and regarded themselves as superior to the equally Spanish creoles, who happened to have been born in Mexico. In addition to the unrest arising from this social stratification, restrictions on trade caused discontent among the small but rising middle class, and official corruption weakened the viceregal government.

These factors did not operate in Texas in quite the same way that they did in the older parts of Mexico. Frontier conditions, even under absolute governments, are conducive to a relative freedom. While many people in Texas were miserably poor, they had no tremendously wealthy neighbors to arouse resentment. Land could be had for the taking, but most people preferred the still easier course of living from the proceeds of the wild cattle and horses which they could lasso on the open plains. Consequently the revolution in Texas, when it came, was no social overturn, and there is no evidence whatever that its leaders were animated by humanitarian or idealistic motives. Probably the most powerful inciting factor was the prospect that a revolutionary government would remove the restrictions on trade with the United States and establish a Texas seaport for traffic with other countries. Added to this, we must consider the never avowed but always powerful motive of personal ambition on the part of the leaders.

Revolutionary fires were fanned by the well-founded hope of potential Mexican insurgents that they might obtain help from the growing young Republic to the North, where both Jefferson and Monroe, to say nothing of innumerable lesser spokesmen, had already expressed ideas of hemispheric solidarity that were to crystallize in the Monroe Doctrine in 1823. Another factor was the overthrow of the legitimate Spanish government at home by Napoleon, who installed his brother on the throne of Spain and sent his agents to foment rebellion against the hereditary king in the Spanish dominions abroad. One of these emissaries, General Octaviano d'Alvimar, turned up in Texas and, although his intentions never became explicit, he was accused of seeking to bring about a revolt in Mexico fully two years before the actual outbreak.

This man, a relative of Napoleon's brother-in-law General Leclerc, was arrested by a Spanish scouting party on the Sabine, August 15, 1808. Feigning amazement at the Spaniards' "effrontery" in arresting him, D'Alvimar declared that he was on his way to Mexico to pursue a mission for Napoleon, a friendly monarch. The case was submitted to the *auditor de guerra* in Mexico City, who decided that D'Alvimar should be considered an enemy, for although Napoleon had seized control of the Spanish government through his brother, Joseph, the viceregal government in Mexico held allegiance to the deposed monarch, Ferdinand VII, in whose name the Duque de Infantado had declared war on Napoleon. Eventually D'Alvimar was sent to San Antonio under guard as a "voluntary" prisoner. But the officials of the region, in council, decided to hold him as a prisoner of war. He was taken into Mexico and finally was sent on an English vessel to Spain, although it was said that in the meantime he had been allowed to communicate with various Mexicans, including Father Miguel Hidalgo y Costilla, later the leader of the first revolutionary outbreak.

Viceroy Iturrigaray was ousted in 1808 by a coup d'etat in the name of King Ferdinand. The following year a creole conspiracy to revolt was nipped in the bud at Valladolid. In the spring of 1810, revolt broke out in South America and spread like the explosion of a string of firecrakcers. But it was not until September 16, 1810, that Hidalgo and his friends, learning that orders had been issued for their arrest, decided to unleash their projected Mexican revolt immediately, three months sooner than they had planned. This bloodless rebellion, which had been intended only to transfer power from the *gachupines* to the creoles, became a social revolution as the landless, shoeless mestizos and Indians swelled the army of Hidalgo and gave expression to the buried resentment of three hundred years as they went about the country burning, looting and killing.

By November, 1810, Dr. John Sibley, the American agent on the Louisiana border, reported hearing that a revolutionary *junta* had been formed in Bexar. In the same month a young blacksmith named José Bernardo Gutiérrez de Lara was spreading the revolution to the northern provinces on the right bank of the Rio Grande. By the beginning of January, discontent among the people of Bexar became so obvious that Governor Manuel de Salcedo called upon the people to pledge their loyalty. On the night of January 15, Lieutenant Antonio Saenz, who had been arrested as a revolutionary emissary from Gutiérrez, escaped from his cell in the Alamo and joined a group of conspirators who were planning to seize the governor and Commandant Herrera and form a provisional government preparatory to turning Texas over to the insurgents. The plot was discovered before it could be carried into execution, but Salcedo became so alarmed that he cancelled a projected march to the Rio Grande with his five hundred troops. He also called a general meeting of the leading citizens, at which he demanded and received a vote of confidence and a pledge of loyalty.

A deceptive calm settled over San Antonio but remained for less than a week. On the afternoon of January 21, Ensign Vicente Flores called on Francisco Travieso, the first *alcalde,* who was disgusted because Salcedo had told him that he, Travieso, would have to command a group of untrained home guards for the defense of Bexar when the troops were ready to leave for the Rio Grande. Flores and Travieso, together, went to another house to call on Captain Juan Bautista Casas, a retired officer of militia who was known to be sympathetic to the insurgents and who, being a former resident of Nuevo Santander, was probably an old friend of Gutiérrez. The plotters stayed with Casas until midnight, interrupted by numerous other visitors whom Casas met outside the door and with whom he talked in whispers. In this way the three chief conspirators agreed upon a plan which they carried out the following morning.

Before dawn, wrapped in long cloaks and with broad-brimmed *sombreros* pulled down over their eyes to avert recognition, Travieso and Flores returned to Casas' house, where they were joined by Sergeant Miguel Reyna and Corporal Tomás Pinedo. Just at the last note of reveille, with the other conspirators hovering in the background, Casas walked into the presidio, made a prisoner of the officer of the guard, and came out to receive the plaudits of the assembled battalion of troops. A little later, Salcedo and Herrera were arrested. The wily Salcedo, feigning that he, like his troops, had been converted to the revolutionary cause, begged to be allowed to serve in the ranks as a common soldier, and reached for the musket of a private who was passing by, but Casas stopped him. Although the troops had followed Casas, it was said that they "instinctively" presented arms when Salcedo and Herrera were led away to be confined under guard in the governor's house.

Meanwhile, though no one in Texas was yet aware of it, the revolutionary armies in Mexico had been severely defeated by the loyalist Brigadier General Féliz María Calleja at the Bridge of Calderón and Hidalgo had been deposed from command by his officers in favor of Ignacio Allende, who was more moderate in his revolutionary aims. The main army then moved northward to join a smaller force which General Mariano Jiménez commanded at Saltillo, and to look for help from the United States, where Gutiérrez would soon go to call on Monroe, the secretary of state.

It will be observed that the coup in San Antonio, whether so planned or not, had important implications for the attempt to bring American aid to the defeated revolutionaries. With Texas in rebel hands, volunteers or organized troops coming from the North would meet no resistance until they had penetrated far into Mexico. In view of the poor communications at this period, it is improbable that the capture of San Antonio was part of any coordinated strategy but if it was an accident it still fitted in perfectly with the plans of the insurgents.

While Allende's army moved painfully northward, Casas released the several revolutionary prisoners in the Alamo and replaced them with *gachupines*. He dissolved the *cabildo* and organized a new governing council in its stead. At the same time he sent emissaries to carry the revolution to La Bahía and Nacogdoches. By February 9, when he received from Jiménez an appointment as brigadier general and governor of Texas, Casas had become so confident that, without regard for the council which he himself had appointed, he proclaimed that he was now authorized to use "all the powers which his judgment might dictate."

Joy reigned in Louisiana when the news of the Texas revolt trickled across the border. Farther east, newspapers predicted that the independence of the Spanish colonies would mean free trade and a new outlet for American enterprise. But in Mexico the loyalists were well aware that the north gate must be closed at any cost.

The gate was closed sooner than anyone expected. Friends and supporters of Casas quickly became disaffected with his arbitrary rule. On the night of March 1, less than six weeks after the first coup, Father Juan Manuel Zambrano, a retired but still vigorous subdeacon, joined with nine other men in persuading the officer in charge of the night watch to turn over the garrison. Before daybreak Zambrano and his friends had organized a new governing *junta,* pledged to support King Ferdinand and his lawful deputies. Next morning, the 400 soldiers of the garrison obediently marched to Casas' house to take him prisoner.

One of the first actions of the new *junta,* which Zambrano was careful to consult at all times, was to dispatch two agents to carry the news of the changed state of affairs to Commandant General Nemesio Salcedo in Chihuahua. These emissaries, Captains José María Muñoz and Luis Galán, were in grave danger of being captured by the forces of the rebel general Jiménez in the vast semi-desert along their way, so they were given only an oral message for Don Nemesio, but they carried letters fom the *junta* to Jiménez, falsely declaring that the counter-coup was not an act against the

Revolution but only against the personal abuses of Casas.

Beyond the Rio Grande at the Presidio of San Fernando de Austria, which was held by the loyalists, the emissaries from Bexar met Lieutenant Colonel Ignacio Elizondo, a former revolutionist who, for reasons of his own, had swung over to covert support of the loyalist cause. They also met Manuel de Salcedo and Herrera, who were virtually at liberty and had, in fact, been rallying the followers of the king in Coahuila while they were still nominally prisoners. It was Don Manuel who had reconverted Elizondo to the loyalist cause—a conversion which was to have far-reaching consequences.

Don Manuel had obtained Elizondo's aid in a shrewd and treacherous plan designed to deal a death-blow to the revolution. The rebel army was known to be on the march across the dusty semi-desert from Saltillo to Monclova. Early on the morning of March 21, Elizondo, whom the revolutionists still believed to be one of them, stationed himself on horseback by the side of the road near the Wells of Baján, an oasis a few miles south of Monclova. Down the dusty road came the rebel army, in small, straggling detachments. As each detachment passed Elizondo, it saluted him and then passed on around a little hill to the place where 300 well-trained loyalist troops lay in ambush to capture them piecemeal. The operation was carried-out with speed and efficiency. The captured soldiers were sent to forced labor, the minor officers were shot immediately, and the leaders were sent away for trial and eventual execution. Disposed of in this way were Hidalgo, Allende and Jiménez, three of the foremost figures of the revolution.

If Manuel de Salcedo had not been sent from Texas in chains by victorious rebels, and if he and Elizondo had not learned from Muñoz and Galán that Texas was again in loyalist hands, ready to cooperate with Coahuila in suppressing the revolt, it is unlikely that the ruse at Baján, which broke the back of the first Mexican revolution, would ever have been thought of. Nor would it have been so decisive had it been tried. When the revolution lost Texas, it lost the chance of recovery from the first setback at the Bridge of Calderón. It would now be ten more years before Spanish power in Mexico could be finally overthrown, and then only by a different set of people, with different motives and objectives than those who answered Hidalgo's Cry of Dolores and fought by his side down to the ultimate disaster at the Wells.

Late in March there was another revolutionary plot at Bexar, but it was discovered before any overt act could be attempted. Several of Casas' friends were sent to Mexico, where they were tried and condemned. Casas himself was tried at San Antonio, beheaded, and his severed head placed on a pole in the plaza for all to see. Herrera and Salcedo returned to their posts, and Texas settled down to a two-year lull before a revolutionary cloud again appeared on the horizon.

The filibuster is a distinctive but not basically abnormal type of person who reached his full flowering in the Mexican and South American revolutions, continuing until the relative pacification of that part of the world less than a generation ago. A few specimens of the genus may still be hatching their plots anywhere between Brownsville and Tierra del Fuego, but if such exist they are probably infected with ideology, whether communist or fascist, and cannot present the symmetrically corrupt efflorescence of pure opportunism that distinguished the true filibuster. The type of man who would once have set out after new empires must now content himself with being a real-estate promoter, a politician, a soldier, or a confidence man. The real filibuster was a combination of all of these, many degrees magnified, and his opportunities were theoretically unlimited, though there is no record of any filibusterer who ever gained a lasting success.

In the Southwest, all the air had been thick with plotting ever since General Wilkinson crossed the Alleghenies in 1784, but it was not until after the outbreak of revolution in Mexico that that country, like a damaged virgin, seemed to become fair game for the filibusters as well as for higher-placed statesmen who saw the manifest destiny of the United States even though the phrase had not yet been invented. The plots had their epicenter in New Orleans, which was the meeting place of the Spanish, French and American elements around the Gulf of Mexico. Unfortunately there were no writers worthy of the name in the western country, and to gain a fair appreciation of what things were like, especially in New Orleans, about 1811, it is necessary to read the O. Henry and Richard Harding Davis stories of revolutionary plotters in the Central American republics almost a century later. Adventurers lacking the price of a meal would buttonhole the rich and powerful with grandiose plans for conquest, outrivaling Cortez, and some of these schemes came within an ace of success. Operating with a hundred dollars or so of borrowed money, Mexican exiles would embark on trips to Washington to see the secretary of state, and sometimes the British ambassador, too. American generals, governors and bankers would be seen huddled with Spanish refugees at café tables in the Vieux Carré, tossing off one straight whiskey after another while they talked in low, conspiratorial tones.

In September, 1811, six months after the revolution had been suppressed in Texas and Northern Mexico, Gutiérrez, the revolutionary blacksmith of Revilla, arrived in Natchitoches with a Texas rebel, José Menchaca, to seek American aid. En route the two men had had a brush with royalists and lost the few hundred dollars they had been carrying. About the same time, José Alvarez de Toledo, a Cuban revolutionary, arrived in Philadelphia with plans of his own.

Though Hidalgo and his immediate associates had been put to death, the revolutionary General José María Morelos controlled large and important area in the South. Gutiérrez, after outlining his plans for making contact with Morelos and other rebel chiefs still fighting in the mountains, obtained funds in Louisiana to continue his trip to Washington. There he met Monroe, then secretary of state, who promised substantial aid (according to Gutiérrez) but refused to put his promises in writing. Monroe saw to it, however, that Gutiérrez obtained enough money to finance his return to the border. Shortly after, Monroe provided Toledo with the means for a conspiratorial trip to Cuba.

Back in New Orleans, Gutiérrez met William Shaler, a special agent of the state department, who was to play an important but ambiguous part in the events that followed. While ostensibly waiting for an opportunity to proceed to his post as consul at Vera Cruz, Shaler became an adviser to Gutiérrez. His almost daily reports to Monroe exhibit an attitude which might be described as sympathetic neutrality. Shaler was an honest, loyal and intelligent public servant, however, and there is no doubt that he believed, probably with good reason, that he was carrying out the policy of the United States.

What was Wilkinson doing in these days? To those who have followed the General's shifty career, it seems incredible that he had no hand in the plottings that centered around the faintly ridiculous figure of Gutiérrez. Actually, however, nothing more than a dim rumor ever connected him with the expedition that was forming in the early months of 1812. In June, just before the expedition jelled, the United States declared war on Great Britain, and Wilkinson may have decided that the time was not right for him to embark on unofficial adventures.

A protege of Wilkinson's was Augustus W. Magee, whom he had recommended for promotion from second lieutenant to first lieutenant. Magee had graduated third in his class at West Point in June, 1808, and was commissioned in January, 1809. Shaler described him in 1812 as "a native of Boston about twenty-four years of age; he is very tall, very robust, of a handsome person and countenance, of a very commanding appearance as an officer and prepossessing manners; he passes for one of the best informed officers of his age in the American Army."

However, there is some evidence that this paragon was a young man of unstable character, and the Washington officials, who refused his promotion, may have been better informed than Shaler and Wilkinson. At any rate, Magee became disgruntled after three years as a second lieutenant, and resigned his commission to organize a filibustering army which would join with forces raised by Gutiérrez in Texas to conquer, not only Texas, but all of Mexico. This undertaking, said one observer, would eclipse all previous dreams of conquest, including the exploit of Cortéz, who captured an empire with five hundred men.

Doing a quick about-face, Magee began organizing the outlaws whom he had recently been pursuing in the Neutral Ground, and who had now been deserted by their revolutionary leader, Menchaca, who was said to have sold out to the royalists. Magee, now a colonel in the revolutionary army under Gutiérrez as the self-appointed general, crossed the Sabine on August 8 and pursued a retreating force of three hundred Spaniards. The general, obviously afraid of the plunge into hostile territory, followed two days later. On the third day, when the filibustering "army" was well into Texas, Governor Claiborne of Louisiana issued a proclamation in which he tardily pointed out that the whole affair was a clear violation of the Neutrality Act of 1797. As the federally appointed territorial governor, of course, Claiborne could have nipped the expedition in the bud if he had cared to. So could Wilkinson, the commander of the Army on the frontier.

After capturing Nacogdoches, the first town on the road through Texas, the invaders increased their force to some seven hundred, including Americans, who continued to follow across the border, and Spanish-Mexican residents of Texas. While Magee and his American associates maintained a fair degree of discipline among their irregular troops, Gutiérrez spent most of his time eating, drinking, and issuing high-sounding proclamations in which he promised to correct various abuses but failed to express any profound philosophy of government. With Nacogdoches as the advanced base, preparations went busily forward for the conquest of the capital, San Antonio. Recruiting meanwhile continued in Louisiana under the averted eyes of Governor Claiborne, who politely brushed aside a protest from the Spanish consul.

In October, leaving a small party to govern the friendly inhabitants of Nacogdoches, the Republican Army of the North, as it was called, moved out on the road to San Antonio. On the way, however, Magee learned that Salcedo had withdrawn his forces from the coast to defend the capital and had taken up a defensive position on the Guadalupe River near present-day New Braunfels, thirty miles from San Antonio. So the Republican Army abruptly changed its direction and confronted La Bahía, taking the place without a struggle on November 7.

Salcedo, remarkably well informed for those days of horse-back communication, learned of the event so quickly that he and his army arrived at La Bahía only six days after the invaders had taken possession. The revolutionary force was sitting snugly in the presidio, which still stands today, a stone enclosure in a commanding position on a little hill beside the San Antonio River. Magee, spoiling for a fight, wrote to Shaler that he had no cause to worry except the treachery of the enemy. "They are," he declared, "a rascally set of treacherous cowards. God never made greater villains. I have tried to get a fight out of them ..." But Don Manuel had other plans. Disposing his forces around the presidio, he sat down to wait until the defenders should be starved out. Meanwhile he acquired reinforcements and Magee became worried over the increasing desertions from the Republican ranks. Before long Magee and his officers, in council, decided on a proposal to withdraw, provided that the Mexicans who had joined with the Americans should be pardoned. But Salcedo refused to agree to this condition.

In December, Magee wrote that he had no more hope of effecting a revolution, but that he could still blast out a way to safety. Gutiérrez told Magee that the United States was welcome to take all Texas if it would only send troops to aid the revolution. Shaler replied that the prospects for such aid would be fair if the patriots would first take San Antonio, and if the United States declared war on Spain, as he expected.

Magee fell ill during the winter and became increasingly despondent. Early in February he ordered a retreat, but when too many of his officers and soldiers objected, the order was withdrawn. At this juncture, on February 6, 1813, Magee died. There is a story, copied by many historians, that he either shot himself or took poison to avoid being shot by his own men, but there is no real evidence that he committed suicide, and he had been ill for weeks before his death.

Soon after Magee died, the royalists were repulsed in two attacks on the fortress. On February 19 Don Manuel ordered his forces to retreat to San Antonio, leaving the whole Province of Texas, except the capital, open to the Republican Army of the North. Battered by the siege and the two attacks, however, the invaders allowed Salcedo's army to retire quietly, without harassment from the rear. Shaler, still interested in taking his post as consul at Vera Cruz, wrote Monroe that he would doubtless soon be able to resume the interrupted journey.

Meanwhile new royalist forces were forming to drive the Republicans out of Texas. The able one-eyed General Joaquín de Arredondo was bringing an army from Nuevo Santander, and General Ignacio Elizondo was preparing to move from his base at Presidio del Norte on the Rio Grande. The Republicans, having allowed their enemies ample time to organize new resistance, moved out on the road to San Antonio exactly a month after Salcedo's retreat. The eight hundred men of the Republican Army were now commanded by "Colonel" Reuben Kemper, who had replaced Magee. At Rosillo Creek, eight miles southeast of San Antonio, on March 29, they were met by 1,200 men under General Simón de Herrera. But the Spanish force was routed in half an hour by a furious attack led by Kemper and another American, "Major" Reuben Ross.

Shaler was happy when he heard of this victory. "The valor and intrepidity of the American volunteers," he wrote to Monroe, "reflects honor on the national character. Several officers particularly Major Ross exhibited in single combat with Spanish officers the most romantic gallantry."

Camping in the Alamo, which was then outside the city, the Republicans demanded unconditional surrender of the capital. After some hesitation, Salcedo gave up on April 2 and became a prisoner with fourteen of his officers, while eight hundred men of the royal army joined the revolution, and three hundred others, with some of their officers, escaped from the city.

Then followed an episode which is still the subject of controversy. The undisputed facts are these: Herrera and Salcedo were formally charged with having bribed Elizondo to betray Hidalgo's army and with having lured Captain José Menchaca to San Antonio to be executed (at the time when Menchaca's followers supposed he had been "bought off"). Twelve royalist officers, besides Herrera and Salcedo, were formally tried on various charges. All were convicted. The fourteen officers were taken out of the city and had their throats cut by soldiers who whetted their sabers on the soles of their shoes.

Most historians, including two of the most scrupulous researchers, Warren and Garrett, report that the Americans, not knowing that the verdict had called for a death penalty, had been told that the convicted officers were being taken to La Bahía, either to remain in prison there or to be taken on board a vessel. When the Americans heard of the treacherous murder of the Spanish officers by other Spaniards, according to this version of the story, they were so incensed that many of them promptly forswore their allegiance to Gutiérrez's revolution and returned to the States.

Castañeda, likewise a thorough scholar, has found contrary evidence to show that the slaughter of the fourteen officers was virtually a lynching, carried out by a mob of one hundred men which included both Mexicans and Americans. Whichever version may be right, it is true that some Americans deserted the expedition when they found that the passions of revolution had led to such a violation of the rules of the game of filibustering as they understood those rules. It is also true that many of the Americans remained faithful to the Republican cause, and there was nothing in the backgrounds of most of these men to make them squeamish about a lynching, whether or not it was clothed with the color of revolutionary legality.

With the capital city safely in his hands, Gutiérrez began to slight his American advisers and had himself elected "President Protector of the Provisional Government of the State of Texas," a title based on a provisional constitution which, while it borrowed many phrases from the writings of Locke, Rousseau and Jefferson, placed heavy restrictions on individual liberty and left no place for freedom of religion, the Catholic Church being established by law. Texas was declared to be an inseparable part of the future Republic of Mexico. Shaler, however, considered the constitutional convention to be "nothing more than an absurd revolutionary farce." He reported that the President Protector had "taken possession of the treasury, and every valuable; he is served in plate, and lives in the style of an Eastern Basha, while everything around him is penury and want."

Apparently feeling that he had little further need of his American allies, Gutiérrez granted furloughs to Kemper and more than a hundred other Americans, who thereupon returned to Louisiana. They found Toledo, the Cuban conspirator, shuttling between Nacogdoches and Natchitoches as a self-appointed and impressively uniformed "general," bursting with revolutionary plans which he confided to any influential person who would listen to him. With Shaler's encouragement, Toledo sent one of his henchmen, Juan de Picornell, to Texas to take command of the Republican Army of the North and prepare for Toledo's own dramatic entry. But Gutiérrez would have none of this, so Picornell, returned as far as Nacogdoches, where Toledo had now set up his headquarters and had assembled a force of volunteers who were urging him to defy Gutiérrez and take charge of the revolution. on May 20, a little more than six weeks after the capture of San Antonio. Here the American agent received confirmation of rumors that Gutiérrez had been dickering for French support. Shaler promptly informed Monroe that Gutiérrez could not remain in command much longer. The American agent also assisted Toledo in establishing and editing the first newspaper circulated in Texas (although it was printed in Natchitoches), the *Gaceta de Texas*.

Meanwhile Arredondo and Elizondo were slowly preparing for

the recapture of Texas. Drawn by a false rumor that Gutiérrez was retreating, Elizondo advanced toward San Antonio in June, against the advice of the shrewd Arredondo. Camping outside the city, Elizondo sent in a flag of truce with a proposal that the Americans retire unmolested, only surrendering Gutiérrez and sixty other Mexican "traitors." Major Ross, informed by his San Antonio Mexican lady-love that the Mexican followers of the Republican Army planned to massacre the Americans and join the enemy, urged a retreat. The other officers refused to agree. Ross thereupon resigned his command and departed for Louisiana. Whether his Mexican Aida accompanied him is not of record.

On the morning of June 20, Captain Perry led an army of nine hundred men to battle against the approximately equal force of Elizondo, which was camped on a small eminence beside Alazan Creek, west of the town. Despite three masses said by the priests in the royalist camp, the rebels continued to advance, and the demoralized army of Elizondo fled in disorder after resisting for less than two hours.

Gutiérrez had been very much in the background during the battle, and the Americans were confirmed in their determination to depose him. The Shaler-Toledo attack on Gutiérrez was now actively promoted by Joseph B. Wilkinson, a son of the general. The latter, by the way, was just now leaving for the front in Canada, after having managed to keep his post on the Texas border for a full year after, one would think, the services of the senior general in the American Army might have been needed in the war with Great Britain. Perhaps as a bribe for doing his duty, Wilkinson at this time was finally promoted from brigadier to major general.

Shaler, actively abetting the aspirations of Toledo to command the Republican Army, explained to Monroe that his interference was necessary because of the sad state of affairs in Texas: "The most deplorable system of terror, rapine and misrule has been followed: arbitrary imprisonments and confiscations, constantly succeed each other; all the resources of the country have been pillaged, and squandered away without any public benefit; and suspicion and discontent are general and at their heigth (sic). It is estimated that more than 1,200 persons have deserted since the reduction of San Antonio, and they are daily disappearing. The Republican force at present consists of about four hundred Americans and eight hundred Mexicans but in about five hundred of the latter little confidence is placed."

Rather surprisingly, for an agent of the United States government, Shaler openly recommended Toledo to the American officers of the Republican Army and wrote to Monroe that "I have pledged my word for his honor and integrity." The filibusters accepted the recommendation and, with the special aid of Joseph Wilkinson, the *junta* of the "State of Texas" was persuaded to send for Toledo.

Shaler himself started for San Antonio about the same time as Toledo but was brought up short by a letter from Monroe which made it clear that this time the American agent had finally overstepped his authority, broad as that authority seems to have been. As against Shaler's open opposition to the Napoleonic royal government, Monroe declared that the United States was at peace with Spain and intended "to preserve that relation with whatever government might exist."

Shaler abandoned his trip to Texas and wrote, "I regret exceedingly having taken any step that does not meet the approbation of the President, as it has ever been my endeavor to conform strictly to the spirit of my instructions. My object has been to keep a vigilant eye on what was passing, and I have never failed to communicate anything to the fullest extent." Shaler evidently believed that it is not always necessary to avoid evil if one can avoid the appearance of evil, for he continued, "The first adventurers in this expedition assembled on the desolate banks of the Sabine. Since that time there has never been within the United States the least appearance of armament, or military preparation, the volunteers went out either singly, or in small bands, usually armed as hunters, and what few supplies have been procured here have been furnished in the common way of trade."

Given larger opportunities, William Shaler might well have become an eminent disciple of Machiavelli. He was not dismissed for his part in the filibuster, but continued in the service of the State Department long afterward. And there is no reason why he should not have been retained or even promoted, for he was doing his duty as he saw it, and he was the one personally disinterested man among all the ambitious figures in this border episode.

It was fortunate for American relations with Spain, however, that Monroe's letter reached Shaler in time to prevent him from carrying out his intention to represent his government in the rebel-held capital of Texas. Early in August, Toledo assumed command of the Republican Army, and President-Protector Gutiérrez, with only three companions and a mule, began a melancholy retirement to the safety of Natchitoches. On August 18 the joined armies of Arredondo and Elizondo, numbering 1,800 men, met the Republican Army of 1,400 at the point where the *Camino Real* crossed the Medina River, seventeen miles south of San Antonio. The rebels were decisively defeated after Samuel Kemper and Miguel Menchaca had refused to obey an order from Toledo to retreat with their men to the shelter of the high banks of the river. The royalists suffered heavy losses, however, so that they could not follow immediately to give the coup de grace to the retreating revolutionaries. A few days later, Arredondo occupied San Antonio and sent Elizondo out to round up the scattering Republican Army.

Elizondo was remarkably lenient with the Americans, sending the captured ones back to the States with passports, horses, and a rifle for every five men. With the Mexicans it was different. Within a week after the Medina victory, 327 Mexican rebel prisoners had been executed without trial. Hundreds fled before Arredondo made his triumphal procession through San Antonio—perhaps the first parade in a city that has since become famous for the pageantry in its streets. In a patio called the *Quinta* (Garden), Arredondo imprisoned several hundred wives and daughters of rebels for fifty-four days, requiring many of them to work from two in the morning until ten at night, grinding corn and baking tortillas for his army, while they looked out and saw their children roaming the streets. Promptly the bodies of Salcedo and Herrera were exhumed and given proper burial.

In search of escaped rebels, Elizondo made a grueling late summer journey through the heart of Texas, capturing a hundred men, an equal number of women, and hundreds of their horses, mules and cattle. In camp on the Brazos River, a captain from Spain, gone mad with the heat and brutality of those weeks, fatally shot Elizondo and killed Elizondo's cousin. The new commander, Colonel Quintero, drove the prisoners to San Antonio like cattle, ordering his men to lash those who fell by the way. He, too, made a triumphal entry into the capital, marching the prisoners between lines of soldiers and townspeople to the presidio, where General Arredondo, with grim humor, taunted them by himself singing a popular *corrido* that some rebel had written about "the one-eyed Arredondo."

The revolution was over and the "State" of Texas had been brought back to the sheltering arms of King Ferdinand VII. By October 10, a little more than a month after the Battle of the Medina, amnesty had been offered to all rebels remaining alive, with certain exceptions, who would present themselves within a specified time. The exceptions included Gutiérrez and Toledo, both of whom were safe in Louisiana, but who had a price of $500 on their heads in Texas.

Arredondo, with tongue in cheek, wrote to Don Luis de Onís, the Spanish envoy to the United States: "... The greater part of those who perished ... were Anglo-Americans. Convinced that the administration of these States has not aided the revolution of Texas, and that its subjects who were found here were nothing but delinquent vagabonds, I hope that if you find it convenient you will inform that government that the vagabonds who attempted to compromise it are punished, according to our laws, for the violation of territory and other trespasses they committed, which should give it satisfaction."

Morphi, the Spanish consul in New Orleans, believed that the defeat at the Medina would forever put a stop to the tendency for Americans to move into the Spanish semi-vacuum in the Southwest. He was wrong, of course. The movement that Gasiot had predicted thirty years before was not to be halted so easily, nor ever in any way at all.

18

The End and the Beginning

The Mexican revolution, which had burned with a low, uneven flame since the betrayal at Baján, was almost extinquished with the capture of the rebel leader Matamoros in January of 1814, but it continued to smoulder like a banked fire under the ministrations of guerrilla chiefs, sometimes indistinguishable from bandits, who maintained the forms of revolutionary government in their mountain fastnesses. Meanwhile the returned leaders of the Gutiérrez-Magee expedition joined with other plotters—American, Mexican and Spanish—to keep alive the hope of intervention in Mexico through an endless series of low-voiced conferences in the taverns of New Orleans and Natchez. These discussions were punctuated with anxious trips to Washington, Philadelphia and Baltimore, the last-named city having become a center for Spanish-American schemes which concerned not only Mexico but the whole of South America.

At the same time that Matamoros was being taken and executed, a Natchez association called the Friends of Mexican Emancipation "authorized" Dr. John Hamilton Robinson, a discharged agent of the State Department, to occupy Texas and prevent its falling into the hands of potential enemies of the United States. This was a pointed reference to the legitimate Spanish monarchy, which was allied with England against Napoleon, while England was at war with the United States.

Toledo was hatching a new plan of his own. In March, 1814, he became Robinson's rival for the support of some four hundred drifters who had been drawn to Natchitoches by reports of Robinson's project. While he went to Natchez in quest of evidence that he hoped would convict Robinson of conspiring with the Napoleonic General Jean Joseph Amable Humbert, Toledo left his forces at Natchitoches in command of Colonel John Smith. While Toledo was still in Natchez, two rival expeditions, headed by Robinson and Smith, crossed the Sabine into Texas. When Toledo himself crossed the Sabine, on May 2, he found the former State Department agent a prisoner in Smith's camp. Four days later, Toledo ordered Robinson released on condition that he support the Mexican revolution. The two expeditions, camped a few miles apart, remained where they were for several weeks, then pulled up stakes and went back to Louisiana.

Meanwhile an American in Natchitoches wrote to a friend: "The situation of the Spanish Provinces is terrible. The Royalists rob and murder those whom they find of the Natives because they are suspected of defection to loyalty. Our Americans go out over the Sabine and rob the poor natives whom they call Quotchipins [*Gachupines*]. It is enough to have property. Robbers & Murders disgrace the Causes—there is no law to restrain them.... As is usual, the prejudices & passions of the people have been awakened 'by the voice of Reason & Liberty,' while the leaders are stimulated by avarice and ambition. Royal Honors, Dukedoms, Principilities [sic] &c are forever rising before them. The guilded Tombs of Mexico are not too remote for their mercenary vision."

In December the Treaty of Ghent concluded the war with England, although the news did not penetrate to the West until after the Battle of New Orleans in January, 1815. In June, Napoleon was finally defeated at Waterloo. Meanwhile Ferdinand VII had been restored to the throne of Spain. Another blow was dealt to the revolution in Mexico when Morelos was captured and shot.

Among the ambitious citizens on the border, plots for the invasion of Texas went on as before. In the summer of 1815 the Spanish envoy, Onís, protested in Washington that Colonel Perry, one of the surviving leaders of the Magee-Gutiérrez fiasco, was openly recruiting for another expedition. President Madison, on September 1, issued a proclamation admonishing all faithful citizens to abstain from such an unlawful enterprise, but this assertion of neutrality had no noticeable effect on Perry's plans. By November, Perry had established himself on Galveston Island, preparing for an attack by land and sea on the Mexican port of Tampico. This expedition soon dispersed, however, when Toledo failed to deliver the financial support he had promised.

Shortly after this time, the concept which has come to be known as the "Good Neighbor Policy" made its first appearance in international discussions. On April 6, 1816, the Viceroy of New Spain, Juan Ruiz de Apodaca, wrote to Onís that he hoped "the laws of good neighborhood may be observed by the citizens of those [United] States." It was 117 years, however, before the Good Neighbor Policy came to be enunciated as the guiding principle of our relations with the countries of the South.

A new figure who became important to Texas in the turbulent period after the War of 1812 was Louis Aury, a former lieutenant in the navy of the revolutionary republic of New Granada. When a Spanish fleet blockaded the port of Cartagena, Aury succeeded in forcing his way out and joining Bolivar and other South American revolutionary leaders at Aux Cayes, Haiti. This group prepared and executed another expedition to South America, but Aury, because of some personal rivalry, stayed behind and eventually became a privateer in the Caribbean, flying the flag of Cartagena. Seeking a better base of operations he took his little fleet, augmented with prize craft, to the coast of Texas in the fall of 1816. After obtaining a set of 14 privateer commissions from the almost non-existent Mexican revolutionary republic, Aury had Galveston declared a legal port. Although half of his Negro crews mutinied and sailed back to Haiti after seriously wounding Aury, he was not too discouraged to establish a formal local government at Galveston on September 17, 1816. From this base Aury's privateers raided enemy shipping on the Gulf, although sometimes they were careless of the distinction between Spanish and other flags.

Fourteen months after Aury had settled at Galveston there arrived another formidable character, Francisco Xavier Mina. Though he was only 27 years old, Mina had already had a long career as a revolutionary leader in Spain, where he had assisted his uncle, General Espoz y Mina, in guerrilla warfare against Napoleon and an unsuccessful revolt against the restored King Ferdinand. Mina was now on his way to carry out, with support from high quarters in England and the United States, an invasion of Mexico, where he hoped to join forces with the rebels who were still holding out in the mountains.

Mina, after establishing fairly amicable relations with Aury, remained at Galveston until he was ready to sail down the coast for his invasion of Mexico, which he did on April 7, 1817. Meanwhile another colorful figure arrived at Galveston in the person of Jean Laffite (more commonly but incorrectly spelled Lafitte), who contemplated ousting Aury's "government" and taking Galveston Island as a base for his own well-known privateering operations.

The two Laffite brothers, of whom Pierre was the more able although Jean attained the greater posthumous fame through the efforts of romatic writers, were of obscure origin but claimed to be the sons of a French father and a Spanish mother. Since 1811 they had directed a fleet of privateers under commissions from the Republic of Cartagena, operating out of Barataria, their private port near the mouth of the Mississippi. Denied permission to import their prize goods legally into the United States, they had become smugglers and so had run afoul of the American authorities. Although the Laffites are known in tradition as pirates, there is no evidence that their activities, other than smuggling and using neutral U.S. territory as a base for privateers, were in any way criminal: that they ever flew the black flag or caused their captives to walk the plank. Nevertheless, the line between privateering and piracy was always a dim one, and the Laffites or their agents may have crossed it on occasion. In any case, the Laffites were not only tolerated but supported financially by the leading citizens of New Orleans. They fraternized with prominent officials like John Randolph Grymes, the U.S. district attorney, and their own lawyer was Edward Livingston, who later became secretary of state under President Jackson.

In spite of their high-placed friends, however, the corsairs of Barataria were scattered by a combined military and naval expedition sent against them by the United States government in September, 1814, after Pierre had been imprisoned for a time in a cell which is still shown to tourists in New Orleans. A few months later, however, the brothers and their followers received a general amnesty from President Madison for their part in the defense of New Orleans against the British. By this time the Laffites had no notion of returning to Barataria, even if they had been permitted to do so. Their eyes were on Texas and the wealth of Mexico.

Aury and Mina sailed away to Mexico on April 7, 1817. The very next day Laffite, ignoring the skeleton government that Aury had left on Galveston Island, set up a state of his own. This might have passed as a routine filibustering move, if it had not been for one fact which, at the time,

219

was known only to the Laffites and two or three others: The Laffite brothers had entered into an agreement with Spanish representatives in New Orleans to betray the revolutionists and put an end for all time to privateering on the Gulf, under whatever flag.

The motives of the Laffites in entering this agreement, and the spirit in which they carried it out, remain obscure even to this day. They asked no reward, and in fact it appears that they were never able to obtain reimbursement for their out-of-pocket expenses. Whether they were sincere in their newfound loyalty to the Spanish king, or whether they merely pretended to act as Spanish agents in order to obtain immunity for their own semi-piratical enterprises, is a question which has not yet been answered positively by those scholars who have made the most through study of this tangled web of intrigue.

Aury conveyed Mina's little army to the mouth of the Santander River in northeastern Mexico, returned and, after a feeble attempt to re-establish himself in Texas, sailed away to new adventures at Amelia Island, on the Atlantic Coast of Florida. Mina, whose 250 men included fifty Americans under Perry, captured the village of Soto la Marina without resistance. Meanwhile a greatly superior force was approaching under the wily Arredondo. After a quarrel with Mina over a question of tactics, Perry marched his fifty men away for a harebrained attack on the Presidio of La Bahía, far away in Texas, which they reached on June 18. The American force, augmented with a few Texas rebels under Vicente Travieso, fled at the approach of Governor Antonio Martínez, but was overtaken and practically wiped out. Perry himself put a bullet through his head. Mina, though he lost most of his men, made his way to the interior, where he joined other revolutionary forces. In October, however, he was captured and shot. By December of that year, 1817, the Mexican revolution was virtually at an end, and would be revived only in a vastly different form three years later. But Texas, its few settlements almost depopulated by revolutionary disorder, still lay wide open to any imperial-minded squatters who might care to walk in.

The next invaders were Frenchmen, friends of Napoleon. But for his vanity, the defeated conqueror himself might have fled to Texas to begin a new empire with the aid of the little Napoleons who infested the Texas border. After Waterloo, but before Napoleon surrendered to the British, his brother Joseph had obtained a passport to go to America. The two brothers closely resembled each other, and Joseph suggested that Napoleon might use his brother's passport to escape to the New World. But Napoleon, unwilling to accept the appearance of ignominious flight, rejected the offer and "threw himself on the generosity of the British nation" by surrendering to Captain Maitland of the *Bellerophon.* So Napoleon was deported to St. Helena and it was Joseph who went to America, where he lived for many years near Bordentown, New Jersey.

Yet the French flag, first raised on these shores by La Salle, was still to fly a second time in Texas. Soon after Waterloo, France began to be flooded with pamphlets advertising a project to establish a colony in the New World for followers of Napoleon who found it expedient to quit their native country. In the romantic tradition of Rousseau, these publications presented an idyllic land, inhabited by gentle savages, where the exiles might find a pure new life uncontaminated with the evils of civilization. Several hundred exiles had reached Philadelphia by December, 1816, including prominent figures such as Charles and Henri L'Allemand, Marshal Grouchy, General Lefebvre-Desnouéttes and General Rigaud. Organized into what was called "The Society for the Cultivation of the Vine and the Olive," the exiles obtained a generous grant of land on the Tombigbee River in western Alabama, but the vine and the olive did not flourish on the Tombigbee, and their colony there was an immediate failure. Meanwhile another group of Napoleonic exiles, headed by General Rigaud, and comprising 150 men with a number of women and children, set sail from Philadelphia in the Schooner *Huntress* on December 17, 1817. The purposes of this expedition have never been made quite clear, but the *Huntress* was reported to carry 600 muskets, 400 sabers, 12,000 pounds of powder, and little or no agricultural equipment. At the same time there were rumors of a plot to install either Napoleon or Joseph Bonaparte as Emperor of Mexico.

General Rigaud's party landed at Galveston, where Jean Laffite, who by now had created a piratical principality with 1,000 men at his command, received them in a friendly manner. Even Laffite's followers, although they were said to be "the scum of the Caribbean," often greeted the exiles with cries of "Vive la liberté!" Meanwhile another party of French exiles was sailing from New Orleans with General Humbert, the drunken deadbeat who had had a finger in every plot on the southwestern border since 1812. The Laffites, despite the really substantial aid they were giving the French colonists at Galveston, entered into a plot with Spanish officials to have the Laffites' own vessel, the *Intrepide,* on which the Humbert party was sailing, captured by a Spanish naval vessel before it reached Galveston. This plan miscarried because Beverly Chew, the collector of the port of New Orleans, would not allow the brig to sail until it had unloaded its arms and powder. Because of this delay, the Spanish vessel failed to find the *Intrepide.*

General Charles L'Allemand arrived at Galveston in March, 1818, with additional colonists, and the combined Rigaud and L'Allemand parties immediately set out for a chosen site on the Trinity River, possibly near the present town of Liberty. Because of a series of blunders, the colonists soon found themselves without food and were reduced to eating a wild plant which made some of them dreadfully ill. Their faith in the teachings of Rousseau was refreshed when a friendly Coushatta Indian came along and healed their sickness with the juice of another herb.

Finally arrived at the destined place, the exiles built on the river bank a cluster of log cabins and blockhouses, more elaborate than the fort that La Salle had established on Garcitas Creek 133 years before. They called the settlement *"Champ d'Asile,"* or "Field of Refuge," and in a manifesto to the world on May 11, 1818, General L'Allemand claimed for his people "the first right given by God to man—that of settling in this country, clearing it, and using the produce which nature never refuses to the patient laborer." The settlers numbered no more than 120, including some Americans, Spaniards and Poles.

L'Allemand disclaimed any warlike intentions, although he promised a firm defense against attack. Property was to be held in common, and the fundamental principle of the local law was to be the obligation of mutual aid and protection. The proclamation was widely reprinted in the United States and Europe. Funds were subscribed and benefit performances for the colonists were given in the theaters of Paris, but not a cent of the money ever reached the cultivators of the vine and the olive. For that matter, it soon became obvious that the vine and the olive could not flourish in Texas any more than in Alabama, so that in deference to reality the wife of one of the officers composed a song, "The Laurel Grows in the Champ d'Asile." Even this was figuratively intended.

A few of the settlers cultivated kitchen gardens, but most of them spent in military maneuvers whatever time and energy they had left from the hard labor of building their rude fortifications. After dark, the men and women gathered around their campfires, where they often heard General L'Allemand telling of his conversations with the now fallen emperor. But by midsummer, only seven months after the French colonists' arrival, friendly Indians brought word that a Spanish army was on the way from San Antonio to expel the exiles. After a discussion in council the colonists decided to withdraw rather than fight.

They rowed their boats down the river to Galveston three months ahead of the dilatory Spaniards, who destroyed their cabins on October 30. At Galveston the Frenchmen became the victims of scurvy, dysentery and fever, and their situation was aggravated by the greed of Laffite's pirates, who charged through the nose for whatever supplies they sold the Frenchmen, although Lafitte himself was still friendly. More trouble arrived in the person of a special agent of the State Department, George Graham, whom President Monroe, aroused by a protest from Onís, had sent to see what was going on at Galveston.

Like Shaler before him, Graham apparently exceeded the letter but not the spirit of his instructions. The Secretary of State, John Quincy Adams, was openly an expansionist who favored an American seizure of Texas, although he was powerless to act on his conviction. Adams must have nodded approvingly when he received a letter from Joshua Child, a citizen of Louisiana, who declared it was high time for the United States to "take possession of their own soil [Texas] and people it with a population that can defend it; thereby placing an imperviable barrier between slavery and the temptations of Mexico."

Graham was directed to warn the Frenchmen that they were occupying territory claimed by the United States. He was also to obtain as much information as he could about the colony and its backers, whoever they might be. On his own account, Graham decided that the spirit of his instructions also required him to look into the case of Jean Laffite and his nest of corsairs. The execution of this double mission proved to be surprisingly easy. It is doubtful if Graham obtained much true information, but he easily persuaded both L'Allemand and Laffite to quit the soil of Texas. This he seems to have accomplished by convincing both men that an American invasion was imminent. He also showed a spirit of friendly co-operation by advising Laffite to give up his privateer commissions from the shadowy Mexican government and obtain new ones from the more firmly established republic of Buenos Aires. As for the Frenchmen, Graham promised to help them obtain relief, and he returned to New Orleans in company with General L'Allemand.

Soon a Spanish agent, too, came to demand that the homeless Frenchmen quit Galveston Island. Most of the Frenchmen—and women and children—then walked the 400 miles overland to New Orleans, supporting themselves by hunting on the way. A few joined the pirates, and another group of 45, including General Humbert, was sent to New Orleans by Jean Laffite in a captured Spanish ship. From Louisiana, most of the colonists made their way back to France, where they long regaled their children and grandchildren with stories of the *Champ d'Asile* in the wilds of Texas. General L'Allemand received a bequest of 100,000 francs from Napoleon, and after the Revolution of 1830 he again became prominent in public life. Rigaud died in New Orleans in 1820, unaware that he too had been named for a 100,000-franc bequest in the will of his master, who outlived him by a year.

The tenuous but persistently argued claim of the United States to the territory between the Sabine and the Rio Grande was finally relinquished in the Florida treaty of February 22, 1819, in which Spain's right to Texas was acknowledged at the same time that Florida was ceded to the United States. The "trading" of Texas for Florida immediately aroused a furore among all the expansionist elements south of the Ohio and west of the Alleghenies. Texas was obviously more valuable than Florida, and it was seriously argued that the government had given away American territory, though in reality the United States had never occupied an inch of either Florida or Texas and the negotiators might have been credited with a good stroke of business in persuading the Spaniards to sign over even that swampy peninsula in exchange for an agreement not to press the U.S. claim to Texas even though they also received a cash payment.

American fire-eaters, however, were not impressed with the obvious advantages of this transaction, which greatly ameliorated the hostility and suspicion that had divided the United States and Spain since the founding of the Republic. To the old individualistic tendencies of adventure and gain that had moved Wilkinson and Nolan and their successors, a new element was now added. The invention of the cotton gin and the introduction of improved varieties of cotton had given slavery a new importance in the South, where proposals for gradual abolition had been popular a few years earlier. Meanwhile the disappearance of slavery in the North had made the "peculiar institution" a sectional issue. The admission of Illinois in 1818 meant that the Union now had eleven free and ten slave states. When Alabama was admitted the following year, the balance of slave and free power in the Senate again became even. While both North and South were uneasy over this precarious division on the slavery question, the Southerners were especially nervous. For the protection of their economic system, which they now regarded as being divinely ordained while northern abolitionists viewed it as the work of the Devil, the Southerners felt the need, if not for a majority in the national government, at least for assurance that no such majority would fall to the North.

Into this situation stepped one of the most remarkable young men who has ever figured in American history—James Long. Born in Virginia and reared in Tennessee, he had won in boyhood the friendly regard of his neighbor, Andrew Jackson. Before he was twenty, he had met the simple requirements of that day for affixing to his name the title of "Doctor of Medicine", and he served honorably as an Army surgeon at the Battle of New Orleans. Soon afterward he met and married a fourteen-year-old schoolgirl, Jane Wilkinson of Natchez, a niece of the doughty General. The wedding, with the permission of her guardian-uncle, took place on May 4, 1815. The young doctor then resigned his commission and resumed his private medical practice. He soon grew restless, decided to become a planter, and accordingly bought a plantation on the site of the future city of Vicksburg, but it was not long before he sold out at a good profit to a clerical land speculator, the Rev. Newell Vick. Back in Natchez, Long engaged in store-keeping for two years. When he learned that the Rev. Mr. Vick was laying out his old plantation in building lots, Dr. Long became infected with the fever of real-estate speculation and, since he had forfeited his chance at Vicksburg, he turned his eyes toward the West.

What more admirable operation could the young doctor perform than, at one stroke, to add a new slave state to the Southern constellation and simultaneously enrich himself and his friends with large slices of the fertile soil of Texas—to say nothing of liberating the downtrodden white people of that Province from their Spanish oppressors?

Long was not alone in his dreams. Natchez was a center of agitation against the Florida treaty. A group of well-known border conspirators, including Gutiérrez, Sibley, Child and Samuel Davenport, met and voted Long a "general" after General John Adair of the U.S. Army had rejected their offer. The sum of $500,000 cash was pledged for an expedition, and every man who would join the party was promised a square league (4,428.4 acres) of Texas real estate.

This expedition, for a change, did not receive the blessing of the American government or its agents. But Long escaped a party sent to arrest him and arrived at Nacogdoches on June 21, 1819, after several advance parties, including one led by a printer, Eli Harris, with his press, had gone on ahead. It was claimed, probably with exaggeration, that Long's force consisted of six hundred Americans and Mexicans, together with a large following of friendly Indians. On the very day of Long's arrival, a temporary government was established, ostensibly by the citizens of Nacogdoches themselves. Long was elected President of the Supreme Council. Two days later, Texas was declared an independent republic. The declaration closely followed the outlines of the American document of 1776.

Under the powers which the supreme council, in adopting the declaration, had conferred on itself, one of its first official acts was to provide for the sale of the most desirable lands in the new Republic at not less than $1 an acre, of which half was to be paid in cash and the remainder in easy installments. The council also decreed that "each private who enters the service before the first of October shall receive ten sections of land as soon as the government is settled."

Two men later to be famous in the Texas Revolution of 1836 first came to public notice as members of Long's government. These were James Bowie, who had already had a chequered career as a gambler, slave-trader and knife-fighter, and who was to meet death in 1836 as co-commander of the force defending the Alamo, and Benjamin Rush Milam, who was killed at the outset of the revolt in 1835 when he led the insurgents into battle with the yell, "Who'll go with Old Ben Milam into San Antonio?"

Whatever may have been Long's merits as a physician and a statesman, he was certainly no military strategist. No sooner had he established himself at Nacogdoches than he scattered his forces, sending four officers with small detachments to four widely separated places. He also betrayed the weakness of his position by writing a letter to Jean Laffite at Galveston, proposing an alliance and offering Laffite letters of marque to cruise under the flag of the new Republic of Texas.

Laffite sent a guarded reply which shows that, while he was not prepared to accept Long's offer, he was willing to keep the Nacogdoches Republic as an ace in the hole for use if anything should happen to break up his friendship with the Spanish monarchy. His own "government" at Galveston seems to have been in abeyance at this time. In his reply to Long he called attention to the failure of previous filibustering expeditions; he declared that "the spirit of liberty is sprouting under my cultivation," and he expressed the hope that the flag which Long had raised in Texas was "the same already existing," by which he meant the flag of the Republic of Mexico. While professing inability to help Long, he politely declared, "However, I shall do everything for you that lies within my power." He concluded with a carefully worded request for detailed information concerning the resources of the Long expedition—information which could very well be sent on to the Spaniards.

When Pierre Laffite heard of this correspondence, he ordered his brother to co-operate with Long. So, on October 9, Galveston became the port of Long's Republic of Texas and Jean Laffite was appointed its governor. Within a few weeks he had flamboyantly used this authority to warn off the U.S. Navy Schooner *Lynx,* which had trespassed upon the coast of the Republic in search of smugglers. Meanwhile Pierre, in his capacity as secret agent, signing himself "No. 19," was sending reports to the Spanish captain general in Havana, advising his excellency that "it would be well to dispose of those gentlemen [Long and his friends] in one way or another." He added, "I foresee the most woeful consequences if they take possession, since it is evident that they are the instruments of a government which seeks means of territorial expansion and is setting them to work as pioneers." Because of just such suspicions, the Spanish government had delayed its ratification of the Florida treaty. Laffite concluded his letter by proposing that a small Spanish fleet be sent to take Galveston, which he promised to deliver at a prearranged signal.

Meanwhile five hundred Spanish troops were massing at San Antonio to repel Long's invasion. Colonel Ignacio Perez led this little army out of the capital on September 27. Indians friendly to Long impeded the Spaniards' progress by setting fire to the prairies, but did not venture to attack. After capturing several small parties of Americans in the open country and killing Long's brother, David, Perez took Nacogdoches on October 28, just after Long and his men had beat a retreat that was compared to a marathon race. In the next month Perez completed the work of "pacification" by burning down some twenty ranch huts and driving away their American occupants.

But the physician-general was not ready to give up, although he underwent, after the flight from Nacogdoches, a period of the utmost hardship which was shared by his young wife and the child who had been born two weeks after he started his expedition. Leaving her two older children with a friend, Jane Long—still a girl in years—had insisted on joining her husband in Texas soon after the youngest was born, and the mother and child spent a hard, lonely winter on the beach at Galveston while Dr. Long sought for aid in the States. The wife again went with her husband on his second sortie into Texas. Just how this expedition was financed at the start is a mystery, for Long had failed in many attempts to obtain money in Louisiana, and at one point he was trading wild venison to Laffite in exchange for powder and ball.

The Laffites' star was setting in the spring of 1820. While they had managed to curry favor with the Spanish consul in New Orleans and the Captain General in Cuba, the viceroy of Mexico had never trusted them. Finally, the Spanish officials refused to have any further dealings with the Laffites. At the same time an American naval brig, the *Enterprize,* arrived with an unequivocal demand that the Laffites evacuate their pirate port of Galveston. When Long arrived there on April 6, he found Jean Laffite preparing to leave. On May 7, Jean sailed away to less profitable fields of endeavor in Yucatan, where it is believed that he eventually died. Pierre, who had stayed in New Orleans all this time to attend to the disposal of the loot, continued to live there for many years in such obscurity that the very date of his death is unknown.

While the Laffites loaded their ships, Long set up his new headquarters at Bolivar Point, across the channel from Galveston Island, where some of his troops had preceded him. But when he called his men to assemble, hardly anyone answered. Leaving one W. W. Walker "in charge," Long returned to New Orleans, where General Humbert and others were attempting to rally support for the new invasion. With considerable difficulty, Long picked up a handful of recruits and obtained money from several prominent citizens. Back at Bolivar Point, on June 4, Long reconvened his Supreme Council, which elected General E. W. Ripley, one of the financial angels, as president of the Republic of Texas, although Ripley never left New Orleans. During the summer the Supreme Council with its less than a hundred soldiers fought off the cannibalistic Karankawa Indians while it attempted to build up its forces for an attack on the royal stronghold of La Bahía.

Nothing decisive happened for more than a year. A fort was built and named "Las Casas." Ripley and Long agreed that one José Félix Trespalacios, a revolutionary schemer from Chihuahua, would be given command of the Republican Army if he could obtain the endorsement of the almost invisible revolutionary government in the interior of Mexico. He did, and was given command. Treasury notes, backed only by the credit of the so-called Republic, were issued to pay the soldiers. Gutiérrez was made vice-president of the Supreme Council, so that the government took on an increasingly Mexican character. Many of the men deserted or became insubordinate when they found the treasury notes worthless. Governor Martínez held the expedition in such contempt that he would not even move against it. In August, 1821, six months late, Long learned that Agustín de Iturbide, a former hatchet-man of the reaction in northern Mexico, had gone over to the Revolution and joined hands with the old revolutionary leader, Guerrero. Under the Plan of Iguala, which Iturbide presented, Mexico was promised an independent monarchy, with the Catholic Church to retain its privileges, and creoles to be granted equality with Spaniards.

Long and his Supreme Council did not much like the Plan, but they decided to go along with it—unless there were truth in the rumor that

228

Iturbide had been captured. Long's expedition, which had started with grandiose plans for creating an empire and eventually righting the balance of power between slave and free states in the American Union, had become a mere annex to the Mexican political revolution. On August 20, Trespalacios and Milam set sail for Vera Cruz, hoping to get in touch with the insurgents or obtain reliable information.

Soon, having learned that Iturbide was marching at the head of a large revolutionary army, Long decided the time was ripe to attack La Bahía. On September 19 he set sail down the coast with three vessels and fifty-two men, almost the whole of his army. They took the rock-walled presidio on the hill without trouble, since the commander had neglected to post sentries. Flushed with the easy victory, Long wrote to Governor Martínez that he was willing to discuss a settlement. Instead of accepting, the governor sent Colonel Perez to demand Long's surrender. Although Long did not know it, the entire Province of Texas had sworn allegiance to the revolution three months before. But the governor did not regard Long as a reliable supporter of the cause.

After a day during which a few bullets spattered harmlessly on the walls of the fort, General Long raised the white flag and surrendered. The captives were taken to Mexico City, where Long was paroled. But on April 8, 1822, when Long was still only 27 years of age, he was shot to death by a Mexican soldier in the capital. We do not know, and probably will never know, whether the fellow was acting under orders or pursuing some personal grievance.

In 1820, as the Spanish regime in the Western Hemisphere drew toward its close, the Province of Texas was in a melancholy state. In the whole Province, larger than Spain itself, there were only two settlements—San Antonio and La Bahía—and their combined population was only 2,516 persons. Nacogdoches, recently a flourishing town of nearly 1,000 souls, had been wholly abandoned as a result of the civil wars and the depredations of bandits who flourished in the restless state of the country. Isolated families were scattered on ranches along the Sabine and Red Rivers, and a few of the Spaniards from San Antonio who had established themselves as cattle-raisers between San Antonio and La Bahía may have remained in possession. The missions of San Antonio were almost in ruins, while the two missions at La Bahía, though still kept up physically, had little influence with the Indians. The garrisons at these two places, unable to obtain supplies, lived by thieving from the citizens. Smuggling went on unchecked.

Into this gloomy scene there now entered a man whose coming was undoubtedly the most important single event in the history of Texas. Moses Austin was a fairly typical Yankee business man, born in Durham, Connecticut, and 59 years old in 1820. Early in life he had engaged in business in Philadelphia and Richmond. By 1796, having become interested in lead mining, he moved to Spanish territory at Ste. Genevieve, Missouri, where rich and almost untapped veins of ore lay within three feet of the surface. For many years he prospered, but after the War of 1812, for reasons which have not been fully explained, his prosperity declined, and in late middle life he found himself almost destitute and in need of new adventures to recoup his fortune. Like others in a similar situation, but with a good New Englander's interest in sound business enterprise rather than armed invasion, Austin now turned his eyes toward Texas.

Riding an old gray horse and accompanied only by one Negro slave, Richmond, on a mule, Moses Austin rode from Little Rock to Natchitoches and there picked up the *Camino Real* into Texas. At Natchitoches two white men joined him—probably dissident members of the Long expedition. From his son, Stephen, the aging Austin had borrowed the Negro, the horse and mule, and $50 in cash for his great adventure.

Before he was allowed to see Governor Martínez, Austin had to submit to a thorough and unfriendly examination by lesser officials at San Antonio. In answering their questions, he subtracted six years from his real age, saying that he was 53. He declared that he was a Catholic, which was at least technically true, since baptism had been requisite to his admission to Spanish territory in Missouri. He flourished his passport of 1796 to prove that he was a Spanish subject, and he declared that the new liberal policies of the Spanish government, of which he had heard, had impelled him to ask permission to settle 300 families of former Spanish subjects from Louisiana in the territory of Texas, fulfilling his Catholic Majesty's desire that his loyal subjects be permitted to settle anywhere in the royal dominions.

But the governor, refusing even to examine Austin's papers, ordered him to leave San Antonio post-haste and to get out of the province as soon as he could reach the border. Austin, his head bent in dejection, walked across Military Plaza to his lodgings. Then occurred one of those accidents that sometimes change the timing of history and the details of its pattern even if they do not alter the larger outline. In the middle of the dusty plaza, where pigs and chickens ran at large, Austin met the Baron de Bastrop, whom he had once known in Louisiana but had not seen or heard of in years. Bastrop, once the holder of a million acres of Louisiana timberland and an associate of Wilkinson and Burr in their grandiose schemes, was now as penniless as Austin, but he retained considerable influence with the Spanish officials, and especially with Governor Martínez. The two old friends embraced, and when Bastrop heard Austin's story, he hastened to intervene with the governor. Martínez soon granted Austin a second interview, consulted the town council, deliberated for three days, and then agreed to forward Austin's petition to the commandant general of the Eastern Interior Provinces, Joaquín de Arredondo, with a favorable recommendation.

What probably tipped the balance was that Austin was able, with Bastrop's aid, to convince the governor that he, Austin, had no connection with Dr. Long and his filibustering expedition. Austin took pains, in fact, to inform the governor regarding the present status of that expedition. He told the governor that Long, abandoned by all but twenty or thirty of his men, was in a desperate position. Austin's two companions, Jacob Forsyth and Jacob Kirkham, who had been longer in Texas, were able to add more information, together with the opinion that American sentiment was opposed to Long's filibustering attempt. Martínez promptly sent this information to the commandant general and the viceroy.

Like his namesake in Exodus, Moses Austin died before he could enter the Promised Land with his colonists. It fell to his son, Stephen, to complete the work he had begun. Before the Austin colony could be established, Spanish power in North America had been driven out forever by the revolution of Iturbide, and the history of Spanish Texas was at an end. What comes after Austin is another story—fifteen years of Mexican rule, ten years of the Texas Republic, and now more than a century of development under statehood. Yet through all the growth, the influences planted in the social soil by three hundred years of Spanish overlordship have necessarily continued to blend their color and flavor with the dominantly Anglo-American civilization of present-day Texas.

19

Texas' Heritage of Spanish Law

Now that we have surveyed three centuries of Spanish development in Texas, with more than a century of actual settlement under Spanish laws and institutions, it should not be surprising to find that the revolt of Texas in 1836 and many later eventualities in the Republic and State to the present day came about largely as a result of these laws and institutions. This fact, though largely unappreciated, should become clear as a result of the evidence embodied in this chapter and the next.

First consider the political character of the American settlers in Texas. Although legitimate immigrants from the United States did not come in large numbers until Austin had received and advertised his empresario grant in 1821, there were a few who came in as early as the last years of the 18th Century, and many more between 1803 and 1820. In giving their reasons to the Spanish authorities for wishing to settle in the king's dominion, these immigrants usually expressed dissatisfaction with the government and policies of the United States. One Daniel Boone, for example, said to be a nephew of the famous Kentucky frontiersman, told the Spaniards that the government of the United States did not "suit" him. Such protestations, though they must be taken with a grain of salt, also contained a modicum of truth. Certainly these people must have been dissatisfied with *something* in the United States, or they would never have taken the trouble to migrate to Texas and establish new homes under a radically different form of government.

As early as 1806 Moses Austin, then living in Missouri, reported to a friend in the East that widespread dissatisfaction had been stirred by the United States government's refusal to recognize many land grants made by Spanish authorities shortly before the cession of Louisiana. These complaints, Austin said, were aggravated by the arbitrary rules established by General Wilkinson, then military governor of the territory, relative to the surveying of claims.

Of the colonists who moved into Texas after 1821, about three fourths came from the states west of the Alleghenies and south of the Ohio and Missouri Rivers, including the State of Missouri. The inhabitants of this region were Andrew Jackson's people, the people from whom Old Hickory sprung and from whose midst he eventually catapulted himself into the White House, where he brought about a revolution in American politics. Many of these people, by the way, were Scotch-Irish, "the contentious Calvinistic advocates of liberty," as Frederick Jackson Turner called them.

The region from which the Texas colonists came was in the later stages of developing from a frontier to a fully settled region. Vast tracts of Indian country separated the areas of white settlement, and while a Virginia-style plantation might adorn the banks of a river, pioneer cabins were still abuilding at the forks of the creek in the hills not far away. According to Turner, "The simplicity of life in this region and these years, together with the vast extent of unoccupied land and unexploited resources, made it easy for this up-country democrat to conceive of equality and competitive individualism as consistent elements of democracy." The pioneer society, Turner points out, has seemed to its socialist critics no so much a democracy as a society of "expectant capitalists." It was based upon the idea of the fair chance for all [white] men, not on the conception of leveling by arbitrary methods and especially by law."

Turner adds on a later page, "The section's Western quality is illustrated by the varied origin and aggressive temper of its public men. The youth of the section; its bold, ardent, adventurous, imperialistic qualities: its will-power, sometimes domineering and usually exhibiting the demand for direct action; the common feeling in the Lower South against any restraints upon the right of the slave-holder to participate on equal terms in the opening of new territories. . . . The spirit of the Western half of the South was that of the Eastern half, but infused with the greater recklessness, initiative, energy and will-power of the West, and more suffused with feeling."

As if in anticipation of these descriptive remarks by the historian, Stephen F. Austin wrote in 1834: "There has been too much of the ardent, impatient and inflamatory [sic] impetuosity of passion in the last three years in Texas. The people of the U.S. are ardent in everything, it is their national character, and what has raised that country to the unparaleled [sic] prosperity it enjoys, and Americans carry the same ardor and enterprise and love of freedom wherever they go." Austin was evidently judging "the people of the U.S." by those he knew best; that is, the people of the western South, whom Turner later described in almost the same words.

It is now too much of a commonplace to need argument that the democracy of early Americans received its earliest and most energetic development on the frontier, remembering that the Atlantic Coast was the frontier when the first colonists landed from England. As conditions became more settled, economic and social stratification reestablished themselves. In the United States generally, the half century following the Declaration of Independence was a period of political struggle between the Federalists, who believed with Alexander Hamilton that government rightfully belongs to the "rich and well born," and the followers of Jefferson, eventually to become the Democratic party, who favored a more broadly based rule of the people. The Democrats predominated in the West, where, as Arthur M. Schlesinger, Jr., says, "orthodox federalism had never discovered a social basis." Schlesinger adds that radicalism in the West was mainly an unconscious process, and there is plenty of evidence that the backwoodsmen assimilated more democracy than they knew. They were deficient in ideology, but the dominant ideas of the time trickled down to them through the stump, the press and the pulpit, sometimes with a rapidity that seems surprising for those days of slow communications. The sources of these ideas lay, first, in political traditions stretching back to the Revolution and before; and, second, in a group of radical writers and speakers who flowered in the Jackson administration in much the same way that similar thinkers, not necessarily approved by the Administration, burst into bloom during the days of the New Deal a century later.

One of the predecessors of Jackson's "kitchen cabinet" of intellectuals was John Taylor, who played an important part in developing the sometimes naive early ideas of Jefferson to a point where they corresponded to the realities of a society that was growing more and more industrial. "Wealth, like suffrage," said Taylor, "must be considerably distributed, to sustain a democratick republick; and, hence, whatever draws a considerable portion of either into a few hands, will destroy it. As power follows wealth, the majority must have wealth or lose power." Taylor then went on to argue in favor of measures to prevent the privileged orders from preying on the people.

In the hard times that followed the panic of 1819, the new mood of radicalism, as it will do at such times, turned its attention to various subjects. Opposition to slavery was one such, although, for reasons unnecessary to discuss, it was mainly confined to the North and was never very popular even there. Much the same can be said of socialism, which appeared in a pre-Marxian and idealistic form at this time. Among more moderate proposals, revision of the old common law through statutory action was a live issue in the United States during the period when Texas was being settled. So was the influence of the clergy in government, which was as widely deplored as it was hotly defended. Imprisonment for debt, still practiced in most of the states in the 1820's, was another target of the reformers. The right to vote, meanwhile, was only gradually being extended to propertyless men.

To its opponents, according to Schlesinger, "The common law seemed an infinite mass of judicial precedents which would always result practically in 'judge-made' law; and it is true that in the hands of judges like Peter Oxenbridge Thacher the common law became a bottomless reservoir of reasons why no one should do anything. The democratic movement to revise and codify the laws thus produced another heated battle line."

The anticlerical movement, though it dated back at least to the Constitution with its ban on an established church, became especially active in the 1820's as a reaction to an attempt by the General Union for Promoting the Observance of the Christian Sabbath to have the federal government prohibit the delivery of mail on Sunday. The editor of a fanatically anti-clerical semi-monthly charged that there existed "among the leaders of a proud and aspiring priesthood, a determination to establish an Ecclesiastical Hierarchy, and to reduce us to worse than Egyptian bondage."

The flow of petitions for a ban on Sunday mail deliveries was routed to a Senate committee headed by Colonel Richard M. Johnson, which answered them with a thundering statement in favor of "religious liberty." A House report along similar lines became so popular that it was printed on satin, framed, and hung in front parlors, barrooms and stage offices across the

235

nation. Johnson, who had been a leader in proposing a law to expunge imprisonment for debt from the federal statute-books, now had also become a champion of religious liberty. He was elected vice-president, (1837-1841).

Meanwhile the settlers in what was then called the Southwest had special problems of their own. For one thing, the expansion of the cotton-growing industry in the South was not a blessing to everyone in that region. According to H. Hale Bellot, summarizing the recent research in this field, "The increased demand for cotton, consequent first upon the growth of the English cotton industry and then upon that of New England, coupled with the introduction of the cotton gin making profitable the growth of the short-staple variety of cotton that alone could be produced on the uplands, led to rapid extension of the cotton area and the extrusion of small farmers by the planters." For those forced out of their former holdings, there were not too many places to go, for, although the public land was immense, its distribution was tied up in a huge complex of national policy. The South, or the more influential representatives of the South, opposed a liberal land policy because their own westward expansion was cut off by Texas and the Indian country of Oklahoma, so that the available lands were most likely to be settled by a majority of non-slaveholding farmers from the North, eventually creating more free states to upset the balance of power in Congress. Capital in the North, on the other hand, opposed free land because it might lead to a labor shortage and higher wages in the northeastern industrial centers.

The general discontent which followed the Panic of 1819 was heightened by a feeling that the panic, followed by widespread hardship, had been brought about by contraction on the part of that great private monopoly, the Bank of the United States, as well as by the action of the government itself in requiring that public lands sold to settlers must be paid for in full cash, even though the basic price was at the same time lowered from $2 an acre to $1.25 an acre. This price, though it seems trifling now, presented real difficulties to the prospective settler who not only had to pay for his land but also had to find money with which to purchase equipment, transport his family to the frontier, and maintain himself for a year or so until the first produce could be marketed. According to Schlesinger, "The new Western states [in the 1820's] felt their development hampered and thwarted by economic and political institutions too much under Eastern control."

The change in the law was mainly responsible for a decline in government land sales from five million acres in 1819 to three quarters of a million acres in 1821. By 1825, the *Missouri Advocate* could angrily declare that the emigration to Texas was due to the difference between "a republic which gives first-class land gratis and a republic which will not sell inferior land for what it is worth." Not until 1862 did the United States government give land free for the asking, and by that time the frontier had receded so far into the regions of little rainfall that it was increasingly difficult for settlers to make a living.

One clue to the reason why the Texas colonists failed to see the inevitability, which now seems obvious, of their eventual absorption into the United States, may be found in a letter which Austin wrote in 1830: "If that [the United States] govt should get hold of us and introduce its land system, etc., etc., thousands who are now on the move and who have not yet secured their titles, would be totally ruined. The greatest misfortune that could befall Texas at this moment would be a sudden change by which many of the emigrants would be thrown on the liberality of the United States of the north—*theirs would be a forlorn hope."*

So the land policy of the United States loomed as a barrier far more formidable than the Sabine River between the Texans and their motherland. The eventual solution of this problem, arrived at by Texas against its will when it retained the disposition of its own public lands in the agreement of annexation, was foreshadowed in some of the events in the United States in 1827 and 1828. In December of the latter year, Governor Ninian Edwards of Illinois presented to his legislature the claim that the public lands within a state were the property of the state rather than of the federal government, and that they should, therefore, be ceded to the state. Duff Green, who was then promoting John C. Calhoun's candidacy for the presidency, commended Edwards on his attitude. "Your position in relation to the public lands," Green wrote, "brings you into company with the South and West and in direct conflict with the East."

The rush for free land in Texas began as soon as Austin's modestly worded announcements appeared in the newspapers of the United States. Americans who were already supplied with unencumbered lands, however, were not generally attracted to the new frontier. The principle at work here had been noted long ago by Hector St. John Crevecoeur, who wrote in 1759, "The rich stay in Europe; it is only the middling and poor that emigrate." Austin similarly wrote in 1828, "The majority of the immigrants to Texas owe debts in the country from which they came, having immigrated with the hope of being able, with time and industry, to accumulate sufficient capital to pay their debts." Both Moses and Stephen Austin, themselves, had failed in business.

Mary Austin Holley, Stephen Austin's sister and a sympathetic observer of the Texas scene at the time of the Revolution, wrote in her book, "Though there are a few who may be styled *nabobs,* as far as wealth is concerned, and others who are worthless and wretches; yet, as a general remark, there are no poor people here, and none rich; that is, none who have much money. The poor and the rich, to use the correlatives where distinction there is none, get the same quantity of land on arrival; and if they do not continue equal, it is for want of good management on the one part, or superior industry and sagacity on the other." This sweet expression of early 19th century liberalism may be partially discounted on the ground that Mrs. Holley was writing to attract settlers, but the evidence for the relative poverty of the Texas colonists, as compared with those who remained in the United States, is so ample that it could be marshalled to the extent of tedium. Even the "nabobs," those who had many slaves, were said to owe large debts at home.

By 1824, Austin began a movement for the relief of Texas colonists who were threatened with suits over debts that they owed before migration. Traditionally, the laws of Spain and Mexico had been far more favorable to debtors than were the laws of either the United States or England. As late as 1830 it was said that five-sixths of the inhabitants of jails in New England had been placed there for debt, although most of them owed less than $20. The first bill to abolish imprisonment for debt was introduced by Martin Van Buren in the New York legislature in 1817, but the process was not expunged from federal law until 1832 or from that of most of the states until 1842.

In Spain as early as 1476, before the discovery of America, a decree of Ferdinand and Isabella forbade the seizure of oxen, other work animals, or tools belonging to farm laborers, except for debts due the king, overlord or owner of the land. A century later the exemption was extended to the cultivated land occupied by the tenant, excepting crown dues, rent to the landlord, or advances made by the landlord to produce the crop. Plough animals were totally exempt from seizure in every case. Similar protection was extended to the tools of urban workmen by new laws in 1683 and 1786. It does not appear that there was any special legislation to prevent these laws from being applicable to the dominions of the king in the Americas.

Austin, having heard of the old Spanish law, proposed in 1824 that the Mexican congress extend similar protection to the Texas colonists. He wrote, "They will however be able by Cultivating Cotton to pay all their debts if time is given them, but if their land and property can be taken for these debts it will ruin them and be of more injury to the improvement of this Country than any thing that could happen."

Austin did not immediately press the point, for as head of the local government in his colony he had, in effect, the power to prevent suits for the collection of debts. Four years later, however, he advocated specifically a law forbidding the forcible collection of foreign debts in the colonies of Texas until 1840, and providing only for the collection of the principal after that date. The prevalence of such debts is indicated by the fact that notes executed by the Texas colonists before their migration were a popular item of merchandise among speculators.

Austin's views met no resistance, but rather general approval, and the law he desired was passed by the legislature of Coahuila and Texas in January, 1829. Protecting lands, farming implements and tools used in a trade, it was more favorable to the debtor than Austin had requested, according to Barker, because in practice the vague provision that payment could only be exacted "in a manner not to affect their attention to their families, to the husbandry or art they possess" would probably have outlawed the debt altogether. The essentials of this homestead exemption law, proposed by Austin and based on a decree of Ferdinand and Isabella, were continued in effect under the Constitution of the Republic of Texas and were superseded on February 5, 1840, by an act of Lamar's administration. The principle is still bodied forth in the Constitution of 1876 and in statutes now in effect and has been adopted by the legislatures of many other states. Texas has gone even farther in the same direction with a law which prohibits the garnishment of wages.

Austin even played with the idea of carrying exemption of property from execution for debt to its logical extreme. He wrote to Edward Livingston in 1832, "By changing the old laws so as to base the credit system up on moral character alone, and not upon wealth and coersive [sic] means— or, in other words, to place the whole credit system upon good faith, and annul all laws (avoiding unjust retroactive effects) for the coersive collection of debts, all landed and personal securities, all imprisonment or process against the person or property for debts." Such a change in the laws would have been revolutionary indeed. Doubtless, upon further reflection, Austin must have become convinced that the proper evaluation of "moral character alone" was a task beyond human power.

Of even more general and positive importance than the protection of debtors, however, was the Spanish-Mexican policy of alloting land in generous quantities for settlement. As compared with the policy in the

United States at any time either in the British colonial or the American national period, the Spanish-Mexican policy was more generous, more consistent, wiser and more realistic. In contrast to the confused policies of the British colonial administration, it was generally true under the Spanish Laws of the Indies that, although the policy varied to some extent from time to time and place to place, land was ordinarily granted direct to the ultimate user by the Sovereign, who owed his title to the highest theological sanctions. Certainly this was true of Texas from the first formal civilian settlement in 1731 to the end of the Spanish regime, and the policy was continued in its essentials by the Mexican government. Under the realistic policy developed during centuries of experience in the semi-arid regions of Mexico, and in sharp contrast to the practice of the United States then and later, the Texas colonists were given land in sufficient amounts to carry on profitable farming or ranching under conditions of low rainfall, the only cost being a nominal tax, deferred for six years, and a service charge of twelve and a half cents an acre, well earned by the empresario for his services as a co-ordinator. The first settlers were each granted "a league and a labor of land," the league amounting to 4,428.4 acres and the labor to 177.14 acres. In a typical instance, the smaller acreage would be well watered, or accessible to irrigation, and suitable for more intensive farming, while the league might be fit only for a cattle ranch.

Spanish and Mexican land grants are the basis of title to 26,280,000 acres of Texas real estate, amounting to approximately one-seventh of the state's land area, and having a probable sale value of several billion dollars, since it includes, in addition to various farm and ranch lands, valuable oil properties, the entire extent of the fertile, irrigated lower Rio Grande Valley, and the entire city of San Antonio as well as other flourishing urban communities. The Spanish royal grants, alone, are estimated at ten million acres.

Titles in these lands are supported by laws reaching back in a direct chain of legal tradition to the ancient Romans. The Roman laws were codified in the Sixth Century in the *Corpus Juris Civilis* (also called the *Codes and Pandects*) of the Emperor Justinian. This *Corpus Juris* was the principal basis of *Las Siete Partidas,* the codification of Spanish law which was accomplished under Alfonso XI, in the 13th Century. This code remained the fundamental law of Spain and the Spanish empire until late in the 19th Century, being supplemented by various decrees of the successive monarchs. The decrees which had special application to the overseas colonies were collected under the general title of *The Laws of the Indies.*

240

Land grants made under these laws generally included the following elements: (1) Title was dependent upon the performance of certain conditions, which usually included use and occupancy for a term of years. (2) Mineral rights were theoretically retained by the king, but in practice the landowners were encouraged to take out gold, silver and other minerals on payment of the "royal fifth." (3) The grantee received full rights to the use of water adjoining or running through his property, often including the right to use water for irrigation to a "reasonable" extent. Even if a piece of property were not contiguous to water, the landowner might command water rights if he had a legal means of access, as by an easement for an irrigation ditch.

The Spanish law remained in effect with no fundamental changes after the revolution of 1821, although the grants were now made by the Mexican states rather than by the central government. The greater part of the area of Texas was now under the jurisdiction of the combined state of Coahuila and Texas, but the region between the Nueces and the Rio Grande belonged to the state of Tamaulipas, successor to the Spanish province of Nuevo Santander.

Colonization laws, adopted by the Mexican nation and the states, established liberal provisions for populating the vast emptiness of Texas. Henderson Yoakum, with a prejudice that is typical of his time, remarks that the Mexicans regarded the land as "without value," hence were willing enough to give it away. But of course, as was pointed out by so early a social philosopher as John Locke, the father of liberalism—"What would a man value ten thousand or a hundred thousand acres of excellent land ready cultivated, and well stocked with cattle, in the middle of the inland parts of America, where he had no hopes of commerce with other parts of the world, to draw money to him by the sale of his product?" It was Locke, also, who pointed out that labor gives value to land—"Nay, the extent of ground is of so little value without labor that I have heard it affirmed that in Spain itself a man may be permitted to plant, sow and reap, without being disturbed, upon land he has no other title to, but only his making use of it." If this custom prevailed in Spain when Locke wrote, about 1690, we may safely assume that it was a practice of immemorial age, which gave the most respectable ancestry to the Spanish-Mexican land policy in Texas. At any rate the Mexicans can hardly be convicted of unwisdom in liberally giving away land which, by that very fact, would eventually become valuable. Austin recognized this when, though with an undertone of pardonable bias, he said at the height of the Revolution in 1836: "The Mexican government have at last discovered that the enterprising people who were induced to move to Texas by certain

241

promises and guarantees, have by their labors given value to Texas and its lands." The Mexicans had also read Locke, however, and there is no reason to believe that their land policy was a piece of inadvertence. Even without Locke, the old Spanish tradition for bringing in *pobladores* would have been enough to account for the policy.

Yoakum illustrates the Spanish procedure in issuing land titles by reference to a typical grant issued to one Luis de la Bega in 1792. The lieutenant governor at that time had announced that he would donate lands to all who had not received them. De la Bega then presented his petition, praying title to a place called *Las Castañas* where he had a herd of mules. The lieutenant governor passed the petition to the *procurador,* who took the grantee ceremonially by the hand, led him to the desired property and granted him possession in due written legal form. The three papers—petition, order and act of possession—constituted De la Bega's title. They were filed in the archives, but the owner could have a certified copy. In another case, the *procurador* stated in his possessory act that he led the grantee by hand to the property, and at each corner of the land, "as a sign of possession, he drove stakes, pulled up weeds and threw stones."

Later, as the country around the few towns in Texas grew more crowded with grants, it became necessary to make investigations or surveys to prevent conflict before titles were issued. Later still, under the Mexican regime, while the increasing number of colonists and the extent of granted land led to the abandonment of such formalities as leading by the hand, the essentials of the Spanish system were preserved. Conditions established by the colonization law were inserted in the decree which became part of the title. Such conditions would typically include setting up permanent landmarks at the corners within one year, the cultivation of the lands, and the payment of the nominal government dues within six years. The three parts of the title were entered into a book, according to their date, and a certified copy *(testimonio)* with a map, was delivered to the colonist as his title. The originals are on file to this day in the General Land Office of the State of Texas.

The simple Spanish-Mexican system of land distribution, though it served well in both the slow-paced development of Texas before 1821 and the rapid settlement by Anglo-Americans after that date, did not, of course, work out perfectly at all times, but its imperfections in practice were due largely to personalities and to a vicious circle of mutual suspicion which grew out of language difficulties and cultural differences. Harbert Davenport, basing his opinion on long experience in the legal examination of old land titles, says that the Spanish-Mexican records can be favorably compared with those kept in the southern American states at the same period. However, it is true that many American settlers filed on land covered by older Spanish grants, either in ignorance or on the supposition that these grants had been forfeited by non-performance of the attached conditions. The informality in the method of settlement, breaking all the bounds of formal rules, contributed to confusion in this regard.

Manuel Mier y Terán, a Mexican government official, wrote in 1828, "Meanwhile the incoming stream of new settlers is increasing; the first news of them comes by discovering them on land already under cultivation, where they have been located for months; the old inhabitants set up a claim to the property, basing their titles of doubtful priority, and for which there are no records, on a law of the Spanish government; and thus arises a lawsuit on which the *alcalde* has a chance to come out with some money."

Stephen Austin's own policy, from beginning to end, was one of single-minded devotion to whatever he considered to be the best interests of his colonies. In this he was followed by all of the more cool-headed and responsible of the colonists. An unfriendly critic, reading the record too hastily, might accuse Austin of being ruled by expediency to the exclusion of all principles, but such an accusation would be unfair. All the evidence shows that Austin was thoroughly American in his political philosophy, and that he maintained the highest standard of personal honor, but that he subordinated all matters of theory to the great enterprise of building a new commonwealth in the almost empty land of Texas.

It is true that his shifts were sometimes remarkable. In November, 1822, when the Emperor Iturbide had just come into power, Austin wrote to a friend, "You must not be frightened at the name of an Imperial government, you like myself have lived under a Monarchy, when Louisiana belonged to Spain and I think we lived as happy then as under the government of the United States. The Emperor has his enemies and in the United States the Democrats will abuse him no doubt, but he is doing the best for his country. These people will not do for a Republic nothing but a Monarchy can save them from Anarchy."

It became evident later, however, that Austin's acceptance of the revolutionary emperor was based entirely on the expectation that Iturbide would provide the stable government that Austin needed for the upbuilding of a colony where the incoming Americans could stand secure on their own land. After Iturbide's fall, Austin wrote in a different tone: "The Emperor has deceived us all—I thought he would have adhered to his oath, and governed according to law—but on the contrary he has violated the one, and trampled on the other—nothing therefore is more just, and more magnanimous than the spirit of indignation and resentment which the nation have manifested and the result I hope and confidently believe will be a Confederated Republic very similar to that of the United States." From various indications which need not be detailed here, it is evident that Austin's conception of a "Confederated Republic" leaned toward a Southern concept of state's rights.

In the same letter just quoted, Austin, writing from Mexico, advised a relative in Texas that "If any questions are asked them [the colonists] as to their opinion of the Government etc. they ought to answer that they moved here to live under the government which the nation may establish they can do themselves no good by meddling in politics and at such a time as this when the government is not yet settled and the nation in a state of political fermentation it is embarking on a doubtful voyage to embrace any party—as foreigners we have a good excuse for remaining neutral without being lyable to suspicions and this is the safe course."

Security of title in the land was one of the continuing cares which Austin had to deal with as the empresario of his colony. Almost as soon as he arrived in Texas after his father's death, he had found it advisable to go to Mexico and have the elder Austin's Spanish grant confirmed by the government of Mexico, so that there would be no question as to the validity of titles, although the local Mexican officials in Texas were permitting the allotment of land under the original arrangement. During Austin's stay in Mexico the Republic gave way to the Empire, and in a few months more the Empire fell, so it was a full year before Austin could have his grant definitely confirmed. On his return he found that many of the colonists, discouraged by his long absence, had returned to the United States, and others who had planned to come to Texas had not done so. He promptly reassured the remaining settlers that their titles were now "perfect and complete for ever." In appealing to the colonists to pay him their empresario fees of twelve and a half cents an acre, which he would accept either in cash or in goods, he went into considerable detail to show that "I have spared neither labor or expence to complete these titles in a way which will render them safe for ever unless forfeited by noncompliance on the part of the settlers with the conditions required as to the Occupancy and improvement of the land."

Although Austin was not wholly convinced of the rightness of slavery, he was inclined to regard it as essential to the success of his colony. Certainly the right to hold slaves was considered by the Southern whites of that period as an inseparable part of their right to work the land without molestation. In spite of his private reservations, Austin headed a committee which addressed a petition to the Mexican government, asking that the three hundred families to be admitted to the colony should be permanently exempted from the operation of an emancipation law which had been passed. "Many of them [the colonists] brought their negro slaves with them as also all their property intending to establish themselves permanently in the Province," the petition declared.

At the same period Austin showed an especially keen interest in learning the details of certain laws of which he had not received copies. He inquired particularly with regard to the laws on settlement of estates; transfer of property between settlers; punishment of criminals, and collection of debts contracted outside of Texas. In a first draft of this letter of inquiry, Austin had also mentioned religious freedom and the possibility of appointing a *juez de letras* to hear appeals from the *alcaldes*, but both of these subjects were dropped before the letter was sent, and a marginal note in Austin's draft indicates that he decided the first subject, at least, was too hot to handle. It does not appear, in any case, that the denial of recognition to any but the Catholic Church was greatly resented by the colonists. They had all gone to Texas deliberately, in full awareness of the law, and those Protestants who felt strongly in sectarian matters had stayed at home in the States.

Austin's interest in obtaining copies of the laws, though natural to a man in his position, may have been heightened by the fact that he was being severely criticized by some of the colonists for alleged arbitrariness in allotting land, and for some of his other actions as a Mexican official. He replied to this criticism frankly and in moderate terms, as was his habit, and he added, "I approve of the principle that every public officer is amendable [sic] to the law for his official acts.—It is the only solid basis upon which free institutions can rest."

Austin himself had become temporarily a victim of the often fatal weakness of personalism in government, which Mexico inherited from Spain and has even now not outgrown. The ideal, in which he believed, was "a government not of men but of laws." But Austin himself, as an official left with too much discretion, had been compelled, willy-nilly, to use that discretion to the displeasure of some of his colonists. In the cases of officials less conscientious and less wise than Austin, this was precisely the situation that piled up a structure of insecurity for the colonists and eventually drove them to revolt.

A premonitory rumble was the so-called "Fredonian War" of

1826-1827, when a small number of American colonists—not connected with Austin—rose in revolt at Nacogdoches because of their dissatisfaction with the manner in which the authorities had settled their title disputes with earlier settlers. Whatever may have been the rights and wrongs of this dispute—and there was right and wrong on both sides—it is evident that the local Mexican authorities had acted under wide discretionary powers which left neither side any means of determining—even to the relative degree that would be possible under a more comprehensive system of law—what rights of theirs would be recognized.

Two of the leaders of the revolt wrote in a manifesto: "We were enticed from our native country under the promise of important advantage to our families, and by a guarantee of our rights and liberties. We have been basely deceived in all these promises, and we know not now, that we have a valid title to one foot of land in the province of Texas. Lands have been granted and taken away at the mere will and pleasure of a corrupt and prejudiced governor without any regard to the forms of justice or the rights of the Judicial Department of this government."

While Austin offered his militia to the Mexican government to suppress his countrymen's rebellion, the people of Dewitt's Colony adopted resolutions of loyalty, in the very first one of which they declared "That the people of this colony came to, and settled in the Mexican nation, by the benign influence of her laws; that as adopted children [they] have full confidence and faith in the equity, justice and liberality in the Federal and State governments of their parent."

Although the two statements just quoted are opposite in spirit as regards the issue of the moment when they appeared, they are firmly in agreement that the signers were brought to Texas by the expectation of being secure in the rights and liberties granted by the laws of Mexico, which for the most part were the laws of Spain as they continued in effect after the political revolution. This point hardly needs further proof after being confirmed from two such variant sources.

More trouble occurred in February of 1831, when a special land commissioner, J. Francisco Madero, reached the lower Trinity River bearing instructions from the governor to issue land titles to the settlers there and farther east, between Nacogdoches and the United States boundary at the Sabine. These people, though they had come as squatters, had made valuable improvements on the lands they occupied. Madero was prevented from carrying out his mission, however, by the violent opposition of the Mexican military commander in the region, the American-born Colonel John Davis Bradburn, who insisted that the issuance of titles would be a violation of the Act of April 6, 1830, which forbade further American immigration into Texas. Mexican officials, other than Bradburn, generally ignored the innumerable violations of this law.

In a speech at Brazoria on September 8, 1835, less than a month before the Texans sprang into an armed revolt with the limited object of establishing a separate state under the Republic of Mexico, Austin looked back with approval to the time when "Under the Spanish government, Texas was a separate and distinct local organization." The union with Coahuila, he declared, was only provisional, and was "always subject to the vested rights of Texas." He continued, "The state, therefore, cannot relinquish those vested rights, by agreeing to the change of government, or by any other act, unless expressly authorized by the people of Texas to do so; neither can the general government of Mexico legally deprive Texas of them without the consent of this people. . . . Texas needs peace, and a local government: its inhabitants are farmers, and they need a calm and quiet life."

As a legal brief, Austin's argument might easily be shot full of holes. During the Spanish regime, of course, Texas was merely a province—an administrative division with no existence as a political entity. It had never been a separate state, and even if it had been, it is doubtful whether a state can be said to have vested rights as the term is used in law, where it is applied to the existing rights of persons as against any contemplated change in the statutes. However, this utterance by Austin doubtless expressed the thoughts and feelings of the American colonists, and it helps to explain the occurrence of the term, "vested rights," in a different context in the first Constitution of the State of Texas in 1845.

20

Spanish Law in the Republic and State

Since land was virtually the only form of wealth among the colonists who began in 1835 to break away from Mexico, it is not surprising that one of the first official documents of the Revolution, the Plan of Government unanimously signed by the members of the Consultative Assembly at San Felipe de Austin on November 13, 1835, implicitly recognized the validity of Mexican and Spanish land titles and continued in effect the Mexican laws then prevailing in Texas. Soon, however, the Texans were compelled to drop their plan for a new state in the Mexican union and turn to independence as the only solution of their problems. Immediately after the Declaration of Independence, in March, 1836, the first steps toward establishing a system of law for the new Republic of Texas were taken at a constitutional convention at Washington-on-the-Brazos. The constitution here adopted was similar in its main outlines to the Constitution of the United States, insofar as the provisions of that Constitution could be made applicable to a unitary nation which did not have to deal with questions of states' rights.

248

In spite of this large omission, the Constitution of Texas was much longer and more detailed than that of the United States. It is in its miscellaneous departures from the United States pattern that we find the best clues to what was in the minds of the leaders of early Texas as they set about giving laws to the people of the Republic. No record of the debates at the convention has come down to us, but the provisions of the Constitution, as adopted, speak very well for themselves.

Article IV, Section 13, provides that "The Congress shall, as early as practicable, introduce, by statute, the common law of England, with such modifications as our circumstances, in their judgment, may require, and in all criminal cases the common law shall be the rule of decision." The Congress finally found it practicable to reduce this provision to statute nearly four years later in the Act of January 20, 1840. From the provision of that law, and from our knowledge of the importance of Spanish laws relating to land tenure, we may safely assume that the makers of the Constitution already had a pretty clear idea what modifications of the common law would be required by the conditions prevailing in Texas. This matter will be examined in more detail when we come to discuss the specific laws which were later adopted. The requirement relating that the common law be applied in criminal cases was, contrariwise, designed to avoid the defects of Mexican law on this subject, especially the denial of trial by jury, although this had recently been granted to the Texas colonists by special legislation.

A direct piece of evidence on the prevalence of American liberal ideas in Texas is provided by Article V, Section 1, which reads as follows: "Ministers of the gospel being, by their profession, dedicated to God and the care of souls, ought not to be diverted from the great duties of their functions, therefore, no minister of the gospel or priest of any denomination whatever shall be eligible to the office of the Executive of the Republic, nor to a seat of either branch of the Congress of the same."

Both from the wording of this section itself, and from the debate which occurred when a similar provision was proposed for the first State Constitution in 1845, it is evident that this ban was directed at Protestant ministers quite as much as at Catholic priests, even though the Texas colonists abhorred "priestcraft," which they associated with the arbitrary political power against which they had revolted. The colonists, however, had had practically no first-hand experience with Catholic priests. Protestant ministers also were few and inconspicuous under the repressive laws of Mexico. The fact that it occurred to the constitution-makers to insert such a provision can only be attributed to the fact that, as we have seen, anti-clerical ideas were popular in Andrew Jackson's United States.

In the Declaration of Rights which was placed at the end of the Constitution (but which was an integral part of the document and not an afterthought like the Bill of Rights added by amendment to the United States Constitution), the Texans went a step farther than the Americans in ensuring the separation of Church and State. We have already seen that clergymen were barred from Congress and the presidency of the Republic. In the Declaration of Rights, Article 3, it is further provided that "No preference shall be given by law to any religious denomination or mode of worship over another, but every person shall be permitted to worship God according to the dictates of his own conscience." This language is much more clearly restrictive than the United States provision that "Congress shall make no law respecting an establishment of religion, or prohibiting the free exercise thereof."

Manhood suffrage, which was a new thing in the United States at that time, was secured to Texas by Article VI, Section 11: "Every citizen of the Republic who has attained the age of twenty-one years, and shall have resided six months within the district or county where the election is held, shall be entitled to vote for members of the General Congress." The term "citizens," needless to say, excluded Negroes. The extension of suffrage even to all white men, regardless of property qualifications, was nevertheless an advanced proposal at the time, and had not yet penetrated to all the states of the Union. It is an odd and seldom realized fact, by the way, that the Constitution of the United States even now, while it prohibits denial of the franchise on grounds of race, color or previous condition of servitude, or because of sex, does not prohibit Congress or the state legislatures from setting up property qualifications for the vote. In fact such qualifications are still established, in Texas and elsewhere, for certain types of elections, such as those in which the voters are asked to approve a bond issue.

The transition from Spanish-Mexican law to Texan law with Spanish modifications was smoothed by the "Schedule" of the Constitution, Section 1, which provided, "That no inconvenience may arise from the adoption of this Constitution, it is declared by this convention that all laws now in force in Texas, and not inconsistent with this Constitution, shall remain in full force until declared void, repealed, altered, or expire [sic] by their own limitation." This is a direct reference to the Spanish-Mexican laws, which had hitherto been kept in force by the "Plan" of the Consultative Assembly. A similar provision was included in the first state constitution in 1845.

Section 7 of the "General Provisions" of the Constitution required that "So soon as convenience will permit, there shall be a penal code formed on principles of reformation, and not of vindictive justice, and the civil and criminal laws shall be revised, digested and arranged under different heads; and all laws relating to land titles shall be translated, revised and promulgated."

Revision of the criminal law was a gradual process, and it is to be feared that the "principles of reformation" are still a pious hope rather than a matter of practice. The most thorough revision of the criminal laws took place pursuant to an act of the legislature of February 11, 1854, and was carried out, under considerable influence from Spanish law, by a commission composed of John W. Harris, O. J. Hartley and James Willie, with the task of revising the criminal portion of law assigned mainly to Willie. The drafts proposed by the commission were adopted by the legislature in 1856.

Continuity of land titles under the new Republic was taken so much for granted by the makers of the Constitution that it was affirmed only by specifying a list of exceptions to the implied rule. The first of these exceptions occurs in Section 8 of the "General Provisions," which prescribes that "All persons who shall leave the country for the purpose of evading a participation in the present struggle, or shall refuse to participate in it, or shall give aid or assistance to the present enemy, shall forfeit all rights of citizenship and such lands as they may hold in the Republic." It is worthy of note that this phraseology includes a virtual equation between citizenship and the ownership of land. This equation is clearly stated in the next section, where it is provided that "All citizens now living in Texas, who have not received their portion of land, in like manner as colonists, shall be entitled to their land in the following proportion and manner: Every head of a family shall be entitled to one league and 'labour' of land, and every single man of the age of seventeen and upwards, shall be entitled to the third part of one league of land."

This was probably the only time in the history of the world that the ownership of land had been recognized as a right to which people are "entitled." The principle thus enunciated was a direct outgrowth of the policy followed from time immemorial by the Spaniards—a policy which had fulfilled the unsatisfield land hunger of the colonists who flowed into Texas from the United States.

Returning to the question of continuity of titles under the changed government, the validity of Spanish-Mexican grants was again given implied recognition in another portion of Section 10 of the "General Provisions," when it was said that "in all cases the actual settler and occupant of the soil shall be entitled, in locating his land, to include his improvement, in preference to all other claims not acquired previous to his settlement, according to the law of the land and this Constitution." The "law of the land," here referred to, was the law of Mexico, and of the State of Coahuila and Texas, which remained in effect.

The Constitution gives further evidence of the paramount importance of the land question in an introductory flourish at the beginning of another paragraph—"And whereas the protection of the public domain from unjust and fraudulent claims, and quieting the People in the enjoyment of their lands, is one of the great duties of this convention . . ."

The Constitution then goes on specifically to annul several large grants, said to amount to a total of 1,100 leagues, which had been given to John T. Mason and others by special acts of the legislature of Coahuila and Texas in 1834 and 1835. These acts were annulled by the Texas constitutional convention on the express ground that they were contrary to certain laws passed by the Mexican Congress in 1824. The same section of the Constitution voided all surveys, locations and titles to land made while the land offices were closed during the confusion of the Texas Revolution, when many prior holders of land, being away at the wars, were unable to prevent acts of possession by newcomers.

Imprisonment for debt, still prevalent in the United States in 1836, was kept out of Texas by Section 18 of the Declaration of Rights, which provided that "No person shall be imprisoned for debt in consequence of inability to pay." It seems probable that this section was motivated by the popularity of such ideas in the United States at the time; by the high proportion of debtors in the Texas population, and by the tradition of lenience toward debtors which had been handed down in Spanish law since Ferdinand and Isabella.

Two other liberal provisions, not found in the Constitution of the United States, are combined in Section 17 of the Texas Declaration of Rights, which reads: "Perpetuities or monopolies are contrary to the genius of a free government, and shall not be allowed; nor shall the law of primogeniture or entailments ever be in force in this Republic." All forms of entail had been abolished by the Spanish Liberal Cortes in 1820 and by the Mexican Congress in 1823. They had also been gradually abolished by the American states.

In sum, it can be said that the Constitution of the Republic of Texas, although built on a framework of traditional American ideas, contains important modifications derived from the popular advanced thinking of the Jacksonian period, on the one hand, and the Mexican tradition of Spanish law on the other. These departures, as well as the more conventional provisions, were of course made effective by acts of the Congress. Later they were generally incorporated in the Constitution and laws of the State of Texas.

While the Republic still ruled, an Act of January 20, 1840, brought about the adoption of the Anglo-American common law in all matters except those relating to land tenure ("colonization and grants of land") which were actually the most numerous and weighty questions dealt with by the courts then and for many years after. A technical analysis of the differences between Spanish and English law would be of little interest, but the Spanish system, besides being bound up to a great extent with the existing property rights of the Texans, was believed to promote justice by its simplicity in theory and practice. It was not case-law, or "judge-made law," but a concise code, which called for no wearisome study of precedents. In the words of Wooten, "The government had it in its power to establish and maintain a simple and direct method of real estate tenures, deriving their validity and incidents immediately from the sovereign political power and burdened with none of the restrictions, technicalities and legal niceties of the feudal and baronial servitudes of the common law titles to realty, instead of complicating our landed system with the black-letter learning of English courts and statutes."

The land law included the Spanish law of waters. In any event the climate of a large part of Texas would have dictated the adoption of a more realistic policy than that handed down from the English common law.

The climate also led the Texans to imitate Spanish liberality in granting tracts of land large enough to support a ranching establishment on the semi-arid plains. Under the Republic, individual or family grants ranged from 640 to 4,605 acres, the latter figure being the equivalent of the Spanish league and labor. At annexation, by the insistence of the United States Congress, Texas luckily retained the right to dispose of its own public lands instead of giving them up to the federal government for disposal under the same policies which had driven the Texans to emigrate. The later land policy of the State continued the tradition of liberality which had been established by the old Spanish government.

With regard to the titles which had their origin in Spanish and Mexican grants, there was great uneasiness in the years following separation from Mexico. In the case of McMullen v. Hodge, Justice Lipscomb explained the pertinent principles at a length and in a manner which indicated that he was writing for public reassurance as much as for the record of the case. Beginning with a discussion of the different kinds of revolutions, he concluded that the Revolution in Texas was simply a change of political control, and he stated emphatically, "This court has repeatedly held, that private rights were not destroyed by the change of government." He quoted Chief Justice Marshall, who said in a case arising in Florida after the annexation of that formerly Spanish territory, "It may be worthy of remark that it is very unusual, even in cases of conquest, for the conqueror to do more than displace the sovereign and assume dominion of the country." Marshall, in turn, had cited very early English decisions in support of his opinion that private rights could not be affected by a change of sovereignty. As late as 1859, however, Chief Justice Wheeler of Texas felt called upon to reaffirm that "There is no more firmly settled or universally approved principle of law, than that a revolution works no change in previously vested rights of property."

Aside from strictly legal considerations, the motives of the early Texas lawmakers in confirming Spanish and Mexican land titles need little discussion. As the courts have stated, the revolt that led to independence in Texas was no social revolution, and there was no reason or intention to interfere with established property relations. Moreover, the men who carried out that revolution were the ones who held most of the privately owned land in Texas. At the date of independence, in fact, almost every citizen of Texas held land under a Spanish or Mexican grant.

Even without court decisions, the continuity of these titles would appear to be sufficiently secured by a section of the first State Constitution, adopted in 1845, which became a part of the agreement of annexation between Texas and the United States. This section was copied in succeeding constitutions, including that of 1876, now in effect, where it forms Section 18 of Article XVI, as follows: "*Vested Rights.*—The rights of property and of action, which have been acquired under the Constitution and laws of the Republic and State, shall not be divested . . ."

Since the rights acquired under Spanish and Mexican land grants, and through other operations of Spanish-Mexican law, were clearly recognized by the Constitutions and laws of the Republic and State, it would seem clear that they are fully confirmed by this section of the Constitution as it now stands. And, in the wildly improbably event that Texas would wish to "divest" these rights, the United States Supreme Court could be asked to intervene on the ground that the guarantee in the Constitution of 1845, through its inclusion in the annexation agreement, has become the supreme law of the United States under Article VI of the federal Constitution.

Significantly, no attempt was made to repeal the "vested

rights" article in a statewide election on constitutional amendments on August 5, 1969, when a large number of articles believed to be obsolete or unnecessary were repealed, including all seven sections of Article XIII and Article 8 of Section XIV, which deal with possible defects in land titles derived from Spanish and Mexican grants. The basic validity of such titles was recognized when the legislature, in a Houst Joint Resolution submitting the question to the voters, added rather unaccountably, " . . . it being specifically understood that the repeal of these sections shall not in any way made any substantive change in our present Constitution."

The Attorney General of Texas, Crawford C. Martin, issued a press statement on July 23, 1969, embodying his "reluctant conclusion" that the catchall amendment should not be adopted, specifically "because of questions relating to land titles."

In a letter to the present writer after the repeal, Mr. Martin said he felt that the repealer might create some difficulties in proving title under certain circumstances, and "Others will make the contention that the adoption of Amendment No. 1 constituted an abrogation of the authority of the State to recover lands of the Public Free School Fund of the State that came to the State as a result of the invalidity of [certain] early Spanish and Mexican grants. . . ." He concluded, however, "I do now and will contend should the question be legally raised in the future that the adoption of Amendment One on August 5, 1969, had no effect on the rights of the people individually or on their rights collectively which are exercised through their sovereign State."

A new case relating to the validity of a land title originally based on a Mexican grant was being heard in the state courts in 1970, after a claimant had alleged that the original grantees had forfeited their property under a provision in the 1836 Constitution of the Republic of Texas that "All persons who shall leave the country for the purpose of evading participation in the present struggle [the Texas War of Independence], or shall refuse to participate in it, or shall give aid or assistance to the present enemy, shall forfeit all rights of citizenship, and such lands as they may hold in the Republic."

The 1970 case was filed in the District Court of San Patricio County by Walter Atchley of Dallas, the Texas Attorney General, and others, against the Superior Oil Company and 204 other defendants. The claimants contend that Felipe de la Portilla and his six sons, who received the grant in 1834, did indeed abandon their seven and a half leagues, or 33,210 acres, in 1836, and that 12,068 acres bordering the Portilla grant are "vacant," or still owned by the State, because of surveying errors. As in several other disputed cases, the acreages are rich in oil.

The recognition of Spanish and Mexican titles, as with any other titles, has always worked both ways. Where the original grant depended on conditions which were not fulfilled by the grantee, such as occupancy for a stated term of years, the Texas courts have held the title forfeited. It is just such questions over the circumstances surrounding the original grant, and not any question as to the general validity of such grants, that have led to sometimes prolonged litigation in numerous cases. In the long-fought Padre Island case, decided as recently as 1945, the Texas Supreme Count upheld the claim of the Balli heirs to an area larger than the original grant, which had been augmented by the gradual piling up of sand from the Gulf against the low, tide-washed island. The Texas attorney general thereupon appealed to the United States Supreme Court, on the ground that the local court was depriving the State of its property without due process of law, but the highest court refused his appeal. According to Harbert Davenport and J. T. Canales, "This is probably the only instance on record where a State, suing as sovereign proprietor in its own courts, has refused to abide by a decision of its own highest tribunal, or has sought, on alleged constitutional grounds, to overturn a solemn judgment of its own Supreme Court."

Another question on accretion was decided by the State Supreme Court on December 10, 1958, when it upheld the rights of a private owner, John Wesley Luttes, against the State, which sought to claim 3,365 acres of mud flats, known to be rich in oil, adjoining his ranch along Laguna Madre in Cameron County. The court upheld Luttes' title under a Mexican grant, even though the State claimed that the mud deposited there was not a natural accretion but had been formed mainly from dirt dredged up in the Intracoastal Canal about a mile offshore. The decision drew some adverse comment in the press since it led to the closing off of numerous beaches in similar situations which had been used by the public for recreation when it was regarded as State property.

Incidentally, Mr. Justice Garwood noted in the decision that "Texas courts' own interpretation of Mexican law as applied to Texas land titles is as binding on the Federal Courts in such a case as is the interpretation of any Texas land law in any matter of Texas land titles."

Another important case on Spanish and Mexican land grants, Valmont Plantations vs. State, was decided as recently as February 14, 1962, after being fought out by imposing batteries of lawyers on both sides. In making this decision the court set aside as an "obiter dictum" (a passing comment and therefore not binding) an opinion expressed by the same court in Motl vs. Boyd (1926), which many lawyers had regarded as definitive.

In the Valmont case, which had numerous subsidiary issues, the State had sued on behalf of itself and several public water districts to gain the right to divert water from the Rio Grande which hitherto had been used by Valmont for irrigation in its extensive properties adjacent to the river. The Supreme Court, adopting in its entirety an earlier decision by the Fourth Court of Civil Appeals which had overruled the District Court in Hidalgo County, held that "Spanish and Mexican grants along the Rio Grande did not have appurtenant riparian irrigation rights in the absence of specific grants of irrigation waters." Many legal experts, upheld by Motl vs. Boyd, had concluded from their study of Roman, Spanish and Mexican law, as distinguished from quite different provisions in English and American law, that the right to the "reasonable" use of water for irrigation was "appurtenant," i.e., ran with the title, to all grants of riparian land.

This case was closely involved in the complicated legal question of the status of lands situated between the Nueces and the Rio Grande, which were formerly part of the Mexican State of Tamaulipas and never belonged to the combined State of Coahuila and Texas. On December 19, 1836, the Congress of the Republic of Texas annexed this area by a legislative act which it lacked the power to enforce. The Texas claim to this region was not made good until General Taylor's American army crossed the Nueces in 1846, at the outset of the Mexican War and after Texas had become a state in the American Union. Thereafter, while both state and federal courts held that the Treaty of Guadalupe Hidalgo, which protects the property rights of Mexican nationals in the territory annexed in 1848, does not apply to lands situated in the former Republic of Texas, the State supreme court has held that the Treaty does apply to the region between the Nueces and the Rio Grande. In the words of Davenport, a lawyer possessed of practical as well as theoretical knowledge in these matters, "The one line of decisions applies to Texas as it existed, prior to 1836, as a member of the Mexican Confederation of States; the other to the area between the Nueces and the Rio Grande, to which Texas first asserted claim by the Act of December 19, 1836, which claim was not admitted by Mexico until the Treaty of Guadalupe Hidalgo of February 2, 1848. The courts of Texas disposed of this technical problem by holding: (a) that from and after December 19, 1836, Texas' claim to the trans-Nueces area was good 'de jure'; that is, as a matter of law, but that Mexico was in control of the greater portion of this area; and (b) that, as between private individuals, the acts of Mexico and of the Mexican State of

Tamaulipas were the acts of the government de facto. The same rule was applied to grants of land. The Texas courts refused to recognize grants of land made by Mexico in this area which *originated* after December 19, 1836; but where proceedings for a grant had been begun by a private individual prior to December 19, 1836, and had progressed to the point where the title would have been perfected, but for the change in sovereignty, under the laws of Tamaulipas, vested private rights had been created which, under the Treaty of Guadalupe Hidalgo, were binding upon the courts as well as upon the political authorities of the State.

It took several acts of the legislature, known as the Relinquishment Acts, to quiet the titles to land between the Nueces and the Rio Grande. Even then, "because of the unsettled condition" of the country, not all of the property owners had been able to take advantage of their rights by 1876, and the new Constitution of that date granted them an additional four years in which to validate their titles. Even then, the uncertainties of the law kept some of the Tamaulipas grants in the courts until our own time, as we have seen, and perhaps the end is not yet.

It is worthy of mention, incidentally, that Spanish units of measurement are still used in determining the metes and bounds of landed property in Texas. These units—as did measurements in all countries before our present age of standardization—exhibited some variability, the length of the basic *vara* or "Spanish yard" having been fixed at anywhere from 32.8748 inches to 35 inches. It was not until 1919 that the legislature fixed the legal length of the vara in Texas at 33-1/3 standard inches. On this basis the labor, 1,000 varas square, becomes 177.14 acres; the league, 5,000 varas square, becomes 4,428.4 acres. A knowledge of these measurements is indispensable to anyone who must deal with real estate titles in a large part of Texas today.

The principle now known as "community property" regulates the property rights of married persons in several Western states under laws derived from the Spanish code, much more favorable to women than the English common law, which inspired the statutes of most American states. The origin of the Texas law in particular is clearly stated by Chief Justice Hemphill, who declared in 1857, "Our laws on marital rights are in substance but a continuation of the rules of Spanish jurisprudence on the same subject."

Under the common law and its statutory offshoots, all property owned by a woman prior to her marriage becomes the property of her husband, as does any wealth accumulated by the couple after their marriage, the wife retaining only a dower right which usually amounts to one-third of the lands acquired after marriage. Under the Spanish and Texan law, the wife's own property is counted as her contribution to the common capital of the marriage. Property acquired after marriage, though subject to the husband's management, is owned equally by husband and wife. As recently as 1948, the existence of such laws in a minority of the states moved Congress to amend the federal income tax law so as to place the residents of all states on a community property basis for income tax purposes, thereby giving them the same advantage that taxpayers in the "community property" states had enjoyed in being able to divide their incomes when computing the tax.

In spite of the advantage to the wife in being able to claim a greater share of property than under the usual American arrangements, the Texas League of Women Voters has found fault with some of the provisions of the community property laws, which place married women in a state of virtual guardianship with regard to the management of property. Just how much these provisions owe to Spanish precedent is a subject of specialized study which cannot be explored here.

Again adapting Spanish laws of ancient respectability, the Texas legislature formulated statutes of descent and distribution which deny the right of a parent to disinherit his children for any cause except a violent attack on the parent or an attempt to defame him by imputing offenses punishable by law.

The distinction between law and equity, which had originated as a progressive step in early English law but had later degenerated into a plaything of formalism, was abolished in Texas in 1840 when the legislature approved an adaptation of the simple Spanish system of pleading cases in court. "Procedure at common law," according to Davenport, "was based on a series of technical 'writs' and 'pleas,' which lawyers moved about like chessmen in an effort to plead their cases into a single issue of law and fact. Under the common law system of pleading, the more clever lawyer, rather than right and justice, was favored to prevail." Under the Spanish system, on the other hand, the plaintiff was required only to tell his troubles to the court in plain and concise language. This simplified system, since its adoption in Texas, has been almost universally introduced in American and even English courts.

Rights to minerals on or under the ground remained vested in the State of Texas under laws which remained in effect for twenty years after annexation, although the State exacted only a five percent royalty instead of the twenty percent demanded by the King of Spain. In 1866, however, an article in the new constitution of that year, ostensibly designed to aid the owners of certain saline deposits, was so worded that it became applicable to all minerals on privately owned lands, including the vast petroleum deposits

259

which then were hardly guessed at. Curtis Bishop has estimated that this one bit of legislation, which he attributes to careless wording, cost the State of Texas a cool billion dollars. Careless or not, the new provision relinquishing the State's right to underground wealth was reaffirmed in the Constitution of 1876.

Although some of the laws formed in early Texas by adapting the principles of the *Siete Partidas* and the Laws of the Indies have been superseded in later years, all of these laws have gone into the making of a body of legal tradition which is still at work in the State. The Tidelands controversy, closely connected with Spanish law in a technical sense, and also animated on its Texas side by a spirit anachronistically resembling that of the early colonists, brought about the announcement that the Governor of Texas would not support the Democratic nominee for president of the United States in 1952.

In addition to the "vested rights" section, numerous other provisions related to Spanish law are embodied in the Constitution of 1876, which is now in effect with numerous piecemeal amendments, and which seems likely to go without serious revision for many years, in spite of the criticism leveled at its highly detailed and cumbersome character. The spirit, if not the letter, of the Spanish laws for the protection of debtors can be seen in a Constitutional ban on garnishment of wages.

What were the motives of the founders of the Republic of Texas in adopting so much of their law from the cast-off governments of Spain and Mexico? To some extent it is true that they followed the line of least resistance, in that it was simpler to take over the old laws bodily than to arrange a transition to a system adopted in its entirety from the Anglo-American tradition. However, this retention of Spanish law was certainly not unavoidable. Even where the doctrine of vested rights decreed confirmation of the acts of the former governments, the future working out of these rights could evidently have been subjected to an altogether different system of law.

It is inescapably significant that the Republic chose to make certain possible changes, and rejected others. Adoption of the Spanish-Mexican law was quite selective, as we have seen. Jury trial and freedom of religion, to cite only two examples out of many, were taken over from American law at the same time that the provisions we have described were taken from the Mexican law. A way to change over to all American laws could certainly have been found if these Spanish-Mexican laws had been repugnant to the people and their legislators. Evidently they were not repugnant but were gladly accepted, in spite of the Texans' hostile feeling toward the government which had formerly administered these laws. We have seen, too, that the inadequacies of the English common law were being recognized in the United States at the same time. So, in forming their first Constitution and the whole framework of their statutory law, the people of the Republic of Texas chose to follow Spanish-Mexican rules in many matters—especially those relating to land tenure—rather than the American laws to which they had been long accustomed before their emigration.

Their reasons for making this choice must be clear to anyone who has followed the foregoing argument. We have seen that the Americans who settled in Texas were identical in background with the people of what was then the Southwestern portion of the United States. Having this background, the Texas colonists would inevitably be attracted to the political and economic doctrines that were prevalent in the United States at the time, with preference, because of their frontier experience and relative poverty, for the more radical of these doctrines. This *a priori* expectation is confirmed by the actual adoption of some of the more advanced American proposals of the time in the Constitution and laws of the Republic of Texas.

The prevalent radicalism was mainly channeled, however, into a desire for freedom and security in the acquisition and undisturbed possession of free land—an ideal which had been sriously frustrated by the land policies of the United States government and the economic conditions prevailing in the United States at the time. To the Texas colonists, land was the philosopher's stone, the universal solvent and the answer to all problems. Where there were such vast expanses of good land to be had for the asking, there was little need for the social reforms on which the rest of mankind might lean for security. The reforms that *were* made in early Texas, for the most part, had to do with control of the land. It is probably that these changes, made by simply adopting large portions of the Spanish-Mexican law, represented in their context as advanced a liberalism as had been shown by any government in the world at that time, even though the text of the changes was derived from the edicts of a paternalistic autocracy.

Under the fortunate circumstance of an apparently unlimited supply of unoccupied land, these laws certainly went farther than any measures adopted in the United States, before or since, to promote the independence of the "little man." The Texan statesmen were not great theoreticians, and their political philosophy was mainly implicit in their actions; but, whether consciously or not, they reduced to reality a far-reaching ideal of favoring the small enterpriser which would have gladdened the heart of Thomas Jefferson. There also are evidences of a struggle between the followers of Jefferson and the breed of Hamilton in the story of the 400-league grants and in later developments, down to the present day. At this time, however, the "big business" element in Texas has a somewhat different complexion than its equivalent in the East. The typical Texas capitalist, plain of appearance and modest in demeanor when not aroused, resents attacks on his vast interests in oil or industry in an absurd analogue of the spirit in which the homespun early Texans fought off any attempt to prevent him from peaceably working his rightfully acquired league and labor of land. Thus the Hamiltonians in Texas today have a strong strain of Jeffersonian blood.

The fact that the liberal laws of Texas were developed under an absolute monarchy need occasion no surprise. Defenders of absolutism have pointed out with some justice that life under such a government may sometimes be freer than life under the tyranny of a majority. The crude theory of divine right, which was developed as a defense for the English monarchs in the 17th Century, never was accepted in Catholic countries like Spain. Rather, the king was made to feel that his right depended on his ruling justly, in accordance with the standards of his time. A disinterested examination of Spanish-American history, at any rate, will show that the king was generally more of a humanitarian than his conquistadores, and he was not entirely above the law. A subject who felt himself threatened with injustice could appeal to the king's judges, who referred to the *Siete Partidas* and the Code of Justinian in much the same way that American judges now refer to the Constitution. It was the king who tried to enforce the laws, or made new ones which had to be in harmony with the old, and the overseas officials who applied, misapplied or ignored them. We may well remember the story of Cabeza de Vaca, who emerged naked from the wilderness to find his fellow-countrymen killing and enslaving the Indians—and who forced them to desist, physically helpless as he was, by simply reminding them that their actions were contrary to the will of the king.

There is nothing in our accepted theory of democracy to deny that some good laws may prevail under an absolute monarchy. Certainly it was under the laws developed by Spain, and taken over without material change by Mexico, that the Texas colonists found the land they desired—land which to them meant freedom.

During the pre-revolutionary period in Texas, the desire to enjoy security on the land showed itself in a willingness to abide by the traditional laws and the Mexican Constitution of 1824—despite their grave denials of civil and religious liberty—as against the vagaries of successive revolutionary leaders. This feeling on the part of the colonists, explicitly described in their writings, explains both the loyalty of the Texans to Mexico for fifteen years and the final break in 1836.

"The general cause of the revolt," says Barker, "was the same [as in the American Revolution] —a sudden effort to extend imperial authority at the expense of local privilege." The historian, of course, is here speaking of the *immediate* cause of the outbreak. In both of the cases mentioned, there were traditions of long growth which explained why the people rose in violent protest when they were threatened with the loss of rights or privileges which they had learned to expect. In the case of Texas, the general American tradition of democracy had been transplanted to Texas soil after taking on the characteristic coloration of the Jacksonian age. What was added under Mexican rule was the reality of free land and the expectation of personal independence to be gained therefrom under stable laws. Only when this personal independence was proximately threatened by the re-centralization of the Mexican government, and other abuses, did the Texas colonists strike out for national independence.

The equation between land and freedom is explicitly stated in the Texas Declaration of Indepencence, when it says, "The Mexican government, by its colonization laws, invited and induced the Anglo-American population of Texas to colonize its wilderness under the pledged faith of a written constitution, that they should continue to enjoy that constitutional liberty and republican government to which they had been habituated in the land of their birth, the United States of America. In this expectation they have been cruelly disappointed, inasmuch as the Mexican nation has acquiesced in the late changes made in the government by General Antonio Lopez de Santa Anna, who, having overturned the constitution of his country, now offers, as the cruel alternative, either to abandon our homes, acquired by so many privations, or submit to the most intolerable of all tyranny. . . ."

Doubtless the movement for complete independence was strengthened by the influx of newcomers—largely adventurers—who had poured in from the United States after the first disorders and who had no feeling of obligation toward Mexico. Although these newcomers were of a more turbulent character than the original settlers brought in by the empresarios, and may have acted in the spirit of Long and Magee rather than in that of Austin, it seems probably that their presence accelerated the revolutionary process without materially changing its outcome or its sequelae.

When independence had been achieved, the security of the colonists still depended upon the maintenance of the rights they had acquired under the Spanish-Mexican laws. Hence they set about establishing a new code which would confirm the existing rights and which would secure for the future the peculiar advantages of both the Anglo-American and the Spanish legal systems, strengthened with improvements derived from the advanced thinking of the time.

The fact that a strenuous devotion to freedom can coexist in the same mind with a belief in slavery or white supremacy should not surprise any objective student of the American mentality, and particularly the Southern mentality, past or present. A slave-owner wrote, and many other slave-owners signed, the Declaration of Independence containing the words: "We hold these truths to be self-evident, that all men are created equal, and are endowed by their Creator with certain unalienable rights; that among these rights are life, liberty and the pursuit of happiness . . ." It would do no good, at this late date, to deplore a similar blind spot in the men who settled Texas.

So, the motivation of the colonists can be summarized in the term "freedom on the land." Like all too-brief summaries, this one is inaccurate, for it takes no account of the overlapping meanings of the terms "freedom," "liberty," "security" and "personal independence." The reader is invited to consider for himself whether a Texas colonist, lord of a league and a labor of land, but lacking a Bill of Rights, had more freedom than a landless American of the same period. Apparently the colonists felt that they had the advantage. Such philosophical questions, however, would lead us too far afield from the main historical theme. The point is that the laws adopted in early Texas provide a key to the motives of the American colonists from the day when Moses Austin first walked across the plaza in San Antonio, through the early difficulties of the empresarios, the Revolution, the organization of the Republic, Annexation, Secession, and many otherwise unrelated events in the later as well as the earlier history of the State. Traditions change more slowly than the circumstances of the times. The traditional character of the Texans, as shown in their struggle for freedom on the land, has its bearings on the present and future of the State of Texas.

SELECTED BIBLIOGRAPHY

Chapters I – II

Bandelier, Fanny (tr.). *The Journey of Alvar Nuñez Cabeza de Vaca, Translated from His Own Narrative.* New York, 1905.

Bishop, Morris. *The Odyssey of Cabeza de Vaca.* New York, 1933.

Castañeda, Carlos E. *The Mission Era.* 6 vols. Austin, 1936-1950.

Hallenbeck, Cleve. *Alvar Nuñez Cabeza de Vaca: The Journey and Route of the First European to Cross the Continent of North America.* Glendale, 1940. Contains Hallenbeck's conclusions regarding the route followed, as well as summaries of previous studies, which vary widely in their results.

Higginson, Thomas Wentworth. *Tales of the Enchanted Islands of the Atlantic.* New York, 1898.

Long, Haniel. *The Power Within Us.* New York, 1943. An imaginative reconstruction of Cabeza de Vaca's spiritual growth.

Parkes, Henry Bamford. *History of Mexico.* Boston, 1960 (Third ed.).

Terrell, John Upton. *Journey into Darkness.* New York, 1962. An account of Cabeza de Vaca's journey.

265

The tale of the Seven Cities is concisely told in Higginson's book. The legend of Roderick has also been used for literary purposes by Washington Irving, Robert Southey, Sir Walter Scott and others. The Parkes work is a convenient summary of Mexican history which I have found valuable as background throughout this book. Details on the explorations of Pineda, Camargo, and Garay can be found in Castañeda, I, Chapters I and II. This vast work, the only complete history of the Spanish colonial period in Texas, will be found cited time after time in succeeding chapters, and I have therefore abbreviated the citation to simply "Castañeda," any further identification being as unnecessary here as it would be in the case of Gibbon or Thucydides in another context.

For the story of Cabeza de Vaca my main source has been his own narrative as translated by Fanny Bandelier. For the route of Cabeza de Vaca, which can only be a matter of conjecture, I have followed Hallenbeck. I cite Long's *The Power Within Us* for its literary and spiritual beauty, not because I believe Long has accurately reconstructed Cabeza de Vaca's mental processes. Morris Bishop's biography has been useful in filling out the story, especially with regard to Cabeza de Vaca's life before and after the Texas episode. With regard to the possible connection between Las Casas and Cabeza de Vaca, I have drawn my own conclusions from my general knowledge of these men and their time. Throughout this book, the sources should not be held responsible for any statements which are evidently matters of opinion, as I have been quite free in drawing my own conclusions from the available evidence.

Chapter III

Bolton, Herbert E. *Coronado: Knight of the Pueblos and Plains.* New York and Albuquerque, 1949.

Hallenbeck, Cleve. *The Journey of Fray Marcos de Niza.* Dallas, 1949.

Hammond, George P., and Rey, Agapito. *Narratives of the Coronado Expedition, 1540-1542.* Albuquerque, 1940. Contains translations of Pedro de Castañeda's narrative and brief reports by several others.

Hodge, Frederick W. (ed.) *Spanish Explorers in the Southern United States, 1528-1543.* New York, 1907. Contains translations of Pedro de Castañeda's narrative of the Coronado expedition; the Gentleman of Elvas' account of the De Soto expedition, and Cabeza de Vaca's *Relación.*

Varner, John and Jeannette (trs.). *The Florida of the Inca.* Austin, 1951.

For the transitional passage relating to Marcos de Niza and Esteban de Dorantes I have, as will be seen from the text, followed Hallenbeck in his commentary on Marcos' account of his journey. In this posthumously published book, Hallenbeck righted an old wrong to the reputation of the first Negro known in American history.

For the Coronado expedition, Bolton's is the definitive work and I have used it for general background as well as for the probable route followed by the expedition, which has been disputed. For descriptive details of Texas as seen by Coronado's men, I have gone to Pedro de Castañeda's first-hand chronicle.

For the De Soto-Moscoso expedition, I have followed the account of one of its members, the anonymous Gentleman of Elvas. The Varners' excellent translation of *The Florida of the Inca,* a compilation made years later from the reminiscences of survivors, was not published until the first draft of this chapter had been written, and I have drawn on the Inca only for a few interesting additional details regarding the first discovery of petroleum in Texas.

The estimate of the number of expeditions known to have entered Texas before La Salle is based on my own analysis of a list in the index to Castañeda, I. Casteñeda's own text, as well as other evidence, shows that the tabulation is far wrong, since it gives full weight to side trips from major *entradas*; to doubtful expeditions; to expeditions which never came near Texas, like that of Ponce de León, and even to mythical sorties like the alleged "Dutch expedition."

Chapter IV

Robles, Vito Alessio. *Coahuila y Texas en la Epoca Colonial.* Mexico, 1938.
Bolton, Herbert E. (ed.). *Spanish Exploration in the Southwest, 1542-1706.* New York, 1916. A collection of translated documents, including a long letter of Fray Damian Manzanet and the itineraries (journals) of the De León expeditions of 1689 and 1690.

The story of the colonization of Northern Mexico, a prerequisite to Spanish occupation of Texas, is derived from Robles, as is the tragic story of Carvajal.

For the Spanish search for La Salle, I have tried to reconcile the often contradictory accounts of Manzanet and De León, translated in Bolton, cited above. Castañeda, I, Chapter XI, has been very helpful in filling out the details.

Chapters V — VI

Bolton, Herbert E. "The Location of La Salle's Colony on the Gulf of Mexico," *Southwestern Historical Quarterly*, XXVII. A classic of historical proof.

Clark, Robert C. *The Beginnings of Texas, 1684-1718*. Austin, 1907.

Cole, E. W. "La Salle in Texas," *Southwestern Historical Quarterly*, XLIX. Disagrees with Bolton on the location of the fort and on other matters.

Dunn, William Edward. *Spanish and French Rivalry in the Gulf Region of the United States, 1678-1702*. Austin, 1917.

Joutel, Henri. *Journal of La Salle's Last Voyage, 1684-1687*. Albany, 1906. The best single source for La Salle's fatal venture into Texas.

Parkman, Francis. *La Salle and the Discovery of the Great West*. Boston, 1927. A great historian's account of La Salle's career. Contains more than 100 pages on the Texas episode, drawing on various original documents from the Margry collection.

For the tragic story of La Salle's colony in Texas, I have relied chiefly on the very complete and obviously honest account of La Salle's lieutenant, Joutel. For what occurred before and after, and for happenings which took place in Joutel's absence, I have turned to Parkman and the documents which he quotes in his admirable book.

Chapters VII — VIII

Espinosa, Isidro Felix. "Diary of 1716," *Preliminary Studies, Texas Catholic Historical Association, I*.

Chabot, Frederick C. *With the Makers of San Antonio*. San Antonio, 1937.

Hackett, Charles W. (tr.). *Pichardo's Treatise on the Limits of Louisiana and Texas*. 4 vols. Austin, 1931.

Hatcher, Mattie Austin (tr.). "The Expedition of Don Domingo Terán de los

Rios," *Preliminary Studies, Texas Catholic Historical Society*, II. A translation of the principal documents, including Terán's journal and a diary kept by the missionaries.

Morfi, Juan Agustin. *History of Texas, 1673-1779*. (Translated and annotated by Carlos E. Castañeda.) Los Angeles, 1935.

Phares, Ross. *Cavalier in the Wilderness*. Baton Rouge, 1952. The only book-length account of St. Denis' entire career.

Ramon, Domingo. "Captain Don Domingo Ramón's Diary of his Expedition into Texas in 1716," tr. by Gabriel Tous, *Preliminary Studies, Texas Catholic Historical Society*, II.

Shelby, Charmion Claire. "St. Denis' Declaration Concerning Texas in 1717," *Southwestern Historical Quarterly*, XXVI.

Tous, Gabriel. "The Espinosa-Olivares-Aguirre Expedition," *Preliminary Studies, Texas Catholic Historical Society*, I.

West, Elizabeth Howard. "Bonilla's Brief Compendium of the History of Texas, 1772," *Quarterly of the Texas State Historical Association*, VII. A translation of an early history.

For the De León expedition of 1690 I have used the De León journal and the Manzanet letter (cited above). The Terán expedition and the abandonment of the missions are well covered in Hatcher, here cited, and in Castañeda, I, Chapter XII. For the general relations between France and Spain at this period, see any standard history of either of these countries. I have used Mary Pratt Parmele, *A Short History of Spain*, New York, 1906. For the expedition of 1709, I have followed Espinosa's diary, making what I believe to be improvements in the Tous translation, as appears in the text.

The most complete accounts of St. Denis are to be found in Castañeda, II, Chapters I-II, and in Phares, cited above. The Phares book is less reliable in that it leans on "tradition" as well as on documentary evidence, but is the only book that covers St. Denis' entire career, in Louisiana as well as in Texas and Mexico. Genealogical information on the St. Denis and Ramón Families can be found in Chabot, *With the Makers of San Antonio*, (cited above). Espinosa's and Ramón's diaries, here cited, are the main sources for my account of the Ramón-St. Denis expedition. Data on the founding of the last two missions, not included in the diaries, is given in Castañeda, II.

Chapter IX

Celíz, Francisco. *Diary of the Alarcón Expedition*. (Tr. by Fritz Leo Hoffman.) Los Angeles, 1930.

Mezquía, Pedro de. "Diary of the Alarcón Expedition into Texas, 1718," (Tr. by Fritz Leo Hoffman), *Southwestern Historical Quarterly,* XLI.

The diaries cited here are the main sources of this chapter. Castañeda, II, Chapter VIII, gives details of the plans projected by Olivares and a condensation of the report of Sevillano de Paredes.

Chapter X

Folmer, Henri. "De Bellisle on the Coast of Texas," *Southwestern Historical Quarterly,* XLIV. An annotated translation of Bellisle's own account of his adventures.

Chapter XI

Buckley, Eleanor Claire. "The Aguayo Expedition into Texas and Louisiana, 1719-1722," *Quarterly of the Texas State Historical Association,* XV.

Peña, Juan Antonio de. "Diary of the Aguayo Expedition " (tr. by Peter P. Forrestal), *Preliminary Studies, Texas Catholic Historical Society,* II.

For the Aguayo expedition itself, my main source has been Peña's diary. The most complete account of the abandonment of the missions and the preliminiaries of the Aguayo expedition is in Castañeda, II, Chapter IV. The preliminaries are also carefully studied in Buckley's article, cited here. The story of the strange happenings at La Bahía is found in Chabot, *With the Makers of San Antonio* (cited above), and in Castañeda, II, Chapter VI, where the reports of Governor Almazán are quoted.

Chapter XII

Cox, Isaac, Joslin. "The Founding of the First Texas Municipality," *Quarterly of the Texas State Historical Association,* II.

————. "The Early Settlers of San Fernando," *Quarterly of the Texas State Historical Association,* V.

270

Dunn, William Edward. "Apache Relations in Texas, 1718-1750," *Quarterly of the Texas State Historical Association,* XIV.

Hatcher, Mattie Austin. "The Municipal Government of San Fernando de Bexar, 1730-1800," *Quarterly of the Texas State Historical Association,* VIII.

Murphy, Retta. "The Journey of Pedro de Rivera, 1724-1728," *Southwestern Historical Quarterly,* XLI.

Descriptions of the Indians of Texas in the 18th Century are derived from Morfi, *History of Texas* (cited above). Since this is the story of the Spaniards in Texas, I describe the Indians as the Spaniards saw them, and I have not seriously attempted to correlate these impressions with modern anthropological knowledge.

Dunn's "Apache Relations" is the source for the Indian troubles described in this chapter.

Chapter XIII

Bolton, Herbert E. *Texas in the Middle 18th Century.* Berkeley, 1915.

Hackett, Charles W. "Policy of the Spanish Crown Regarding French Encroachments from Louisiana, 1721 1762," in vol. I, *New Spain and the Anglo-American West,* 2 vols., Los Angeles, 1932.

Pierce, Frank Cushman. *A Brief History of the Lower Rio Grande Valley.* Brownsville, 1917.

Sanford, Trent E. *The Architecture of the Southwest.* New York, 1950.

The complicated story of the troubles of Governor Sandoval is told in Hackett, *Pichardo's Treatise,* III, Chapter XIII (cited above), which contains translations of many of the letters exchanged by Sandoval, St. Denis and others during the controversy.

The younger St. Denis' success with the Indians is attested by Governor Ripperdá in a letter quoted in Chabot, *With the Makers of San Antonio* (cited above). Further data on Spanish-French relations during this period can be found in Hackett, *Policy of the Spanish Crown,* here cited. The murder of Father Ganzabal is recounted in Bolton, *Texas,* here cited, and in Castañeda, III, Chapter VIII. The present condition of the Nueces Valley missions is a matter of personal observation.

The boundaries of Spanish Texas are discussed in exhaustive detail in

Hackett, *Pichardo's Treatise,* cited above. My brief summaries of the histories of the lower Rio Grande Valley and the El Paso region (no part of Texas in Spanish times) are derived respectively from Pierce and Sanford, cited above. Sanford's excellent book is not limited by its title, but could very well be called a history of the Southwest with the emphasis on architecture.

Chapter XIV

Blackmar, F. W. *Spanish Institutions of the Southwest.* Baltimore, 1891. Valuable for general background though it has little information on Texas specifically.

Bolton, Herbert E. *Athanase de Meziéres and the Louisiana-Texas Frontier, 1768-1789.* Cleveland, 1914.

————. "The Spanish Abandonment and Reoccupation of East Texas," *Quarterly of the Texas State Historical Association,* IX.

Pagés, Pierre-Marie-Francois de. *Travels Round the World in the Years 1767-1771.* Translated from the French. 2 vols. Dublin, 1791.

Solís, Gaspar José de. "Diary of a Visit of Inspection of the Texas Missions Made by Fray Gaspar José de Solís in the Year 1767-68," translated by Margaret Kenney Kress with introductory note by Mattie Austin Hatcher, *Southwestern Historical Quarterly,* XXXV.

The reports of Rubí and La Fora on conditions in Texas in 1767 are used here as condensed in Castañeda, IV, Chapter V. The reports on the Bishop of Guadalajara and Captain Menchaca are found in Castañeda, IV, Chapter I. The report of Father Fernández de Santa Ana is quoted in Castañeda, III, Chapter II. The descriptions of the missions in 1762 are as given by the Bishop of Guadalajara. The quoted comments by Dr. Bolton are found in his *Texas in the Middle 18th Century* (cited above). Father Morfi's praise of San José Mission is in his *History of Texas,* (cited above). Father Solís' description of San José and La Bahía in 1768 are from the *Diary* here cited. The "New Regulations of the Presidios" and their results are summarized in Castañeda, IV, and by Bolton in *De Meziéres.*

Chapter XV

Quintero, J. A. "Philip Nolan and His Companions," *Texas Almanac,* 1867. Contains translation of Lt. Múzquiz's journal.

Brown, William Horace. *The Glory Seekers: The Romance of Would-Be Founders of Empire in the Early Days of the Southwest.* Chicago, 1906.

Garrison, George P. *Texas: A Contest of Civilizations.* Boston and New York, 1903.

Hale, Edward Everett. *Philip Nolan's Friends.* New York, 1876. Preface explains how Hale came to write this novel to make amends for misusing the name of Philip Nolan in "The Man Without a Country."

Hay, Thomas Robson, and Werner, M. R. *The Admirable Trumpeter: A Biography of General James Wilkinson.* New York, 1941. Highly informative although it bogs down in a futile effort to suspend judgment regarding Wilkinson's character.

Hatcher, Mattie Austin. "The Louisiana Background of the Colonization of Texas, 1763-1803," *Southwestern Historical Quarterly,* XXIV.

————. "Conditions Affecting the Colonization Problem, 1795-1801," *Southwestern Historical Quarterly,* XXV.

Jefferson, Thomas, et al. "Concerning Philip Nolan," *Quarterly of the Texas State Historical Association,* VII. The Jefferson-Clark correspondence, with letters to Jefferson from William Dunbar and General Wilkinson, all relating to Nolan.

Pike, Zebulon Montgomery. *Exploratory Travels Through the Western Territories of North America.* 2 vols. London, 1811.

Yoakum, Henderson. *History of Texas.* New York, 1856. 2 vols. (Facsimile edition, Austin, 1935.) Appendix gives Ellis P. Bean's colorful account of the Nolan expedition and Bean's later adventures in Mexico.

Weems, John Edward. *Men Without Countries.* Boston, 1969. The latest research on Wilkinson, Nolan and Bean.

Lay, Bennet. *The Lives of Ellis P. Bean.* The University of Texas Press, Austin, 1960.

My account of the early career of General Wilkinson and his relations with Nolan is based on Brown and on Werner and Hay, cited above, which are also the main sources for Nolan's career prior to his last expedition. The connection between Nolan and Jefferson is displayed in the Jefferson-Clark correspondence. Nolan's last expedition, up to his encounter with Múzquiz, is told here as described in Bean's memoir. The Múzquiz expedition and the death of Nolan are documented by Múzquiz's diary. Pike's remarks on the wild horses of Texas are quoted from this book, which has gone through numerous later editions.

Chapter XVI

Hatcher, Mattie Austin. *The Opening of Texas to Foreign Settlement, 1801-1821*. Austin, 1927.

McCaleb, Walter F. *The Aaron Burr Conspiracy*. New York, 1903. Contains much material on Wilkinson as well as on Burr.

Ramos de Arizpe, Miguel. *Report* (tr. by Nettie Lee Benson). Austin, 1950. Another translation was published at Philadelphia in 1814. This pamphlet gives concise facts on Texas and Northern Mexico as of 1812.

Gasiot's prophecy is translated in Castañeda, V, Chapter I. Other data on Spanish fears of American attack can be found in Hatcher, the works cited in this and the preceding chapter. Hatcher, *The Opening of Texas,* here cited, describes in detail the Spanish policy on immigration. Information regarding the new settlements of this period is in Ramos de Arizpe's report. McCaleb's excellent work is my main source for the Burr conspiracy and Wilkinson's activities on the Sabine. Pike's descriptions of Texas and the Mexican life of the period are summarized from his book (cited above).

Chatper XVII

Chabot, Frederick C. (ed.). *Letters of 1811*. San Antonio, 1938.

Garrett, Julia Kathryn. *Green Flag Over Texas*. New York and Dallas, 1939. Best published source for the 1811 revolt.

Warren, Harris Gaylord. *The Sword Was Their Passport*. Baton Rouge, 1943. Best published source for the filibusters, 1813-1820.

For the general Mexican revolution and the conditions that preceded it, see Parkes (cited above) or any standard history of Mexico. A convenient tabulation of dates, which I have used in correlating events in Texas with those in Mexico proper, is contained in Alfonso Teja Zabre, *Historia de Mexico,* Mexico, 1948. Castañeda, VI, Chapter V, gives evidence for a discrepant version of the execution of fourteen Spanish officers in San Antonio in 1813, as noted in the text. Also see Brown, *The Glory Seekers* (cited above).

Chapter XVIII

Barker, Eugene C. *Life of Stephen F. Austin.* New York, 1927.

Faye, Stanley. "The Great Stroke of Pierre Laffite," *Louisiana Historical Quarterly,* XXIII.

————. "Commodore Aury," *Louisiana Historical Quarterly,* XXIV.

Hartmann et Millard. *Le Texas, ou Notice Historique sur le Champ d'Asile.* Paris, 1819.

Hatcher, Mattie Austin. "Texas in 1820," *Southwestern Historical Quarterly,* XXIII.

———— (tr.). "Letters of Antonio Martinez, the Last Spanish Governor of Texas, 1817-1822," *Southwestern Historical Quarterly,* XXXIX.

Wooten, Dudley G. (ed.). *A Comprehensive History of Texas.* Dallas, 1898. Contains Stephen Austin's account of Moses Austin's visit to San Antonio.

Also see Castañeda, VI; Brown, *The Glory Seekers,* and Warren, *The Sword Was Their Passport* (cited above).

Chapter XIX

On the characteristics of the Americans who settled Texas see the following:

Hatcher, Mattie Austin. *The Opening of Texas to Foreign Settlement, 1801-1821.* Austin, 1927.

Barker, Eugene C. (ed.). *The Austin Papers.* Washington and Austin, 1924-1926. 3 vols.

Harman, Samuel Lowrie. *Culture Conflict in Texas, 1821-1835.* New York, 1932.

Turner, Frederick Jackson. *The United States, 1830-1850: The Nation and Its Sections.* New York, 1935.

Schlesinger, Arthur M., Jr. *The Age of Jackson.* Boston, 1946.

Bellot, H. Hale. *American History and American Historians.* Norman, 1952.

On the history of Texas for the period in question see:

Barker, *The Austin Papers, above cited.*

Barker, Eugene C. *Mexico and Texas, 1821-1835.* Dallas, 1928.

Barker, Eugene C. *Life of Stephen F. Austin.* (Second edition.) Austin, 1949.
Holley, Mary Austin. *Texas.* Lexington, Kentucky, 1836. Facsimile edition, Austin, 1935.
Yoakum, Henderson. *History of Texas.* 2 vols. New York, 1855.
Wooten, Dudley G. *A Comprehensive History of Texas.* Dallas, 1898.

Chapter XX

For the laws of Spain, Mexico, Texas and the United States pertinent references are found in the following:

Webb, Walter Prescott. *The Great Plains.* New York, 1931. Especially Chapter IX, "New Laws for Land and Water."
Texas Constitution of 1876, reprinted, as amended, in biennial editions of the *Texas Almanac and State Industrial Guide,* published by the Dallas News.

The early constitutions and laws of the Republic and State of Texas are printed in:

Gammel, J. N. *Laws of Texas.* 10 vols. Austin, 1891.
Early Spanish laws applicable to Texas can be found in:

Novisima Recopilación de las Leyes de la España. Madrid, 1805.
Recopilación de Leyes de las Reynos de las Indias. Madrid, 1774.

Partial texts of Spanish and Mexican laws can be found in Gammel, above cited, and in:

Sayles, J. and J. H. *Early Laws of Texas.* 3 vols. Kansas City, 1891.
Davenport, Harbert, and Canales, J. T. *The Texas Law of Flowing Waters, with Special Reference to Irrigation from the Lower Rio Grande.* Brownsville, 1949.

Texas laws now in effect are published in:

Vernon's Texas Statutes. Decisions of the Texas Supreme Court are compiled in *Reports of Cases Argued and Decided in the Supreme Court of the State of Texas*, usually cited as *Texas Reports*, and in the *South Western Reporter*.

On mineral rights see:

Hawkins, Walace [sic]. *El Sal Del Rey*. Austin, 1947.

In the preparation of these two chapters I owe a great debt to the late Harbert Davenport of Brownsville for advice and assistance based on his unique combination of historical knowledge and practical experience as a lawyer who for more than fifty years specialized in cases which involved principles carried over from the old Spanish law.

Recent interpretations and other references on Spanish law:

On recent Supreme Court decisions, see:

South Western Reporter, Second Series, Vol. 324, Texas Edition. West Publishing Company, St. Paul. Contains text of the Texas Supreme Court decision in Luttes vs. Texas.

San Antonio Express, May 28, 1959. Contains an article by Jon Ford on the Luttes case and its implications.

South Western Reporter, Second Series, Vol. 355. West Publishing Company, St. Paul. Contains text of Texas Supreme Court decision on the Valmont case.

South Western Reporter, Second Series, Vol. 346. West Publishing Company, St. Paul. Contains text of Fourth Court of Civil Appeals decision in the Valmont case.

Collection of Roman, Spanish and Mexican Laws and Commentaries. Prepared by Plaintiffs' Attorney in State of Texas, et al., vs. Valmont Plantations. Austin, 1960. Contains text and/or facsimilies of the original editions of many of these documents and "Reproduces virtually all of the legislation that throws light on the nature of irrigation rights in New Spain."

Miscellaneous references for further study:

Ashford, Gerald. "Jacksonian Liberalism and Spanish Law in Early Texas," *Southwestern Historical Quarterly*, LVII. Contains much the same information as Chapter XIX-XX in the present work as the matter stood at the time of writing, but without the changes made necessary by later decisions and constitutional amendments. The Quarterly article does carry footnotes giving more detailed documentation of the sources.

Dobbins, Betty Eakle. *The Spanish Element in Texas Water Law*. Austin, 1959. A valuable study, only a small part of which is outdated by recent decisions and amendments.

Vance, John Thomas. *The Background of Hispanic American Law: Legal Sources and Juridical Literature of Spain*. New York, 1943.

Ernest Wallace, editor, with the assistance of David M. Vigness. *Documents of Texas History*. Austin, 1963. Contains the Texas Declaration of Independence, the Constitution of 1836, and 124 other documents, many of which throw light on the motives of the revolt in Texas as well as on events in the Spanish period and in more recent history.

Yarbrough, Donald B., compiler. *Texas Water Development Board 89: Laws and Programs Relating to Water and Related Land Resources*. Austin, December, 1968; reprinted May, 1969.

Texas Jurisprudence: Second Edition, Vol. 60. By the editorial staffs of the publishers. Bancroft-Whitney Company, San Francisco—The Lawyers Cooperative Publishing Company, Rochester, N.Y., 1964.

General

Anonymous. *History of the Archdiocese of San Antonio*. San Antonio, 1950. An official history, published by the Archdiocese.

Belden, Joe and Associates. *The Latin-American Population in Texas*. Austin, 1951.

Brooks, Charles Mattoon. *Texas Missions: Their Romance and Architecture*. Dallas, 1936.

Corner, William. *San Antonio de Bexar: A Guide and History*. San Antonio, 1890.

Habig, Fr. Marion A., O.F.M. San Antonio, 1968. *San Antonio's Mission San José: State and National Historical Site, 1720-1968*. San Antonio, 1968. Recounts the entire history of this mission, from its founding to recent restorations, along with much valuable information on other missions. Includes a thorough bibliography.

Hansen, Harry, editor. *Texas: A Guide to the Lone Star State*. New revised edition; originally compiled by the Federal Writers, Program of the Works Projects Administration in the State of Texas; American

Guide Series. New York, 1969.

McCaleb, Walter F. *The Spanish Missions of Texas.* San Antonio, 1954 and 1961.

Ramsdell, Charles. *San Antonio: A Historical and Pictorial Guide.* Austin, 1959; revised edition, 1968.

Saunders, Lyle. *The Spanish-Speaking Population of Texas.* (Inter-American Education Occasional Papers V.) Austin, 1949.

Sibley, Marilyn McAdams. *Travelers in Texas, 1761-1860.* Austin and London, 1967.

Simpson, L. B., editor; Paul D. Nathan, translator. *The San Saba Papers: A Documentary Account of the Founding and Destruction of the San Saba Mission.* San Francisco, 1959.

Webb, Walter Prescott, and Carroll, H. Bailey, editors. *The Handbook of Texas.* 2 vols. Austin, 1952. An encyclopedic reference work.

Weddle, Robert S. *The San Saba Mission: Spanish Pivot in Texas.* Austin, 1964.

————. *San Juan Bautista: Gateway to Spanish Texas.* Austin and London, 1968. Includes a thorough bibliography of published and unpublished material on Spanish Texas, with special reference to the Rio Grande border in the 18th Century.

Ximenes, Ben Cuellar. *Gallant Outcasts: Texas Turmoil, 1519-1734.* San Antonio, 1963.

ILLUSTRATIONS

San Jose Mission

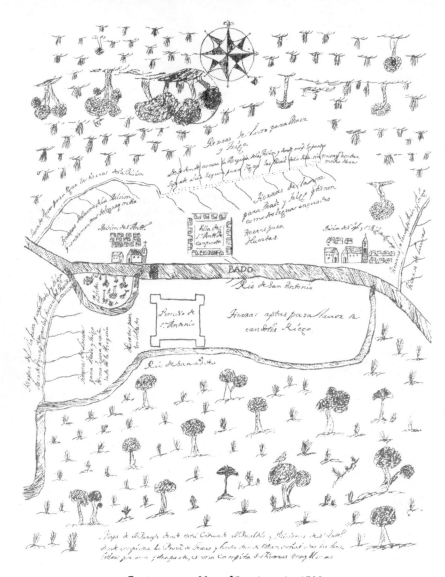

Contemporary Map of San Antonio, 1730.

*Early picture of the buffalo,
first discovered by Cabeza de Vaca.*

Coronado on the Trail

Father Margil de Jesus

Robert Cavalier De La Salle.

Two
early views
of
Mission Concepcion.

La Bahia del Espiritu Santo.

Index

Urdinola, Francisco de, 46, 125
Urdinola, Luis de, 46
Urrutia, Joseph de, 89, 93, 98, 145, 146
Urrutia, Toribio de, 145-147

Vallejo, Father Francisco, 153
Valmont Plantations v. State, 256
Van Buren, Martin, 238
Vergara, Father, 146
Viana, Father Mariano Francisco de
    Dolores y, 156, 198
Vick, Rev. Newell, 225
Vidal, Jose, 184
Villa of San Marcos de Neve, 192
Villa of Santisima Trinidad de Salcedo,
    192
Vitry, Father Pierre, 150, 151, 153

Walker, W. W., 228
Washington-on-the-Brazos, 248
Webb, Walter Prescott, 2
Wells of Bajan, 205
Wheeler, Justice, 254
Wilkinson, Gen. James, 174, 177-184,
    188, 192-197, 207, 233
Wilkinson, Jane, 225, 227
Wilkinson, Joseph B., 212, 213
Willie, James, 251

Xaromes (Indians), 107
Ximenez, Father Diego, 157

Yanaguana, 85, 86, 99
Ybarbo, Antonio Gil, 172
Yoakum, Henderson, 241, 242

Zambrano, Father Juan Manuel, 204
Zerbin, Doctor, 198
Zevallos, Juan Joseph, 155, 156
Zuniga, Father Garcia de, 158